AT HOME
with the WORD®
2019

Sunday Scriptures and Scripture Insights

YEAR C

Catherine A. Cory, PHD
Rev. Patrick J. Hartin
Susan Gleason Anderson, MA
Tanya Rybarczyk, MA, MAPM

ALSO AVAILABLE IN A LARGE PRINT EDITION

LITURGY
TRAINING
PUBLICATIONS

Nihil Obstat
Reverend Mr. Daniel G. Welter, JD
Vicar for Canonical Services
Archdiocese of Chicago
March 2, 2018

Imprimatur
Very Reverend Ronald A. Hicks
Vicar General
Archdiocese of Chicago
March 2, 2018

Prayers in the introductions to each liturgical time are adapted from *Prayers for Sundays and Seasons, Year C* by Peter Scagnelli, Chicago: Liturgy Training Publications, 1997.

At Home with the Word® 2019 © 2018 Archdiocese of Chicago: Liturgy Training Publications, 3949 South Racine Avenue, Chicago, IL 60609; 800-933-1800; fax 800-933-7094; email: orders@ltp.org; website: www.LTP.org. All rights reserved.

This book was edited by Mary G. Fox. Kris Fankhouser was the production editor, Anna Manhart was the designer, and Kari Nicholls was the production artist.

The cover art for this year's *At Home with the Word*® is by James B. Janknegt. The interior art is by Kathy Ann Sullivan.

Printed in the United States of America

ISBN 978-1-61671-382-9

AHW19

Welcome to At Home with the Word® 2019

The Authors of the Introductions

Marielle Frigge, OSB, taught Scripture and theology for thirty-three years at Mount Marty College in Yankton, South Dakota, and is now formation director for Sacred Heart Monastery. Michael Cameron teaches Scripture and history of Christianity in the theology department at the University of Portland in Oregon.

Scripture Readings

For each Sunday, you will find the three readings and Responsorial Psalm from the *Lectionary for Mass*, from which readings are proclaimed in Roman Catholic churches in the United States.

Scripture Insights

Two authors have written Scripture Insights for 2019. Catherine A. Cory is associate professor of theology at the University of St. Thomas in St. Paul, Minnesota. She received her doctoral degree in Christianity and Judaism in antiquity from the University of Notre Dame, and has taught at the undergraduate and graduate level since 1991. She is coeditor of *The Christian Theological Tradition* (Routledge, 2008) and wrote some of its chapters. She is also the author of *Revelation* (Liturgical Press, 2006) and other works on the New Testament. Dr. Cory wrote Scripture Insights from the First Sunday of Advent through the Fourth Sunday of Easter.

Father Patrick J. Hartin a priest of the Diocese of Spokane, Washington, taught New Testament studies and Christian spirituality at Gonzaga University from 1995 to 2016. His doctorate in New Testament is from the University of South Africa (Pretoria). His books include *James*, in the Sacra Pagina Series (2003), *Exploring the Spirituality of the Gospels* (2010), and *A Window into the Spirituality of Paul* (2015), all from Liturgical Press. Father Hartin wrote the Scripture Insights from the Fifth Sunday of Easter through the end of the liturgical year.

Practice of Faith, Hope, Charity

Two authors wrote the Practice of Faith, Hope, or Charity. Susan Gleason Anderson is a parish director of religious education and has served in catechetical ministry for nearly twenty years. Her master of arts degree is from the University of Chicago Divinity School, where she studied theology. She wrote the practices for the First Sunday of Advent through the Fourth Sunday of Easter.

Tanya Rybarczyk holds master's degrees in pastoral ministry from the University of Portland and English from Binghamton University, New York. She is a Catholic adult faith formation educator, specializing in classes and retreats on meditative Catholic prayer practices. Her writing has been featured in *America* magazine. She wrote the practices from the Fifth Sunday of Easter through the Solemnity of Our Lord Jesus Christ, King of the Universe.

Additional Downloadable Questions and Activities

Download additional questions and activities for three audiences: families, Christian initiation groups, and other adult groups. The link http://www.ltp.org/ahw will take you to the At Home with the Word® Extra Content page. Click on the desired audience, Adult Faith-Sharing Groups, Christian Initiation Groups, or Families.

Weekday Readings

See the opening of each liturgical time for a list of Scripture texts read at Mass on weekdays and on feasts falling on weekdays.

Art for 2019

On the cover, James B. Janknegt. from Elgin, Texas, has illustrated the crossing of the Red Sea. Moses stands on a rock with arms raised, the people, having just reached safety, huddle below him, and the Egyptians are about to be engulfed by the walls of water that have allowed the people to pass. This is the third of several scenes from salvation history to appear on the covers of *At Home with the Word®* in coming years. The reading, from Exodus 14:15—15:1, is proclaimed during the Easter Vigil. In the interior art, Kathy Ann Sullivan uses a scratch board technique to evoke the liturgical seasons, from our ancestors on the Jesse tree to the oil lamps for Ordinary Time in the fall. Kathy Ann designed the scenes in the baptismal font at St. Mary's Cathedral in Colorado Springs.

Table of Contents

The Lectionary

by Marielle Frigge, OSB

WHAT IS A LECTIONARY?

The word *lectionary* comes from the Latin word *legere*, "to read," and names a collection of Scripture readings from both the Old and New Testaments that are proclaimed throughout the liturgical year in a particular order. Christian lectionaries were in use already in the fourth century, but before the invention of the printing press in the mid-fifteenth century, readings differed from place to place. Printing allowed for a more standardized lectionary, so that Catholics around the world could hear the same Bible readings at Mass on any given day.

However, in the four centuries before the Second Vatican Council (1963–65), the lectionary had a somewhat limited ability to touch the faith lives of Catholics. Most could not understand what was read because Scripture readings as well as the prayers of the Mass were proclaimed in Latin. Further, because the lectionary of that time used only particular selections from the Bible repeated year after year, Catholics received a restricted exposure to the riches of Scripture.

GIFTS OF THE SECOND VATICAN COUNCIL

After the Second Vatican Council, not only were the biblical readings made available in the language of the people, but the structure of the lectionary was expanded as well. These changes resulted from a fresh understanding of the role of Scripture in the liturgy. Returning to the ancient understanding that Christ is present in the Scriptures, the Council Fathers further emphasized that the Eucharist nourishes God's people at two tables: the proclaimed Word of God and the Eucharistic banquet. For this reason, the revised Lectionary includes much more Scripture. Rather than repeating a yearly pattern, it includes a three-year cycle for Sundays and a two-year cycle for weekdays. Through this expanded array of selections, it aims to present the broad sweep of the salvation story, arranged purposefully around the liturgical year with the four major liturgical seasons of Advent, Christmas Time, Lent, and Easter Time punctuating the many weeks of Ordinary Time.

These great liturgical seasons instruct the faithful in the most significant aspects of salvation history. The liturgical year begins with Advent, expressing the ancient longing and hope of God's covenant people for redemption. Christmas Time celebrates the Incarnation of the Lord, God's Word of salvation fully present and active in the world, made flesh in Jesus the Christ. During Lent, the Scripture readings call Christians to deeper conversion: to amend their ways of failing to respond to God's saving Word, to cultivate greater intimacy with God, and to rejoice that he never ceases to offer life-changing mercy. These Scriptures about conversion speak powerfully to those preparing for initiation. Easter Time proclaims the Paschal Mystery, the redeeming Death and Resurrection of Jesus Christ. That mystery leads us into life in divine Spirit, poured out upon all the faithful at Pentecost, sending us out to serve. In addition to highlighting the liturgical seasons, the Lectionary illuminates other key mysteries of Catholic faith in solemnities such as the Most Holy Trinity, the Most Holy Body and Blood of Christ, the Assumption of the Blessed Virgin Mary, and in feasts such as the Presentation of the Lord and the Exaltation of the Holy Cross.

FOUR SUNDAY SCRIPTURE SELECTIONS

At Home with the Word® provides all four Scripture passages of each Sunday: a selection from the Old Testament (except during Easter Time when we hear from Acts of the Apostles); a Responsorial Psalm or canticle; a New Testament reading from one of the letters, Acts of the Apostles, or Revelation; and, most important, a Gospel passage. Each year of the three-year cycle draws from a particular Gospel account: Matthew in Year A, Mark in Year B, and Luke in Year C. The Gospel of John, so highly symbolic and profound, is heard in the liturgical seasons. The Lectionary includes readings from John on several Sundays of Lent, during the sacred Triduum, and most Sundays of Easter Time. Because Mark is the shortest Gospel account, some Sundays of Ordinary Time in Year B use passages from John.

The pattern of today's Catholic Lectionary has served as a model for lectionaries of several other Christian churches. As a result, Catholics and many Protestants hear the same Scripture passages proclaimed on Sundays. The biblical Word of God thus draws them closer.

Understanding how the four Scripture passages of each Sunday are related can help us appreciate how the Lectionary invites Christians to understand, ponder, and integrate the message of God's Word. The First Reading from the Old Testament usually bears some connection to the Gospel passage, often by means of a significant person, event, or image. Rooted in the ancient practice of the Jewish synagogue, the Responsorial, which follows the First Reading, is usually from a psalm and represents the people's response to God's Word in the First Reading. In this way the first two Scripture passages mirror a theme woven throughout the Bible: God always takes the initiative to address humankind, speaking a Word that invites a response from God's people. The Responsorial may also illustrate or clarify what the First Reading proclaims, or may be related to the liturgical season, and thus is intended to foster meditation on the Word of God.

Frequently the Second Reading, always from the New Testament, follows the ancient practice of *lectio continua* (Latin for "continuous reading"), so that on each Sunday we hear important selections in order from a particular book. For example, the Second Reading is often an excerpt from one of the letters of St. Paul, and by continuous reading over several Sundays, the Lectionary presents some of his major theological insights in a particular letter.

During Ordinary Time the Lectionary presents continuous reading in the Gospels also, allowing us to see each evangelist's distinctive way of unfolding the Gospel story. For example, in Year A, from the Fourteenth Sunday of Ordinary Time to the end of the liturgical year in November, we hear the Gospel of Matthew from chapter 11 through chapter 25. Not every verse of Matthew is included, and occasionally a Sunday solemnity or feast requires a reading from a different Gospel, but continuous reading relates major aspects of Matthew's narrative, just as it does for Mark's in Year B and Luke's in Year C. Over time, through continuous reading, we can become familiar with the particular content and qualities of each Gospel account.

THE LECTIONARY AS A VISUAL SIGN

The Lectionary nourishes us with its words proclaimed in the liturgy—the Lord's own voice speaking to his people. It also nourishes us as a visual sign of the Lord's presence among us. The United States Conference of Catholic Bishops reminds Catholics that gestures and physical objects used in liturgy are "signs by which Christians express and deepen their relationship to God" (*Built of Living Stones: Art, Architecture, and Worship,* 23). Although the Lectionary's proper place during the liturgy is on the ambo (the special podium from which readings are proclaimed), a part of the Lectionary—the Gospel readings—has been made into a separate Book of the Gospels. That book, often richly decorated, may be carried in the entrance procession on Sundays and holy days. It is placed on the altar at the beginning of Mass and then, when the assembly rises to sing the Alleluia, the Gospel reader may processes with the book to the ambo, accompanied by servers holding candles. In response to the deacon or priest's introduction to the Gospel Reading, the people respond, signing their forehead, lips, and heart with a small cross. Observing such signs and ceremonies, one could not miss the special reverence we give to the Word of God—especially in the Gospel.

In the bishops' teaching about the ambo, from which the Scriptures are proclaimed, we find an apt crystallization of the Church's conviction about the role of Scripture in the Mass. Urging that the ambo should be of a size and placement that draws attention to the sacred Word, the document says, "Here the Christian community encounters the living Lord in the word of God and prepares itself for the 'breaking of the bread' and the mission to live the word that will be proclaimed" (*Built of Living Stones,* 61).

Introduction to the Gospel according to Luke

by Michael Cameron

The Gospel according to Luke, together with its sequel, the Acts of the Apostles, presents a breath-taking narrative of early Christianity, from Gabriel announcing the birth of John the Baptist in Jerusalem to the Apostle Paul announcing the Gospel of Jesus in Rome. This majestically conceived, magnificently crafted epic makes up about a quarter of the New Testament.

Luke was a second-generation Christian who may have been a Gentile admirer of Judaism before his conversion. He was well educated, traveled widely, wrote excellent Greek, and was influenced by contemporary modes of writing history. He echoes the atmosphere, the language, and at times even the style of the Old Testament. Luke tells us directly that he is handing on what contemporaries of Jesus have reported (1:1–4). Writing about fifty years after Jesus' time, he incorporates many stories and sayings from Mark, from a source also known to Matthew, and from his own traditions. Nevertheless, he shapes the traditions according to his own rich perspective.

Luke is a theologian with a historical bent, possessing a strong sense of the salvation story's development through three phases of time. *The time of Israel* is the period of "the law and the prophets" (16:16) from the creation to the appearance of John the Baptist. The entire Old Testament portrayed Israel growing in the knowledge of God and awaiting the future "redemption of Jerusalem" (2:38). Luke's account represents this time poetically through the infancy narrative (chapters 1 and 2), with its unforgettable characters who represent Old Testament piety at its best. *The time of Jesus* encompasses his baptism to his Ascension (chapters 3 to 24), when salvation is definitively accomplished in the words and works of the Messiah, especially his Death and Resurrection in Jerusalem (24:44–47). Luke accentuates the dramatic immediacy of salvation by a strategic use of the word *today* (fulfillment "today," 4:21; salvation "today," 19:9; paradise "today," 23:43). *The time of the church* stretches from Pentecost until Jesus returns. Anticipated in 24:48, this period begins to unfold in the 28 chapters of Acts of the Apostles.

Luke's work has a distinctive, sweet air, a beautiful mildness. His naturally humane outlook finds deep resonance with Jesus' concern for people's healing and salvation. In contrast to Mark's rough prophet, Matthew's wise teacher, and John's mystical divine, Luke's Jesus is the herald of healing peace. From the early scene announcing "liberty to captives" (4:17–19) to the last healing of the slave of the high priest who arrested him (22:50–51), Luke's Jesus is the good and gentle Savior. At the same time, Luke is blunt about Jesus' severe demands on those who become his disciples (14:25–33; 17:7–10), who must take up their cross daily (9:23) and leave *everything* to follow him, a favorite idea (5:11, 28; 14:33).

Luke is an exquisite storyteller, with a keen eye for deep characters, pungent storylines, poignant ironies, and heartwarming endings. As with all such masters, his pen's slightest stroke speaks volumes, as when Jesus agonizes while the disciples sleep "from grief" (22:45), or Peter denies Jesus a third time and "the Lord turned and looked at Peter" (22:61). Luke's arresting vignettes anticipate the stained glass storytelling of great medieval cathedrals. It is not accidental that artists have often rendered Luke as a portrait painter, or that the Church has made Luke patron saint of artists.

Luke contains certain features that the other Gospel accounts omit or mention only in passing. Joy is a distinct emphasis (1:14, 47; 2:10; 10:17, 21; 15:7, 10; 19:37; 24:41), as are prayer (3:21; 6:12; 11:5–8; 18:1–8; 23:46), the Holy Spirit (1:15, 41, 67; 2:27; 4:18; 10:21; 11:13), Jesus' friendships with women (7:36–50; 8:2–3; 10:38–42; 23:27–31; 23:55), and his teaching on hospitality (9:49–50; 10:25–37; 14:12–14; 15:4) and right attitude about wealth (6:24–25; 12:13–21; 16:19–31). If Luke's account of the Gospel had somehow not survived, our loss would be incalculable.

Luke alone gives us the stories of Jesus' infancy narrative, including the birth of John the Baptist, the angel Gabriel's Annunciation to Mary (1:26–38), and her visitation to Elizabeth (1:39–45); the liturgical songs of Mary (1:46–55, the Magnificat)

and Zechariah (1:67–79, the Benedictus); he draws *images* of the crowded inn at Bethlehem, Jesus lying in the manger, shepherds frightened by angels singing "Peace on Earth" (2:1–20), hoary Simeon exclaiming his praise (2:28–32, the *Nunc Dimittis*), old Anna prophesying redemption, (2:36–38), the young Jesus cross-examining the scholars (2:46), and Mary keeping in her heart the mysteries about her son (2:19, 51).

Luke's memorable *characters* include the judgmental Pharisee Simon (7:39–47), the hungry learner Mary (10:39), the repentant taxman Zacchaeus (19:1–10), and the distraught disciple Cleopas (24:18–24). Special *dramas* abound: Jesus raised up a widow's only son at his funeral, then "gave him to his mother" (7:11–17), healed the woman bent double for eighteen years (13:10–17), and cured ten lepers among whom the Samaritan alone returned to say thanks (17:11–19). He painted a host of affecting *scenes*: Jesus reading in his home synagogue (4:16–20), Peter repenting at Jesus' knees (5:8), the woman bathing Jesus' feet with her tears (7:38), Jesus praying with sweat "like drops of blood" (22:44).

Further, Luke transmitted many unique *sayings* of Jesus: "One's life does not consist of possessions" (12:15). "Do not be afraid any longer, little flock" (12:32). "The kingdom of God is among you" (17:21). "Father, forgive them, they know not what they do" (23:34). "Today you will be with me in Paradise" (23:43). And many well-known parables are found only in Luke: the Good Samaritan (10:29–37), the Woman's Lost Coin (15:8–10), the Prodigal Son (15:11–32), the Rich Man and Lazarus (16:19–31), the Widow and the Unjust Judge (18:1–8), the Pharisee and the Tax Collector (18:9–14).

Luke's first sentences in the prologue (1:1–4) address an otherwise unknown figure named Theophilus (the name means "God's friend"), who symbolizes any Christian seeking a deeper understanding of Jesus. For each reader who takes up his "orderly sequence" with serious intent, Luke has a single stirring aim. Literally translated, it reads, "that you may come to know a deep assurance about the teachings you have received."

Introduction to the Gospel according to John

by Michael Cameron

This Gospel has no year of its own in the Lectionary's three-year cycle, but it is strongly represented *every* year during Christmas, Lent, and Easter Time; it also appears in Ordinary Time in Mark for Year B, Sundays 17–21. John shares some features of the first three Gospels (called "synoptic" for "seeing together"). Some stories overlap, characters seen in the Synoptics reappear, and John clearly voices the evangelistic, instructional purpose of all the Gospels: that you may believe and receive life in Jesus' name (20:31).

But its vision stands majestically apart, like the eagle that became this Gospel's symbol. It is rooted in the teaching of a mysterious unnamed figure, the "disciple whom Jesus loved" (13:23; 19:26; 20:2; 21:7, 20), who authenticates this Gospel's "testimony" (19:35; 21:24). It uniquely portrays the divine Word acting with God and as God to create all things (1:1–5), taking human flesh to reveal the Father's glory (1:1, 14–18).

John communicates in distinctive ways. The Synoptics tell Jesus' story in compact vignettes; John constructs chapter-long dramas (see especially chapters 4, 9, and 11). The first three Gospels contain pithy, memorable sayings about God's Kingdom; John's Jesus speaks hypnotically repetitive discourses focused on eternal life (for example, 6:22–59; 10:1–18; chapters 14–17). The Synoptics' homespun parables pique curiosity about Jesus' message; the Johannine Jesus poetically develops elements like water (4:7–15), bread (6:25–35), and light (3:19–21; 9:4–5; 12:35–36) into metaphors for contemplating divine truth.

John tells unique stories about Jesus: He changes water into wine (2:1–11), disputes with Nicodemus (3:1–21), engages the Samaritan woman at the well (4:4–26), heals a man born blind (9:1–41), raises dead Lazarus (11:1–45), chides the doubting Thomas (20:24–29), and cooks post-Easter breakfast for the disciples (21:1–14). John also varies details from some familiar synoptic stories, among which Jesus "cleanses the Temple" early in his ministry rather than late (2:13–22); the Synoptics' Passover meal ("the Last

Supper") is a meal *before* Passover where Jesus washes the disciples' feet (13:4–15); the synoptic Jesus anguishes before death, but in John goes to the Cross with serenity (12:27; 18:11); and unlike the Synoptics, John has Jesus die on the day of preparation for Passover when the Passover lambs are sacrificed. These repeated references to Passover heighten the sacrificial symbolism of Jesus' death. Likewise, a strong liturgical symbolism makes Jesus' death the true Passover lamb sacrifice (1:29), his risen body the true Temple (2:21), and his sacramental Body and Blood the true food and drink of Israel's wilderness journey (6:53–58).

John's hallmark strategies of indirectness and double meanings entice characters to move from surface earthly meanings to encoded heavenly meanings. Some catch on, like the woman at the well (4:4–26), but others miss the point, like Nicodemus, (3:3–10), the crowds (7:32–36), and Pilate (18:33–38). This indirectness separates truly committed disciples from the half-hearted window shoppers (2:23–25). Jesus performs "signs" (not "miracles") that lure people up the new ladder of Jacob arching from earth's pictures to heaven's glory (1:51; Genesis 28:12). This imagery of signs ends in a plain revelation about Jesus' divinity not found in the Synoptic Gospels. His seven solemn "I AM" statements (6:35; 8:12; 10:7; 10:11; 11:25; 14:6; 15:1) recall God's revelation to Moses as "I AM" (Exodus 3:14) and testify to Jesus as the only source of life. So the inner truth of the blind man seeing is, "I am the light of the world" (9:5), and of the dead man rising, "I am the resurrection and the life" (11:25).

Jesus' signs hint at his divine glory (2:11) to be fully revealed at his "hour" (2:4; 7:30; 8:20; 13:1). Like the disciples, readers put things together only after the Resurrection (2:22); then we realize that as Jesus was "lifted up" for crucifixion by the Romans, he was lifted up to glory by his Father (3:14; 8:28; 12:32). He mounted his Cross like a king ascending his throne, as Pilate's placard unwittingly proclaimed (19:19–22). The Son's mission was to reunite the world to its source of eternal life in God (3:16; 4:34; 17:4). He died with satisfaction that this work was accomplished, and announced, "It is finished!" (19:30).

In the Gospel according to John, God the Father is unseen and mostly silent, but pervasively present. The Father sent the Son, loves him (5:20; 15:9), bears him witness (5:37; 8:18), glorifies him (8:54), and dwells with him (14:11). The Father grants the Son to have life in himself, to judge the world, and to raise the dead (5:19–30). Father and Son together gave life to the world at creation (1:1–2), and continue to do so (5:17). God the Son in human flesh has "explained" the Father, literally "brought God into the open" (1:18). The Son does this so completely that Jesus says, "Whoever has seen me has seen the Father" (14:9; 12:45).

But divine life emanates from a third mysterious presence, "the Spirit of truth" (14:17). The Father and the Son together send the Spirit (15:26), who teaches the disciples about what Jesus said and who he was (14:26; 16:13). By the Spirit's indwelling, divine life flows through them like a river (7:38–39; 14:17).

John depicts the disciples as fruitful vine branches that the Father lovingly tends (15:1–5). Omitting all other ethical instruction, this Gospel says that the only measure of the disciples' fruitfulness is their love for one another (13:34–35; 15:12–17).

True to character, this Gospel is sometimes one-sided. John's sense of Jesus' real humanity is relatively weak; and though teaching that "salvation is from the Jews" (4:22), it can be hostile toward Judaism (8:21–26, 37–59). John must be balanced by the rest of the New Testament and the Church's later teaching. But its profound spiritual theology of the Word made flesh (1:14) has decisively shaped Christian theology, spirituality, and art, ever since it was written in the late first century.

Introduction to St. Paul and His Letters

by Michael Cameron

Paul's Conversion

Saul of Tarsus was born about the same time as Jesus, to a pious Jewish family in Tarsus, in the Roman province of Cilicia (modern eastern Turkey). Well-educated and extremely religious, this son of Roman citizens was a member of the strict Pharisees (Philippians 3:5–6). In Christianity's earliest days, he says, "I persecuted the church of God beyond measure and even tried to destroy it" (Galatians 1:14–15). But then came the sudden turning point of his life: just outside Damascus, a brilliant flash of light blinded his eyes, buckled his legs, and altered his mind about God's design for human salvation (Acts 9:1–19). Christ's last known post-Resurrection appearance suddenly brought the Pharisee to birth as an Apostle, as "one born abnormally" (1 Corinthians 15:8).

Since Moses had said that anyone hanged on a tree was cursed by God, the crucified Christ had been a stumbling block to Saul, the Jew. But God revealed to Paul (Saul's Greek name) the awesome truth that this crucified man was God's power and wisdom (1 Corinthians 1:24). Christ's Death and Resurrection had turned the page of world history and unleashed the powers and blessings of the Age to Come. In that knowledge, Paul discounted everything that went before in his life as "rubbish" in comparison to knowing Christ, even his prized Jewish pedigree. Paul's blockbuster insight was that, for Jews and Gentiles alike, saving faith in Jesus Christ alone, not the works of Moses' Law, made one a part of God's people (Philippians 3:5–10).

Paul's Mission and Teachings

That insight released a mighty energy in Paul to announce Christ to the whole world. So began Paul's thirty-plus-year missionary ministry. He suffered beatings, imprisonments, and repeated brushes with death, but by the mid-60s of the first century, he had planted a network of vibrant Christian communities throughout the eastern Mediterranean basin. Concerned to stay in touch with his churches, to feed them with sound teaching, and to protect them from poachers, he wrote letters that eventually became part of our New Testament. Their profound theology, breathless style, and stirring imagery have kindled and rekindled Christian faith ever since.

Paul never knew the earthly Jesus, and he speaks little of stories familiar to us from the Gospels (though he knew Peter and the Apostles personally, used their traditions, and quotes Jesus' words at the first Eucharist). Paul's thinking flows almost exclusively from the reality of the Lord's Death and Resurrection—the moment when God's power decisively defeated sin and inaugurated the Age to Come.

Paul explains that event with an outpouring of vivid metaphors. His imagery of "justification" imagines a scene at the Judgment Day when Christ's Death acquits us of breaking the Law of Mount Sinai (Romans 3:21–31). His liturgical concept of "sanctification" pictures Christ giving believers the holiness needed to approach God in purity (1 Corinthians 6:11). Paul connects to economic imagery when he speaks of "redemption," portraying Christ's costly Death buying us back from slavery to sin (Romans 3:24; 1 Corinthians 6:20). His political-military picture envisions humanity's ancient and chronic warfare with God brought to an end in "reconciliation" (Romans 5:10–11). He evokes the family with his "adoption" image, conveying our change of status when Christ made us over from slaves to children of God (Romans 8:14–15; Galatians 4:4–7).

Christians behave not according to external laws, Paul teaches, but by the force of the Holy Spirit, who produces in believers the many fruits of the new life (Galatians 5:22–23), the greatest of which is love (1 Corinthians 13:13). The same love of God displayed in Christ's Death pours forth into our hearts through the Holy Spirit (Romans 5:5–8). The Spirit remakes us in the image of Christ: "all of us, gazing with unveiled face on the glory of the Lord, are being transformed into the same image from glory to glory, as from the Lord who is the Spirit" (2 Corinthians 3:18).

Christ somehow joined us to himself at his Cross so that when he died, we died (2 Corinthians 5:14). Christians "baptized into Christ's death" die to their old selves and rise to newness of life (Romans 6:3–4). In this new humanity, which leaves behind old identities, the oneness of Christ knows "neither Jew nor Greek, slave nor free, male nor female" (Galatians 3:28). All drink of the same Spirit who makes them the mystical "Body of Christ" (1 Corinthians 12:12–27), the Church, whose members offer worship to God while humbly serving one another. In Christ we are "the new creation: the old things have passed away; behold, the new things have come" (2 Corinthians 5:17).

But the new life emerging in Christians conflicts with the world as it is. Paul leaves social change to God while urging Christians to live patiently within the structures of society as they stand until the new age takes over. So slaves do not seek freedom, the unmarried do not seek marriage, and Gentiles do not seek circumcision, because "the world in its present form is passing away" (1 Corinthians 7:17–31).

For the time being we see God, the world, and ourselves in a blur, but one day we will understand everything (1 Corinthians 13:12). Bodily death is pure gain: we depart to "be with Christ" (Philippians 1:23)—Paul does not say more—and await the resurrection of the body, when Christ "will change our lowly body to conform with his glorious body" (Philippians 3:21). We will be radically different, but somehow still ourselves, just as wheat stalks are both different from, and the same as, the tiny seeds they come from (1 Corinthians 15:36–49). When that moment comes, Christ's work will be done, and God will be "all in all" (1 Corinthians 15:28).

But for Paul and his readers, including us, the present remains the time for work. With the hope of the Resurrection constantly drawing us on, Paul says, we must "be firm, steadfast, always fully devoted to the work of the Lord, knowing that in the Lord your labor is not in vain" (1 Corinthians 15:58).

Studying and Praying Scripture

by Michael Cameron

A recent study claimed that only 22 percent of American Catholics read the Bible regularly, and just 8 percent are involved in Scripture groups. Not many know how profoundly biblical the Roman Catholic Church has been from her very roots, having "always venerated the divine scriptures as she venerates the Body of the Lord" (*Dei Verbum* [*Dogmatic Constitution on Divine Revelation*], 21). How may Catholics learn to read Scripture? This essay sketches a path for seekers.

PREPARING TO READ

Become an apprentice to the Bible. Ordinary people can reach a good level of understanding, but at a cost: the Bible yields its riches to those who give themselves to the search for understanding. Start by reading daily, even if only for a few minutes. Join a group that reads and discusses Scripture together.

You will need tools. Think of yourself as a prospector for the Bible's gold. Nuggets on the ground are easily picked up, but the really rich veins lie beneath the surface. Digging requires study, commitment, and skills.

Invest in tools that reap the harvest of others' labors. Buy a study Bible with introductions, explanatory notes, and maps. Use another translation for devotional reading and comparison. Get access to a Bible dictionary with detailed information on biblical books, concepts, geography, outlines, customs, and so forth. Bible concordances will help you find all occurrences of particular words. A dictionary of biblical theology will give guidance on major theological ideas. A Bible atlas will give a sense of the locations and movements in the biblical stories. Recent Church documents on the Bible offer rich instruction to seekers.

READING FOR KNOWLEDGE

Get to know historical contexts suggested by a passage. Learn all you can about the Bible's basic story line, its "salvation history," beginning with Israel and continuing in the Church. Salvation by God's grace, obedience to God's will, and judgment on sin are basic to both Old and New Testaments. Learn about the covenants with Abraham and David that emphasize God's grace. The covenant with Moses presumes God's grace and emphasizes obedience. Both covenant traditions reemerge and are fulfilled in the New Covenant in Jesus, who pours out his life to save all people (grace) but is extremely demanding of his disciples (obedience).

Read entire books of the Bible in order to gain a sense of the "whole cloth" from which the snippets of the Sunday Lectionary are cut. Try to imagine what the books meant for their original authors and audiences. Ask how and why a book was put together: What is its structure, outline, main themes, literary forms, overall purpose?

Get to know the Old Testament narratives and psalms, but learn the Gospel accounts especially. The Lectionary's yearly focus on Matthew, Mark, or Luke offers an opportunity to learn each one. John is the focus during the Church's special seasons.

READING FOR WISDOM

Read as one who seeks God, like the writer of Psalm 119. Ask what the text is asking you to believe, do, or hope for. Jesus' powerful proclamation in Mark 1:15 gives a strong framework: "This is the time of fulfillment" (now is the time to be attentive and ready to act); "the kingdom of God is at hand" (God is about to speak and act); "repent" (be willing to change your mind and move with fresh direction); "believe in the gospel" (embrace the grace that has already embraced you).

Read books straight through, a self-contained section at a time, carefully, slowly, and meditatively. Stop where natural breaks occur at the end of stories or sequences of thought.

Beware the sense that you already know what a text is going to say. Read attentively, asking what God is teaching you through this text at this minute about your life or about your communities—family, church, work, neighborhood, nation. Trust the Holy Spirit to guide you to what you need.

READING FOR WORSHIP

The goal of reading the Bible is not learning new facts or getting merely private inspiration for living, but entering into deeper communion with God. Allow the Bible to teach you to pray by giving you the words to use in prayer. The psalms are especially apt for this, but any part of the Bible may be prayed. This practice, dating back more than fifteen hundred years, is called *lectio divina*, Latin for "sacred reading."

Read Scripture in relation to the Eucharist. The Bible both prepares for Jesus' real presence and helps us understand it. The same Jesus who healed the lepers, stilled the storm, and embraced the children is present to us in the Word and in the Sacrament.

The Bible is a library of spiritual treasures waiting to be discovered. The Church intends that this treasury be "wide open to the Christian faithful" (*Dei Verbum* [*Dogmatic Constitution on Divine Revelation*], 22).

RESOURCES

Brown, Raymond E., ss. *101 Questions and Answers on the Bible.* Mahwah, NJ: Paulist Press, 2003.

Casey, Michael. *Sacred Reading: The Ancient Art of Lectio Divina.* Liguori, MS: Liguori, 1997.

Frigge, Marielle, OSB. *Beginning Biblical Studies.* Winona, MN: Anselm Academic, 2013.

Hahn, Scott. *Catholic Bible Dictionary.* New York: Doubleday, 2009.

Magrassi, Mariano. *Praying the Bible.* Collegeville, MN: Liturgical Press, 1998.

New Collegeville Bible Commentary Series. Collegeville, MN: Liturgical Press. (Short books on individual books of the Bible, various dates.)

Paprocki, Joe. *The Bible Blueprint, A Catholic's Guide to Understanding and Embracing God's Word.* Chicago: Loyola Press, 2009.

The Bible Documents: A Parish Resource. Chicago: Liturgy Training Publications, 2001.

The Catholic Study Bible, 3rd Edition. General editor, Donald Senior, CP. New York: Oxford, 2016.

Advent

Prayer before Reading the Word

In this and every year,
in this and every place,
O God everlasting,
your Word resounds in the wilderness of Advent,
calling us to stand upon the height
and to behold the splendor of your beauty.

Fill in the valleys of our neglect;
bring low our mountains of self-centeredness.
Prepare in our hearts
your way of righteousness and peace.
Let our love become a harvest of goodness,
which you will bring to completion
for the day of Christ Jesus,
who was, who is, and who is to come,
your Son who lives and reigns with you
in the unity of the Holy Spirit,
one God, for ever and ever. Amen.

Prayer after Reading the Word

God of holiness,
whose promises stand through all generations,
fulfill the longings of a humanity
weighed down by confusion and burdened
            with fear.

Raise up our heads and strengthen our hearts,
that we may proclaim to all people
the Good News of your presence in our midst.
May we delight to share with them
your peace, which surpasses all understanding.

We ask this through our Lord Jesus Christ,
            your Son,
who lives and reigns with you
in the unity of the Holy Spirit,
one God, for ever and ever. Amen.

Weekday Readings

December 3: *Isaiah 2:1–5; Matthew 8:5–11*

December 4: *Isaiah 11:1–10; Luke 10:21–24*

December 5: *Isaiah 25:6–10a; Matthew 15:29–37*

December 6: *Isaiah 26:1–6; Matthew 7:21, 24–27*

December 7: *Isaiah 29:17–24; Matthew 9:27–31*

December 8: Solemnity of the Immaculate Conception of the Blessed Virgin Mary
Genesis 3:9–15, 20; Ephesians 1:3–6, 11–12; Luke 1:26–38

December 10: *Isaiah 35:1–10; Luke 5:17–26*

December 11: *Isaiah 40:1–111; Matthew 18:12–14*

December 12: Feast of Our Lady of Guadalupe
Zechariah 2:14–17; Luke 1:26–38

December 13: *Isaiah 41:13–20; Matthew 11:11–15*

December 14: *Isaiah 48:17–19; Matthew 11:16–19*

December 15: *Sirach 48:1–4, 9–11; Matthew 17:9a, 10–13*

December 17: *Genesis 49:2, 8–10; Matthew 1:1–17*

December 18: *Jeremiah 23:5–8; Matthew 1:18–25*

December 19: *Judges 13:2–7, 24–25a; Luke 1:5–25*

December 20: *Isaiah 7:10–14; Luke 1:26–38*

December 21: *Song of Songs 2:8–14 or Zephaniah 3:14–18a; Luke 1:39–45*

December 22: *1 Samuel 1:24–28; Luke 1:46–56*

December 24: *Morning: 2 Samuel 7:1–5, 8b–12, 14a, 16; Luke 1:67–79*

December 2, 2018 FIRST SUNDAY OF ADVENT

READING I *Jeremiah 33:14–16*

The days are coming, says the LORD, when I will fulfill the promise I made to the house of Israel and Judah. In those days, in that time, I will raise up for David a just shoot; he shall do what is right and just in the land. In those days Judah shall be safe and Jerusalem shall dwell secure; this is what they shall call her: "The LORD our justice."

RESPONSORIAL PSALM
Psalm 25:4–5, 8–9, 10, 14 (1b)

R. To you, O Lord, I lift my soul.

Your ways, O LORD, make known to me;
   teach me your paths,
guide me in your truth and teach me,
   for you are God my savior,
   and for you I wait all the day. R.

Good and upright is the LORD;
   thus he shows sinners the way.
He guides the humble to justice,
   and teaches the humble his way. R.

All the paths of the LORD are kindness
     and constancy
   toward those who keep his covenant and
     his decrees.
The friendship of the LORD is with those who
     fear him,
   and his covenant, for their instruction. R.

READING II *1 Thessalonians 3:12—4:2*

Brothers and sisters: May the Lord make you increase and abound in love for one another and for all, just as we have for you, so as to strengthen your hearts, to be blameless in holiness before our God and Father at the coming of our Lord Jesus with all his holy ones. Amen.

Finally, brothers and sisters, we earnestly ask and exhort you in the Lord Jesus that, as you received from us how you should conduct yourselves to please God—and as you are conducting yourselves —you do so even more. For you know what instructions we gave you through the Lord Jesus.

GOSPEL *Luke 21:25–28, 34–36*

Jesus said to his disciples: "There will be signs in the sun, the moon, and the stars, and on earth nations will be in dismay, perplexed by the roaring of the sea and the waves. People will die of fright in anticipation of what is coming upon the world, for the powers of the heavens will be shaken. And then they will see the Son of Man coming in a cloud with power and great glory. But when these signs begin to happen, stand erect and raise your heads because your redemption is at hand.

"Beware that your hearts do not become drowsy from carousing and drunkenness and the anxieties of daily life, and that day catch you by surprise like a trap. For that day will assault everyone who lives on the face of the earth. Be vigilant at all times and pray that you have the strength to escape the tribulations that are imminent and to stand before the Son of Man."

Practice of Hope

New beginnings invite us to look to the future and call us to a renewed attentiveness to the present moment. As we begin the liturgical year, we are reminded that it is here and now that we find signs of hope for a time of fulfillment and promised redemption that is not yet fully known. In this season of anticipation, we make ready to receive the Lord when he appears. ◆ Be attentive to the news today and look for signs of hope even in the most troubling events. Pray that those who are most affected by these events may find strength and hope. ◆ Investigate the legislative advocacy work of your state Catholic Conference (a directory of websites can be found at http://www.nasccd.org/directory/index.html). Identify a current focus issue and take the recommended action. ◆ Pray the Lord's Prayer with extra care. Consider especially the significance of the words: "thy kingdom come, thy will be done on earth as it is heaven."

Download more questions and activities for families, Christian initiation groups, and other adult groups at http://www.ltp.org/ahw.

Scripture Insights

On this First Sunday of Advent, the reading from Jeremiah provides a prophecy of restoration and healing for Judah and the promise of a salvific king from the line of David. This prophecy also notes that Jerusalem will be called by a new name, "the LORD our Justice." The Hebrew *yhwy tzidqenu* is a play on the name *tzidqi-yahu* or Zedekiah, a "puppet" king of Judah who, against the warnings of Jeremiah, revolted against the Babylonians and brought about the destruction of Jerusalem in 587/6 BC. Zedekiah is remembered as the last king of the Davidic line.

For Christians, Zedekiah is not the last king of Judah. In today's Gospel, we hear of the glorious Son of Man, the Risen Christ, whose return will be announced with cosmological signs and who will come in power so great that it will shake the heavens. Those who wait for him need not cower in fear. Instead, they should stand tall because it is the dawn of redemption for those who practice faithful endurance. Yes, the faithful will suffer difficulties, but soon they will experience the justice, mercy, and compassion of God in the presence of the Son of Man.

In the Second Reading, Paul echoes these thoughts about the coming Son of Man and adds an admonition for how we should live in the meantime. Perhaps not surprisingly, he says love is the rule. We are called to grow in love for everyone and thereby have the ability to stand blameless before God when Christ returns.

◆ What does the metaphor of a shoot being raised up from David suggest to you about God's promised king? (First Reading)

◆ How can love strengthen the heart for the coming of Christ? (Second Reading)

◆ How can you remain vigilant for the coming of the Lord? (Gospel)

READING I *Baruch 5:1–9*

Jerusalem, take off your robe of mourning
   and misery;
 put on the splendor of glory from
   God forever:
wrapped in the cloak of justice from God,
 bear on your head the mitre
 that displays the glory of the eternal name.
For God will show all the earth your splendor:
 you will be named by God forever
 the peace of justice, the glory
  of God's worship.

Up, Jerusalem! stand upon the heights;
 look to the east and see your children
gathered from the east and the west
 at the word of the Holy One,
 rejoicing that they are remembered by God.
Led away on foot by their enemies they left you:
 but God will bring them back to you
 borne aloft in glory as on royal thrones.
For God has commanded
 that every lofty mountain be made low,
and that the age-old depths and gorges
 be filled to level ground,
 that Israel may advance secure in the glory
  of God.
The forests and every fragrant kind of tree
 have overshadowed Israel at God's
  command;
for God is leading Israel in joy
 by the light of his glory,
 with his mercy and justice for company.

RESPONSORIAL PSALM
Psalm 126:1–2, 2–3, 4–5, 6 (3)

R. The Lord has done great things for us; we are
  filled with joy.

When the LORD brought back the captives of Zion,
 we were like men dreaming.
Then our mouth was filled with laughter,
 and our tongue with rejoicing. R.

Then they said among the nations,
 "The LORD has done great things for them."

The LORD has done great things for us;
 we are glad indeed. R.

Restore our fortunes, O LORD,
 like the torrents in the southern desert.
Those who sow in tears
 shall reap rejoicing. R.

Although they go forth weeping,
 carrying the seed to be sown,
they shall come back rejoicing,
 carrying their sheaves. R.

READING II *Philippians 1:4–6, 8–11*

Brothers and sisters: I pray always with joy in my every prayer for all of you, because of your partnership for the gospel from the first day until now. I am confident of this, that the one who began a good work in you will continue to complete it until the day of Christ Jesus. God is my witness, how I long for all of you with the affection of Christ Jesus. And this is my prayer: that your love may increase ever more and more in knowledge and every kind of perception, to discern what is of value, so that you may be pure and blameless for the day of Christ, filled with the fruit of righteousness that comes through Jesus Christ for the glory and praise of God.

GOSPEL *Luke 3:1–6*

In the fifteenth year of the reign of Tiberius Caesar, when Pontius Pilate was governor of Judea, and Herod was tetrarch of Galilee, and his brother Philip tetrarch of the region of Ituraea and Trachonitis, and Lysanias was tetrarch of Abilene, during the high priesthood of Annas and Caiaphas, the word of God came to John the son of Zechariah in the desert. John went throughout the whole region of the Jordan, proclaiming a baptism of repentance for the forgiveness of sins, as it is written in the book of the words of the prophet Isaiah: / *A voice of one crying out in the desert: / "Prepare the way of the Lord, / make straight his paths. / Every valley shall be filled / and every mountain and hill shall be made low. / The winding roads shall be made straight, / and the rough ways made smooth, / and all flesh shall see the salvation of God."*

Practice of Faith

In today's Psalm response, we rejoice in all the good things God has done for us. Among those good things is the grace we receive in the Sacrament of Baptism that allows us to share in God's divine life and to act out of God's love. When we fail to allow God to work in us for the good, we seek forgiveness in the Sacrament of Penance and are restored to grace. ◆ Celebrate the Sacrament of Penance during Advent, at a parish communal Penance service or at individual confession. ◆ In the Angelus on December 6, 2015, Pope Francis asked his audience to question whether they feel as Christ does and accept apologies without retribution. Reflecting on today's Gospel, he asks them to consider whether they have opened their hearts to receive the salvation God offers. Consider reading the pope's reflection as your examination of conscience: w2.vatican.va/content /francesco/en/angelus/2015/documents/papa -francesco_angelus _20151206.html. ◆ Set aside time for journaling and quiet prayer, making a list of the great things the Lord is doing for you. Rejoice in the Lord's goodness.

Download more questions and activities for families, Christian initiation groups, and other adult groups at http://www.ltp.org/ahw.

Scripture Insights

In today's First Reading, the author of Baruch addresses personified Jerusalem, who is grieving over her people in exile in Babylon. He attempts to console her, telling her to take off her mourning garments and wrap herself in the robe of God's justice. The crown of God's glory that she receives is probably Aaron's priestly crown with its engraving, "Sacred to the LORD" (Exodus 28:37). In addition, she will receive a new name, "the peace of justice, the glory of God's worship." In other words, Jerusalem will become the priest of God's temple, and she will rejoice as her people come back to her in pilgrimage. What an amazing image of God's care and protection!

The Gospel describes a scene in which John the Baptist is called by God in the wilderness and responds by proclaiming a "baptism of repentance for the forgiveness of sins." This is not the Baptism that those becoming Christian seek. Rather, John is calling the people to commit themselves to an immersive experience of repentance. Yet God is a gracious God, and the reward will be great for those who accept the challenge. Quoting Isaiah, John says that the valleys will be filled and the mountains made low to make straight the way so all may know God's salvation.

The Second Reading echoes many of the same themes, especially joy at the recognition of God's care and protection and the call to be pure and blameless when at last we stand before God when Christ returns in glory.

◆ How does the author of the First Reading show God extending consolation?

◆ When you have needed consolation, how were paths made straight and valleys filled so that you could feel whole again?

◆ Following the pattern of today's Responsorial Psalm, write a personal prayer of lament-turned-to-trust.

December 16, 2018 THIRD SUNDAY OF ADVENT

READING I *Zephaniah 3:14–18a*

Shout for joy, O daughter Zion!
　　Sing joyfully, O Israel!
Be glad and exult with all your heart,
　　O daughter Jerusalem!
The LORD has removed the judgment
　　　　against you,
　　he has turned away your enemies;
the King of Israel, the LORD, is in your midst,
　　you have no further misfortune to fear.
On that day, it shall be said to Jerusalem:
　　Fear not, O Zion, be not discouraged!
The LORD, your God, is in your midst,
　　a mighty savior;
he will rejoice over you with gladness,
　　and renew you in his love,
he will sing joyfully because of you,
　　as one sings at festivals.

RESPONSORIAL PSALM
Isaiah 12:2–3, 4, 5–6 (6)

R. Cry out with joy and gladness:
　　for among you is the great and Holy One
　　　　of Israel.

God indeed is my savior;
　　I am confident and unafraid.
My strength and my courage is the LORD,
　　and he has been my savior.
With joy you will draw water
　　at the fountain of salvation. R.

Give thanks to the LORD, acclaim his name;
　　among the nations make known his deeds,
　　proclaim how exalted is his name. R.

Sing praise to the LORD for his
　　　　glorious achievement;
　　let this be known throughout all the earth.
Shout with exultation, O city of Zion,
　　for great in your midst
　　is the Holy One of Israel! R.

READING II *Philippians 4:4–7*

Brothers and sisters: Rejoice in the Lord always. I shall say it again: rejoice! Your kindness should be known to all. The Lord is near. Have no anxiety at all, but in everything, by prayer and petition, with thanksgiving, make your requests known to God. Then the peace of God that surpasses all understanding will guard your hearts and minds in Christ Jesus.

GOSPEL *Luke 3:10–18*

The crowds asked John the Baptist, "What should we do?" He said to them in reply, "Whoever has two cloaks should share with the person who has none. And whoever has food should do likewise." Even tax collectors came to be baptized and they said to him, "Teacher, what should we do?" He answered them, "Stop collecting more than what is prescribed." Soldiers also asked him, "And what is it that we should do?" He told them, "Do not practice extortion, do not falsely accuse anyone, and be satisfied with your wages."

　　Now the people were filled with expectation, and all were asking in their hearts whether John might be the Christ. John answered them all, saying, "I am baptizing you with water, but one mightier than I is coming. I am not worthy to loosen the thongs of his sandals. He will baptize you with the Holy Spirit and fire. His winnowing fan is in his hand to clear his threshing floor and to gather the wheat into his barn, but the chaff he will burn with unquenchable fire." Exhorting them in many other ways, he preached good news to the people.

Practice of Charity

"What should we do?" To each who asked this question, crowds, tax collectors, and soldiers, John gives a specific response. Each person is called to a conversion of heart expressed in the circumstances of their lives. As we open our hearts to the Lord's presence among us, the fruit of conversion is shown through our lives of joyful service. ◆ Show that you are ready to welcome the Lord into your midst by beginning each day with a prayerful commitment to serve the Lord with joy in all you do. ◆ Reflect on the example of St. Thérèse of Lisieux (see http://www.saint-therese.org/about-therese/) who served her heart's desire to be a missionary by offering her prayers from the cloister and, in so doing, became a patron saint of missionaries. ◆ Focus your prayer this week on the Psalm response: "Among you is the great and Holy One of Israel." Praying Scripture phrases or short prayers often throughout the day reminds us that God is always near.

Download more questions and activities for families, Christian initiation groups, and other adult groups at http://www.ltp.org/ahw.

Scripture Insights

Good news! Let us rejoice in anticipation! This theme is evident in today's readings. In the First Reading, we hear that on that final day when God's justice is fully manifest, he will take away Jerusalem's shame and give her cause for great rejoicing. "Daughter Zion" is a personification of the ideal city of Jerusalem where God, the king of Israel, can dwell as its savior and lover. Today's Responsorial Psalm closely parallels this notion of the exultant "Daughter Jerusalem," even though the phrase is not used.

Likewise, in the Second Reading, Paul exhorts his readers to rejoice in the nearness of the Lord and not to be anxious, but always to act with kindness (Greek *epieikés*, meaning "mildness, forbearance, fairness, moderation"). Then, when they make their requests known to God, they will experience the fullness of God's peace.

Today's Gospel describes a scene in which John the Baptist preaches repentance in anticipation of the coming messiah. When John tells the crowds that they must live righteously, they are so enamored of his words that they think he is the long-awaited messiah. He lays that idea to rest, saying, "one mightier than I is coming. . . . He will baptize you with the Holy Spirit and fire." The Greek *baptizo* means "to dip or submerge, as in a ritual." With that, John continues to preach the "good news" to the people. One may wonder how the crowds could consider a baptism "with the holy Spirit and fire" to be good news?

◆ What does the First Reading tell us about the nature of God and God's relationship toward the chosen ones?

◆ As you reflect on the Second Reading, consider how acting with kindness and offering gratitude to God in prayer has brought you a sense of God's peace.

◆ What does it mean to you to be baptized "with the Holy Spirit and fire"?

READING I *Micah 5:1–4a*

Thus says the LORD:
You, Bethlehem-Ephrathah,
    too small to be among the clans of Judah,
from you shall come forth for me
    one who is to be ruler in Israel;
whose origin is from of old,
    from ancient times.
Therefore the Lord will give them up,
       until the time
    when she who is to give birth has borne,
and the rest of his kindred shall return
    to the children of Israel.
He shall stand firm and shepherd his flock
    by the strength of the LORD,
    in the majestic name of the LORD, his God;
and they shall remain, for now his greatness
    shall reach to the ends of the earth;
    he shall be peace.

RESPONSORIAL PSALM
Psalm 80:2–3, 15–16, 18–19 (4)

R. Lord, make us turn to you; let us see your face
    and we shall be saved.

O shepherd of Israel, hearken,
    from your throne upon the cherubim,
        shine forth.
Rouse your power,
    and come to save us. R.

Once again, O LORD of hosts,
    look down from heaven, and see;
take care of this vine,
    and protect what your right hand has planted,
    the son of man whom you yourself
        made strong. R.

May your help be with the man of your
        right hand,
    with the son of man whom you yourself
        made strong.
Then we will no more withdraw from you;
    give us new life, and we will call upon
        your name. R.

READING II *Hebrews 10:5–10*

Brothers and sisters:
When Christ came into the world, he said:
  "Sacrifice and offering you did not desire,
    but a body you prepared for me;
  in holocausts and sin offerings you took
        no delight.
Then I said, 'As is written of me in the scroll,
behold, I come to do your will, O God.'"

First he says, "Sacrifices and offerings, holocausts and sin offerings, you neither desired nor delighted in." These are offered according to the law. Then he says, "Behold, I come to do your will." He takes away the first to establish the second. By this "will," we have been consecrated through the offering of the body of Jesus Christ once for all.

GOSPEL *Luke 1:39–45*

Mary set out and traveled to the hill country in haste to a town of Judah, where she entered the house of Zechariah and greeted Elizabeth. When Elizabeth heard Mary's greeting, the infant leaped in her womb, and Elizabeth, filled with the Holy Spirit, cried out in a loud voice and said, "Blessed are you among women, and blessed is the fruit of your womb. And how does this happen to me, that the mother of my Lord should come to me? For at the moment the sound of your greeting reached my ears, the infant in my womb leaped for joy. Blessed are you who believed that what was spoken to you by the Lord would be fulfilled."

Practice of Faith

In today's Gospel, we find inspiration in the encounter between two women of faith as they recognize God's faithfulness to them and respond by trusting in God's will. Like the Blessed Virgin Mary and St. Elizabeth, we try to be open to the Word that God speaks to us. ◆ Where in your life are you being challenged to follow God's will? Ask for the grace to respond to this challenge with trust in God's faithfulness. ◆ The gift of faith leads us to seek out God's will when facing decisions. Seek to do that through the practice of prayerful discernment as taught by St. Ignatius of Loyola: www.ignatianspirituality.com/making-good-decisions/discernment-of-spirits. ◆ Who helps you to know God's will in your life? Spend some time in prayerful reflection of the Visitation, using an image from the encounter of Mary and Elizabeth. Perhaps an image can be found in your Bible or you can find one online, for example, this painting by a seventeenth-century artist, Philippe de Champaigne: www.bing.com/images/search?q=The+Visitation+by+Philippe+De+Champaigne&FORM=IDINTS.

Download more questions and activities for families, Christian initiation groups, and other adult groups at http://www.ltp.org/ahw.

Scripture Insights

Today's Scripture readings are filled with joyful expectation in the face of incredible odds. In the First Reading, the prophet issues an oracle of hope to a people whom he had been railing against for their failure to act justly. Though they must pay the price for their sins now, in God's time, a messiah-king will be raised up from among the least of them. This messiah-king will act in peace and *be peace*! Bethlehem was David's hometown. Hence, the messiah-king will be of the lineage of David. The woman of whom he speaks is the mother of this long-awaited messiah-king, but she remains nameless.

In the Gospel, we are privileged to imagine the tender and private encounter of two seemingly insignificant women. Both would have been the target of much gossip—one because she was pregnant before her marriage was finalized and the other because she had been denied children for all the years of her marriage. The former would become the mother of the messiah-king and the latter the mother of John the Baptist, whom God chose to announce the long-awaited reign of God.

As today's Second Reading reminds us, however, salvation and God's reign of peace come at a cost. The author of this reading imagines the incarnate Christ praying from Psalm 40 and committing himself to do God's will, even to the point of replacing the sin offerings of the temple with his body, which will be sacrificed on the cross. Thus, we are consecrated to God once and for all time.

◆ What attributes does Micah provide that would describe God's ideal king?

◆ Today's Responsorial Psalm uses two images to reflect on God's relationship to humanity—the shepherd and the vineyard owner. What images would you use?

◆ What would you like to learn from Mary and Elizabeth?

Christmas Time

Prayer before Reading the Word

By the light of a star, O God of the universe,
you guided the nations to the Light of the world.

Until this Redeemer comes again in glory,
we, with the Magi, seek the face of the Savior.
Summon us with all those who thirst now
to the banquet of love.
May our hunger be filled and our thirst
           be quenched
with your Word of truth.

We ask this through our Lord Jesus Christ,
           your Son,
who lives and reigns with you
in the unity of the Holy Spirit,
one God, for ever and ever. Amen.

Prayer after Reading the Word

In the beginning, O God, was your Word,
and now in time your Word becomes flesh.
The Light that shines unconquered
through the darkness of the ages,
and has made his dwelling place among us,
transforming earth's gloom into heaven's glory.

As we behold upon the mountains
the messenger who announces your peace,
touch our lips as well that we may lift up
           our voices
as bearers of Good News and heralds
           of salvation.

We ask this through our Lord Jesus Christ,
Emmanuel, God-with-us,
your Son, who lives and reigns with you
in the unity of the Holy Spirit,
God, for ever and ever. Amen.

Weekday Readings

December 25: Solemnity of the Nativity of the Lord
   Day: Isaiah 52:7–10; Hebrews 1:1–6; John 1:1–18
December 26: Feast of St. Stephen
   Acts 6:8–10; 7:54–59; Matthew 10:17–22
December 27: Feast of St. John, Apostle and Evangelist
   1 John 1:1–4; John 20:1a, 2–8
December 28: Feast of the Holy Innocents
   1 John 1:5—2:2; Matthew 2:13–18
December 29: Fifth Day within the Octave
   of the Nativity of the Lord
   1 John 2:3–11; Luke 2:22–35

December 31: Seventh Day within the Octave of the
   Nativity of the Lord
   1 John 2:18–21; John 1:1–18
January 1: Solemnity of Mary, the Holy Mother of God
   Numbers 6:22–27; Galatians 4:4–7; Luke 2:16–21
January 2: *1 John 2:22–28; John 1:19–28*
January 3: *1 John 2:29—3:6; John 1:29–34*
January 4: *1 John 3:7–10; John 1:35–42*
January 5: *1 John 3:11-21; John 1:43–51*
January 7: *1 John 3:22—4:6; Matthew 4:12–17, 23–25*

January 8: *1 John 4:7–10; Mark 6:34–44*
January 9: *1 John 4:11–18; Mark 6:45–52*
January 10: *1 John 4:19—5:4; Luke 4:14–22a*
January 11: *1 John 5:5–13; Luke 5:12–16*
January 12: *1 John 5:14–21; John 3:22–30*

READING I *Isaiah 52:7–10*

How beautiful upon the mountains
    are the feet of him who brings glad tidings,
announcing peace, bearing good news,
    announcing salvation, and saying to Zion,
    "Your God is King!"

Hark! Your sentinels raise a cry,
    together they shout for joy,
for they see directly, before their eyes,
    the LORD restoring Zion.
Break out together in song,
    O ruins of Jerusalem!
For the LORD comforts his people,
    he redeems Jerusalem.
The LORD has bared his holy arm
    in the sight of all the nations;
all the ends of the earth will behold
    the salvation of our God.

RESPONSORIAL PSALM
Psalm 98:1, 2–3, 3–4, 5–6 (3c)

R. All the ends of the earth have seen the saving
    power of God.

Sing to the LORD a new song,
    for he has done wondrous deeds;
his right hand has won victory for him,
    his holy arm. R.

The LORD has made his salvation known:
    in the sight of the nations he has revealed
        his justice.
He has remembered his kindness and
        his faithfulness
    toward the house of Israel. R.

All the ends of the earth have seen
    the salvation by our God.
Sing joyfully to the LORD, all you lands;
    break into song; sing praise. R.

Sing praise to the Lord with the harp,
    with the harp and melodious song.
With trumpets and the sound of the horn
    sing joyfully before the King, the LORD. R.

READING II *Hebrews 1:1–6*

Brothers and sisters:

In times past, God spoke in partial and various ways to our ancestors through the prophets; in these last days, he has spoken to us through the Son, whom he made heir of all things and through whom he created the universe, / who is the refulgence of his glory, the very imprint of his being, / and who sustains all things by his mighty word. / When he had accomplished purification from sins, / he took his seat at the right hand of the Majesty on high, / as far superior to the angels / as the name he has inherited is more excellent than theirs.

For to which of the angels did God ever say:
    You are my son; this day I have begotten you?
Or again:
    I will be a father to him, and he shall be a son
        to me?
And again, when he leads the firstborn into the world, he says:
    Let all the angels of God worship him.

GOSPEL *John 1:1–18*

Shorter: John 1:1–5, 9–14

In the beginning was the Word, / and the Word was with God, / and the Word was God. / He was in the beginning with God. / All things came to be through him, / and without him nothing came to be. / What came to be through him was life, / and this life was the light of the human race; / the light shines in the darkness, / and the darkness has not overcome it. / A man named John was sent from God. He came for testimony, to testify to the light, so that all might believe through him. He was not the light, but came to testify to the light. The true light, which enlightens everyone, was coming into the world. / He was in the world, / and the world came to be through him, / but the world did not know him. / He came to what was his own, / but his own people did not accept him.

    But to those who did accept him he gave power to become children of God, to those who believe in his name, who were born not by natural generation nor by human choice nor by a man's decision but of God. / And the Word became flesh / and made his dwelling among us, / and we saw his glory, / the glory as of the Father's only Son, / full of grace and truth. / John testified to him and cried out, saying, "This was he of whom I said, 'The one who is coming after me ranks ahead of me because he existed before me.'" From his fullness we have all received, grace in place of grace, because while the law was given through Moses, grace and truth came through Jesus Christ. No one has ever seen God. The only Son, God, who is at the Father's side, has revealed him.

Practice of Hope

On this day, we ponder and celebrate the mystery of God's great love. The glory of God is revealed in his Son, who took on flesh so that we might become children of God. Our churches are bright with the lights of Christmas as we worship God, who brings light to our darkness and saves us. ◆ Notice the brightness of the lights decorating your church, your neighborhood and your home. Take steps to ensure that these lights continue to shine brightly throughout the Christmas season as a sign of God's glory and our salvation. ◆ Read the pope's Urbi et Orbi message for Christmas on the Vatican website: http://w2.vatican.va/content /vatican/en.html. ◆ Light a candle near the crèche in your home as you pray with a Christmas carol, such as "O Little Town of Bethlehem" or "It Came Upon a Midnight Clear." Ask God to show you where the light of his glory is shining in your life.

Download more questions and activities for families, Christian initiation groups, and other adult groups at http://www.ltp.org/ahw.

Scripture Insights

Today we celebrate in joy the incarnate Word of God. The First Reading provides a backdrop in three parts: (1) a voice that announces a messenger coming over the mountains, bringing the Good News of God's enthronement as king of Zion/ Jerusalem; (2) the guards responsible for watching over the ruins of Jerusalem see God returning to Jerusalem with the people who had been exiled many years before; and (3) a song of thanksgiving, which celebrates the way God has redeemed Jerusalem's inhabitants. In summation, this reading is a reversal of the story of the Babylonian exile.

Today's Gospel reading is the prologue of the fourth Gospel, in which Jesus is portrayed as the Word that comes forth from God's mouth, revealing God to the world. This Word was with God in the beginning, and creation came into being through him. Yet when he came into the world among his own, his own rejected him. Pay attention to the central part of this poem, in which God declares those who accept the Word and believe in him to be children of God by God's will alone. This Word came to dwell (literally, "pitched his tent") among us, and we—the believers—have seen his glory as the Father's only Son.

Likewise, the Second Reading from the Letter to the Hebrews depicts the Son as the climax and fullness of God's revelatory words to the world. Some of the descriptors, such as "refulgence of [God's] glory" and "imprint of his being" are reminiscent of personified Wisdom in Wisdom 7:26. The phrase "accomplished purification from sins" refers to Jesus' Crucifixion.

◆ Compare the Second Reading and the Gospel. Find the similarities and differences in their descriptions of the Son. What surprises you about what you found?

◆ As you reflect on the First Reading, imagine yourself joining the procession into Jerusalem led by God the king. What are your impressions?

◆ How have you experienced the Word having "pitched his tent" among us?

READING I *1 Samuel 1:20–22, 24–28*

Alternate reading: Sirach 3:2–6, 12–14

In those days Hannah conceived, and at the end of her term bore a son whom she called Samuel, since she had asked the LORD for him. The next time her husband Elkanah was going up with the rest of his household to offer the customary sacrifice to the LORD and to fulfill his vows, Hannah did not go, explaining to her husband, "Once the child is weaned, I will take him to appear before the LORD and to remain there forever; I will offer him as a perpetual nazirite."

Once Samuel was weaned, Hannah brought him up with her, along with a three-year-old bull, an ephah of flour, and a skin of wine, and presented him at the temple of the LORD in Shiloh. After the boy's father had sacrificed the young bull, Hannah, his mother, approached Eli and said: "Pardon, my lord! As you live, my lord, I am the woman who stood near you here, praying to the LORD. I prayed for this child, and the LORD granted my request. Now I, in turn, give him to the LORD; as long as he lives, he shall be dedicated to the LORD." Hannah left Samuel there.

RESPONSORIAL PSALM
Psalm 84:2–3, 5–6, 9–10 (see 5a)

Alternate Psalm: Psalm 128:1–2, 3, 4–5 (see 1)

R. Blessed are they who dwell in your house,
    O Lord.

How lovely is your dwelling place,
    O LORD of hosts!
  My soul yearns and pines for the courts
    of the LORD.
My heart and my flesh cry out for the
    living God.   R.

Happy they who dwell in your house!
  Continually they praise you.
Happy the men whose strength you are!
  Their hearts are set upon the pilgrimage.   R.

O LORD of hosts, hear our prayer;
  hearken, O God of Jacob!
O God, behold our shield,
  and look upon the face of your anointed.   R.

READING II *1 John 3:1–2, 21–24*

Alternate reading: Colossians 3:12–21 or 3:12–17

Beloved: See what love the Father has bestowed on us that we may be called the children of God. And so we are. The reason the world does not know us is that it did not know him. Beloved, we are God's children now; what we shall be has not yet been revealed. We do know that when it is revealed we shall be like him, for we shall see him as he is.

Beloved, if our hearts do not condemn us, we have confidence in God and receive from him whatever we ask, because we keep his commandments and do what pleases him. And his commandment is this: we should believe in the name of his Son, Jesus Christ, and love one another just as he commanded us. Those who keep his commandments remain in him, and he in them, and the way we know that he remains in us is from the Spirit he gave us.

GOSPEL *Luke 2:41–52*

Each year Jesus' parents went to Jerusalem for the feast of Passover, and when he was twelve years old, they went up according to festival custom. After they had completed its days, as they were returning, the boy Jesus remained behind in Jerusalem, but his parents did not know it. Thinking that he was in the caravan, they journeyed for a day and looked for him among their relatives and acquaintances, but not finding him, they returned to Jerusalem to look for him. After three days they found him in the temple, sitting in the midst of the teachers, listening to them and asking them questions, and all who heard him were astounded at his understanding and his answers. When his parents saw him, they were astonished, and his mother said to him, "Son, why have you done this to us? Your father and I have been looking for you with great anxiety." And he said to them, "Why were you looking for me? Did you not know that I must be in my Father's house?" But they did not understand what he said to them. He went down with them and came to Nazareth, and was obedient to them; and his mother kept all these things in her heart. And Jesus advanced in wisdom and age and favor before God and man.

Practice of Charity

Just as Jesus, Mary, and Joseph worshipped God together with their faith community, we, too, gather in God's house with one another as the family of God. Today is an opportunity to reflect on the blessed gift of worshipping together as one family in faith. The example of the Holy Family of Nazareth shows us that praying together with others strengthens us to face daily challenges. ◆ Invite members of your own family or a family close to you to join you at Mass or for another shared time of prayer. Read *The Joy of Love* (Amoris laetitia), paragraphs 65–66 and 315–318, on family life and prayer: https://w2.vatican.va/content/dam /francesco/pdf/apost_exhortations/documents /papa-francesco_esortazione-ap_20160319 _amoris-laetitia_en.pdf. ◆ Meditate on this verse from today's Second Reading: "Beloved, we are God's children now. . . ." Pray for your family, giving thanks for each one as they are now and lifting up their hopes for the future, praising God for what each may yet become.

Download more questions and activities for families, Christian initiation groups, and other adult groups at http://www.ltp.org/ahw.

Scripture Insights

Today we are invited to reflect on what it means to be part of God's family. In the First Reading, we encounter the elderly Hannah, who had been grieving over and dealing with the shame that came with having no children. In desperation, she prayed to God for a son, whom she promised to consecrate to God for life, and indeed Hannah gave birth to a son. When it was time to take him to the temple at Shiloh, the family offered the appropriate sacrifice, and then Hannah—this oppressed woman who had no voice—spoke! Careful attention should be given to her words.

In the Gospel, we learn that the Holy Family went to Jerusalem for Passover. They journeyed in a caravan, because it was the safest way to travel through the countryside. On their way home, when Mary and Joseph realize that their son was not with the caravan, they return to Jerusalem in a panic, only to find him teaching the elders in the Temple. Making the situation even more bizarre, Jesus tells them, "Did you not know that I must be in my Father's house?" In the ancient world and in some cultures today, childhood stories are regarded as predictors of the child's destiny.

The Second Reading invites us to reflect on our status as God's children and what it means for us when the salvation story reaches its end. The author of the First Letter of John reminds us that we are already, in this moment, children of God, but, when all is fulfilled, we will experience the incomprehensible. We will see God face-to-face!

◆ Carefully reread the Gospel and look for indications that Jesus was raised to be a faithful Jew. How did his parents accomplish this task? What relevance, if any, does this story have for Christians today?

◆ Prayerfully reflect on the First Reading and see if you can identify with Hannah. What do you imagine she was feeling as she gave up her son?

◆ What does it mean to you to be called a child of God? How does this realization affect the way you live day to day?

January 6, 2019 THE EPIPHANY OF THE LORD

READING I Isaiah 60:1–6

Rise up in splendor, Jerusalem! Your light
    has come,
  the glory of the Lord shines upon you.
See, darkness covers the earth,
  and thick clouds cover the peoples;
but upon you the LORD shines,
  and over you appears his glory.
Nations shall walk by your light,
  and kings by your shining radiance.
Raise your eyes and look about;
  they all gather and come to you:
your sons come from afar,
  and your daughters in the arms of their nurses.

Then you shall be radiant at what you see,
  your heart shall throb and overflow,
for the riches of the sea shall be emptied out
    before you,
  the wealth of nations shall be brought to you.
Caravans of camels shall fill you,
  dromedaries from Midian and Ephah;
all from Sheba shall come
  bearing gold and frankincense,
  and proclaiming the praises of the LORD.

RESPONSORIAL PSALM Psalm 72:1–2, 7–8, 10–11, 12–13 (see 11)

R. Lord, every nation on earth will adore you.

O God, with your judgment endow the king,
  and with your justice the king's son;
he shall govern your people with justice
  and your afflicted ones with judgment. R.

Justice shall flower in his days,
  and profound peace, till the moon be no more.
May he rule from sea to sea,
  and from the River to the ends of
    the earth. R.

The kings of Tarshish and the Isles shall offer gifts;
  the kings of Arabia and Seba shall
    bring tribute.
All kings shall pay him homage,
  all nations shall serve him. R.

For he shall rescue the poor when he cries out,
  and the afflicted when he has no one to
    help him.
He shall have pity for the lowly and the poor;
  the lives of the poor he shall save. R.

READING II Ephesians 3:2–3a, 5–6

Brothers and sisters: You have heard of the stewardship of God's grace that was given to me for your benefit, namely, that the mystery was made known to me by revelation. It was not made known to people in other generations as it has now been revealed to his holy apostles and prophets by the Spirit: that the Gentiles are coheirs, members of the same body, and copartners in the promise in Christ Jesus through the gospel.

GOSPEL Matthew 2:1–12

When Jesus was born in Bethlehem of Judea, in the days of King Herod, behold, magi from the east arrived in Jerusalem, saying, "Where is the newborn king of the Jews? We saw his star at its rising and have come to do him homage." When King Herod heard this, he was greatly troubled, and all Jerusalem with him. Assembling all the chief priests and the scribes of the people, he inquired of them where the Christ was to be born. They said to him, "In Bethlehem of Judea, for thus it has been written through the prophet:

And you, Bethlehem, land of Judah, / are by no means least among the rulers of Judah; / since from you shall come a ruler, / who is to shepherd my people Israel."

Then Herod called the magi secretly and ascertained from them the time of the star's appearance. He sent them to Bethlehem and said, "Go and search diligently for the child. When you have found him, bring me word, that I too may go and do him homage." After their audience with the king they set out. And behold, the star that they had seen at its rising preceded them, until it came and stopped over the place where the child was. They were overjoyed at seeing the star, and on entering the house they saw the child with Mary his mother. They prostrated themselves and did him homage. Then they opened their treasures and offered him gifts of gold, frankincense, and myrrh. And having been warned in a dream not to return to Herod, they departed for their country by another way.

Practice of Faith

On Epiphany, we celebrate Christ made known to all people. Attentive to the signs and seeking to know God more fully, the Magi followed the star and worshipped as a king the child they found with Mary. May we have eyes to see the signs given to us that will lead us to know Christ manifest in our lives. ◆ Following the example of the Magi, who opened their treasures in homage, share a gift that God has given to you in service to another. ◆ Consider how interreligious dialogue recognizes humanity's common desire for God and community by reading the text of Nostra aetate, the *Declaration on the Relation of the Church to Non-Christian Religions*. What opportunities do you have to work together with people of all faiths for the common good? ◆ Recognizing Christ manifest to us in the Eucharistic presence, pray the Anima Christi, before the Blessed Sacrament if possible.

Download more questions and activities for families, Christian initiation groups, and other adult groups at http://www.ltp.org/ahw.

Scripture Insights

Epiphany is one of the oldest feasts of the Christian calendar, and, as its name suggests, it is a celebration of the manifestation of Christ to the world. The Greek *epiphaneia* means "manifestation," especially as it relates to the manifestation of a deity.

Today's First Reading is about the reestablishment of Jerusalem after the Babylonian exile. The prophet issues a double imperative. He tells them to arise and then to allow their light to shine, because God's glory has dawned on them and radiates forth in the city to such an extent that they become the light to the nations. The Hebrew word *kabowd*, translated here as "glory," is also used to describe God's presence in the Holy of Holies. During the exile, God's glory left the Temple, but now it will return in full radiance!

Compare this song, to the Gospel that tells the story of the Magi who come from the East, perhaps Persia or Arabia, to seek out the newborn King of the Jews. Scholars of the esoteric sciences (for example, dream interpretation and astrology), these men also represent the Gentile nations who come to see this great king. However, this manifestation is also fraught with danger as we see in Herod's treacherous activity. The Magi's gifts of gold and frankincense are also mentioned in today's First Reading, but myrrh is a strange gift to give a mother and baby, since it was used as a painkiller and for burial. Is it an omen of the future?

In the Second Reading, we are told that God planned from the beginning that the nations (Greek *ethne*, also translated "Gentiles") would be coheirs of the one body in Christ. Thus, we celebrate the manifestation of Christ to the world.

◆ Reread the First Reading and create a picture in images or words of how this vision of the new Jerusalem might manifest itself. What new insights did you glean about the significance of this text?

◆ When and how have you experienced God's *kabowd*, or glory, in your life?

◆ Prayerfully reflect on the Gospel, and converse with Mary about "all these things in her heart." What did you discover in prayer?

READING I   *Isaiah 40:1–5, 9–11*

Alternate reading: Isaiah 42:1-4, 6-7

Comfort, give comfort to my people,
    says your God.
Speak tenderly to Jerusalem, and proclaim
    to her
      that her service is at an end,
      her guilt is expiated;
indeed, she has received from the hand of
      the LORD
    double for all her sins.

    A voice cries out:
In the desert prepare the way of the LORD!
    Make straight in the wasteland a highway
      for our God!
Every valley shall be filled in,
    every mountain and hill shall
      be made low;
the rugged land shall be made a plain,
    the rough country, a broad valley.
Then the glory of the LORD shall be revealed,
    and all people shall see it together;
    for the mouth of the LORD has spoken.

Go up onto a high mountain,
    Zion, herald of glad tidings;
cry out at the top of your voice,
    Jerusalem, herald of good news!
Fear not to cry out
    and say to the cities of Judah:
    Here is your God!
Here comes with power
    the Lord GOD,
    who rules by a strong arm;
here is his reward with him,
    his recompense before him.
Like a shepherd he feeds his flock;
    in his arms he gathers the lambs,
carrying them in his bosom,
    and leading the ewes with care.

RESPONSORIAL PSALM   *Psalm 104:1b–2, 3–4, 24–25, 27–28, 29–30 (1)*

Alternate Psalm: Psalm 29:1–2, 3–4, 3, 9–10 (11b)

R. O bless the Lord, my soul.

O LORD, my God, you are great indeed!
    You are clothed with majesty and glory,
robed in light as with a cloak.
    You have spread out the heavens like
      a tent-cloth.   R.

You have constructed your palace upon the waters.
    You make the clouds your chariot;
you travel on the wings of the wind.
    You make the winds your messengers,
and flaming fire your ministers.   R.

How manifold are your works, O LORD!
    In wisdom you have wrought them all—
the earth is full of your creatures;
    the sea also, great and wide,
in which are schools without number
    of living things both small and great.   R.

They look to you to give them food in due time.
    When you give it to them, they gather it;
when you open your hand, they are filled with
      good things.   R.

If you take away their breath, they perish and
      return to the dust.
    When you send forth your spirit, they
      are created,
and you renew the face of the earth.   R.

READING II   *Titus 2:11–14; 3:4–7*

Alternate reading: Acts 10:34–38

Beloved: The grace of God has appeared, saving all and training us to reject godless ways and worldly desires and to live temperately, justly, and devoutly in this age, as we await the blessed hope, the appearance of the glory of our great God and savior Jesus Christ, who gave himself for us to deliver us from all lawlessness and to cleanse for himself a people as his own, eager to do what is good.

When the kindness and generous love
of God our savior appeared,
not because of any righteous deeds we had done
but because of his mercy,
he saved us through the bath of rebirth
and renewal by the Holy Spirit,
whom he richly poured out on us
through Jesus Christ our savior,
so that we might be justified by his grace
and become heirs in hope of eternal life.

GOSPEL *Luke 3:15–16, 21–22*

The people were filled with expectation, and all were asking in their hearts whether John might be the Christ. John answered them all, saying, "I am baptizing you with water, but one mightier than I is coming. I am not worthy to loosen the thongs of his sandals. He will baptize you with the Holy Spirit and fire."

   After all the people had been baptized and Jesus also had been baptized and was praying, heaven was opened and the Holy Spirit descended upon him in bodily form like a dove. And a voice came from heaven, "You are my beloved Son; with you I am well pleased."

Practice of Charity

The baptism of Jesus is a moment of transparent grace, a time when the communion of the Father, Son, and Holy Spirit are revealed. Through the grace of Baptism, we share in the divine life of the Blessed Trinity. ◆ Look for, or recall, a moment of grace in which you were affirmed as a beloved child of God. How can you help another to recognize this affirmation in his or her life? ◆ Reflect on the mystery of our communion with the Blessed Trinity as you read paragraphs 257–260 of the Catechism of the Catholic Church: www.vatican .va/archive/ENG0015/__P17.HTM. ◆ Seek out and pray with an icon of the Baptism of Jesus, giving thanks that you share the divine life of the Blessed Trinity through your Baptism.

Download more questions and activities for families, Christian initiation groups, and other adult groups at http://www.ltp.org/ahw.

Scripture insights

On this Feast of the Baptism of the Lord, today's Scriptures invite us to be confident in and mindful of the presence of the divine in our midst.

   In the First Reading, the prophet urges personified Jerusalem to shout out from its place on the mountaintop, "Here is your God," because its people's long exile in Babylon is about to come to an end. Note that God is depicted as a shepherd carrying the lambs in the fold of his garment, close to his heart (Hebrew *cheq*, meaning "at breast"), and carefully leading the nursing ewes (Hebrew *ul*, meaning "to give suck") as they make their way to God's holy city.

   Today's Gospel juxtaposes John the Baptist with Jesus in a most remarkable scene. The crowds were listening to John, who was preaching a baptism of repentance, and were eager to learn whether he might be the messiah. Yet John tells them that he is only the messenger. Someone greater was coming, he said, one who would baptize with the Holy Spirit and fire. The scene quickly shifts to the crowd, who had participated in John's ritual of repentance and to one in their midst who is manifest to the world through a heavenly voice and a descending Holy Spirit as God's beloved Son.

   The Second Reading invites us to reflect on our Christian Baptism, which the author describes as a "bath of rebirth" and a "renewal by the Holy Spirit." He reminds us that it was given to us as grace (Greek *charis*, meaning "kindness" or "gift"), not because we earned it, but because God is merciful, generous, and loving.

◆ Study the First Reading, looking for its many descriptors of God. What do they tell you about the nature of God and God's relationship to humanity?

◆ As you reflect on today's Gospel, what message might we glean from the presentation of a crowd captivated by John's celebrity even while God's beloved Son stood unnoticed among them?

◆ As you pray over the Second Reading, ask how God wants you to respond to the generous gift you have been given in the "bath of rebirth."

Prayer before Reading the Word

In you, O Lord our God,
we find our joy,
for through your Law and your Prophets
you formed a people in mercy and freedom,
in justice and righteousness.
You call us with your voice of flame.
Give us ears to hear,
lives to respond,
and voices to proclaim the Good News
            of salvation,
which we know in our Savior Jesus Christ,
who lives and reigns with you and the Holy Spirit,
one God, now and forever. Amen.

Prayer after Reading the Word

In your Word, Lord God,
you reveal your power to heal and save us.
Let this Good News echo throughout the world,
in every tongue and in every culture,
so that people everywhere may gladly embrace
the salvation and life you offer to all.
We ask this through our Lord Jesus Christ,
            your Son,
who lives and reigns with you
in the unity of the Holy Spirit,
one God, for ever and ever. Amen.

Weekday Readings

January 14: *Hebrews 1:1–6; Mark 1:14–20*
January 15: *Hebrews 2:5–12; Mark 1:21–28*
January 16: *Hebrews 2:14–18; Mark 1:29–39*
January 17: *Hebrews 3:7–14; Mark 1:40–45*
January 18: *Hebrews 4:1–5; Mark 2:1–12*
January 19: *Hebrews 4:1–5, 11; Mark 2:13–17*

January 21: *Hebrews 5:1–10; Mark 2:18–22*
**January 22: Day of Prayer for the Legal Protection
of Unborn Children
1 Samuel 24:3–21; Mark 3:13–19**
January 23: *Hebrews 7:1–3, 15–17; Mark 3:1–6*
January 24: *Hebrews 7:25—8:26; Mark 3:7–12*
**January 25: Feast of the Conversion of St. Paul the Apostle
Acts 22:3–16 or 9:1–22; Mark 16:15–18**
January 26: *2 Timothy 1:1–8 or Titus 1:1–5; Mark 3:31–35*

January 28: *Hebrews 9:15, 24–28; Mark 3:22–30*
January 29: *Hebrews 10:1–10; Mark 3:31–35*
January 30: *Hebrews 10:11–18; Mark 4:1–20*
January 31: *Hebrews 10:19–25; Mark 4:21–25*
February 1: *Hebrews 10: 32–39; Mark 4:26–34*

**February 2: Feast of the Presentation of the Lord
Malachi 3:1–4; Hebrews 2:14–18;
Luke 2:22–40 or 2:22–32**
February 4: *Hebrews 11:32–40; Mark 5:1–20*
February 5: *Hebrews 12:1–4; Mark 5:21–43*
February 6: *Hebrews 12:4–7, 11–15; Mark 6:1–6*
February 7: *Hebrews 12:18–19; Mark 6:7–13*
February 8: *Hebrews 13:1–8, Mark 6:14–29*
February 9: *Hebrews 13:15–17, 20–21; Mark 6:30–34*

February 11: *Genesis 1:1–19; Mark 6:53–56*
February 12: *Genesis 1:20—2:4a; Mark 7:1–13*
February 13: *Genesis 2:4b–9, 15–17; Mark 7:14–23*
February 14: *Genesis 2:18–25; Mark 7:24–30*
February 15: *Genesis 3:1–8; Mark 7:31–37*
February 16: *Genesis 3:9–24; Mark 8:1–10*

February 18: *Genesis 4:1–15, 25; Mark 8:11–13*
February 19: *Genesis 6:5–8, 7:1–5, 10; Mark 8:14–21*
February 20: *Genesis 8:6–13, 20–22; Mark 8:22–26*
February 21: *Genesis 9:1–13; Mark 8:27–33*
**February 22: Feast of the Chair of St. Peter the Apostle
1 Peter 5:1–4; Matthew 16:13–19**
February 23: *Hebrews 11:1–7; Mark 9:2–13*

February 25: *Sirach 1:1–10; Mark 9:14–29*
February 26: *Sirach 2:1–11; Mark 9:30–37*
February 27: *Sirach 4:11–19; Mark 9:38–40*
February 28: *Sirach 5:1–8; Mark 9:41–50*
March 1: *Sirach 6:5–17; Mark 10:1–12*
March 2: *Sirach 17:1–15; Mark 10:13–16*

March 4: *Sirach 17:20–24; Mark 10:17–27*
March 5: *Sirach 35:1–12; Mark 10:28–31*

READING I *Isaiah 62:1–5*

For Zion's sake I will not be silent,
    for Jerusalem's sake I will not be quiet,
until her vindication shines forth like the dawn
    and her victory like a burning torch.

Nations shall behold your vindication,
    and all the kings your glory;
you shall be called by a new name
    pronounced by the mouth of the LORD.
You shall be a glorious crown in the hand
        of the LORD,
    a royal diadem held by your God.
No more shall people call you "Forsaken,"
    or your land "Desolate,"
but you shall be called "My Delight,"
    and your land "Espoused."
For the LORD delights in you
    and makes your land his spouse.
As a young man marries a virgin,
    your Builder shall marry you;
and as a bridegroom rejoices in his bride
    so shall your God rejoice in you.

RESPONSORIAL PSALM
Psalm 96:1–2, 2–3, 7–8, 9–10 (3)

R. Proclaim his marvelous deeds to all the nations.

Sing to the LORD a new song;
    sing to the LORD, all you lands.
Sing to the LORD; bless his name.   R.

Announce his salvation, day after day.
Tell his glory among the nations;
    among all peoples, his wondrous deeds.   R.

Give to the LORD, you families of nations,
    give to the LORD glory and praise;
    give to the LORD the glory due his name!   R.

Worship the LORD in holy attire.
    Tremble before him, all the earth;
say among the nations: The LORD is king.
    He governs the peoples with equity.   R.

READING II *1 Corinthians 12:4–11*

Brothers and sisters: There are different kinds of spiritual gifts but the same Spirit; there are different forms of service but the same Lord; there are different workings but the same God who produces all of them in everyone. To each individual the manifestation of the Spirit is given for some benefit. To one is given through the Spirit the expression of wisdom; to another, the expression of knowledge according to the same Spirit; to another, faith by the same Spirit; to another, gifts of healing by the one Spirit; to another, mighty deeds; to another, prophecy; to another, discernment of spirits; to another, varieties of tongues; to another, interpretation of tongues. But one and the same Spirit produces all of these, distributing them individually to each person as he wishes.

GOSPEL *John 2:1–11*

There was a wedding at Cana in Galilee, and the mother of Jesus was there. Jesus and his disciples were also invited to the wedding. When the wine ran short, the mother of Jesus said to him, "They have no wine." And Jesus said to her, "Woman, how does your concern affect me? My hour has not yet come." His mother said to the servers, "Do whatever he tells you." Now there were six stone water jars there for Jewish ceremonial washings, each holding twenty to thirty gallons. Jesus told them, "Fill the jars with water." So they filled them to the brim. Then he told them, "Draw some out now and take it to the headwaiter." So they took it. And when the headwaiter tasted the water that had become wine, without knowing where it came from—although the servers who had drawn the water knew —, the headwaiter called the bridegroom and said to him, "Everyone serves good wine first, and then when people have drunk freely, an inferior one; but you have kept the good wine until now." Jesus did this as the beginning of his signs at Cana in Galilee and so revealed his glory, and his disciples began to believe in him.

Practice of Faith

Jesus' first miracle at the wedding feast of Cana is a sign of God's abundant generosity. Not only was water made the choicest of wines, it was offered in extraordinary amounts: six jugs, twenty to thirty gallons each, filled to the brim! We, too, receive a lavish feast in the Word and Eucharist we celebrate at Mass and so are sent forth to offer lives of generous service to others. ◆ Practice generosity this week by showing extravagant care for someone who needs extra care and attention. As you do this, recall that God loves you this much, and more. ◆ Consider the effects of the abundant gift we receive in the Eucharist while reading paragraphs sixteen to twenty of Pope John Paul II's encyclical Ecclesia de eucharistia: http://www.vatican.va/holy_father/special_features/encyclicals/documents/hf_jp-ii_enc_20030417_ecclesia_eucharistia_en.html. ◆ Pray the Pange Lingua, St. Thomas Aquinas' prayer celebrating the gift of Eucharist, using a recording of Gregorian chant, for example, https://www.youtube.com/watch?v=Qw1Izxp_gdY.

Download more questions and activities for families, Christian initiation groups, and other adult groups at http://www.ltp.org/ahw.

Scripture Insights

During Ordinary Time, we are called to reflect on the life of Jesus and try to conform our lives to his. Ordinary Time also has a forward motion, inviting us to eagerly await the salvation and redemption of God's holy people.

This theme of eager awaiting is vividly presented in the First Reading, when the prophet says that he is compelled to proclaim a message of hope to God's chosen as they return from the Babylonian exile and struggle to renew the holy city. Personified Jerusalem, we are told, will be given a new name as her salvation is made known to the world.

The Second Reading reminds us that we cannot earn our salvation. Rather, it comes to us by our cooperation in effecting the gifts of the Holy Spirit for the benefit of the community. No matter the gifts an individual possesses, Paul says, everything comes from God and is the work of God for the common good.

In today's Gospel, we learn how Jesus saves the day by miraculously providing choice wine for a poorly planned wedding feast, but the deeper message of this story is signaled by Jesus' cryptic response to his mother's request for help. The time (of Jesus' death) had not yet come, but the abundance of water into wine is a sign (Greek *semeion*, meaning "an indication" or "a mark") of the great wedding banquet (Isaiah 62:4–5; cf. Isaiah 54:4–8) that was expected to accompany the restoration of God's holy people at the end time.

◆ What do the descriptors of Zion and Judea in the First Reading tell us about God's relationship with the Jewish people after the exile?

◆ If you could have a dialogue with each character in the Gospel, what would they tell you about what they had experienced?

◆ As you pray and reflect over the Responsorial Psalm, what words of praise would you like to add?

READING I *Nehemiah 8:2–4a, 5–6, 8–10*

Ezra the priest brought the law before the assembly, which consisted of men, women, and those children old enough to understand. Standing at one end of the open place that was before the Water Gate, he read out of the book from daybreak till midday, in the presence of the men, the women, and those children old enough to understand; and all the people listened attentively to the book of the law. Ezra the scribe stood on a wooden platform that had been made for the occasion. He opened the scroll so that all the people might see it—for he was standing higher up than any of the people—; and, as he opened it, all the people rose. Ezra blessed the LORD, the great God, and all the people, their hands raised high, answered, "Amen, amen!" Then they bowed down and prostrated themselves before the LORD, their faces to the ground. Ezra read plainly from the book of the law of God, interpreting it so that all could understand what was read. Then Nehemiah, that is, His Excellency, and Ezra the priest-scribe and the Levites who were instructing the people said to all the people: "Today is holy to the LORD your God. Do not be sad, and do not weep"—for all the people were weeping as they heard the words of the law. He said further: "Go, eat rich foods and drink sweet drinks, and allot portions to those who had nothing prepared; for today is holy to our LORD. Do not be saddened this day, for rejoicing in the LORD must be your strength!"

RESPONSORIAL PSALM *Psalm 19:8, 9, 10, 15 (see John 6:63c)*

R. Your words, Lord, are Spirit and life.

The law of the LORD is perfect,
　　refreshing the soul;
the decree of the LORD is trustworthy,
　　giving wisdom to the simple.   R.

The precepts of the LORD are right,
　　rejoicing the heart;
the command of the LORD is clear,
　　enlightening the eye.   R.

The fear of the LORD is pure,
　　enduring forever;
the ordinances of the LORD are true,
　　all of them just.   R.

Let the words of my mouth and the thought
　　　　of my heart
　　find favor before you,
O LORD, my rock and my redeemer.   R.

READING II *1 Corinthians 12:12–14, 27*

Longer: 1 Corinthians 12:12–30

Brothers and sisters: As a body is one though it has many parts, and all the parts of the body, though many, are one body, so also Christ. For in one Spirit we were all baptized into one body, whether Jews or Greeks, slaves or free persons, and we were all given to drink of one Spirit. Now the body is not a single part, but many. You are Christ's body, and individually parts of it.

GOSPEL *Luke 1:1–4; 4:14–21*

Since many have undertaken to compile a narrative of the events that have been fulfilled among us, just as those who were eyewitnesses from the beginning and ministers of the word have handed them down to us, I too have decided, after investigating everything accurately anew, to write it down in an orderly sequence for you, most excellent Theophilus, so that you may realize the certainty of the teachings you have received.

Jesus returned to Galilee in the power of the Spirit, and news of him spread throughout the whole region. He taught in their synagogues and was praised by all.

He came to Nazareth, where he had grown up, and went according to his custom into the synagogue on the sabbath day. He stood up to read and was handed a scroll of the prophet Isaiah. He unrolled the scroll and found the passage where it was written:

The Spirit of the Lord is upon me, / because he has anointed me / to bring glad tidings to the poor. / He has sent me to proclaim liberty to captives / and recovery of sight to the blind, / to let the oppressed go free, / and to proclaim a year acceptable to the Lord.

Rolling up the scroll, he handed it back to the attendant and sat down, and the eyes of all in the synagogue looked intently at him. He said to them, "Today this Scripture passage is fulfilled in your hearing."

Practice of Hope

This week's readings invite us to renew our appreciation for the immeasurable gift of God's Word and the power it has to show us how to direct our lives according to God's will. ◆ Set aside a place in your home to enthrone the Bible, showing reverence by placing candles, flowers, or sacred images nearby. Gather with others to celebrate the power of God's Word in your life as you pray today's Responsorial Psalm. ◆ Learn more about the importance of Scripture in the life of the Church by reading paragraph twenty-one of the *Dogmatic Constitution on Divine Revelation*, Dei verbum, found at http://www.vatican.va/archive/hist _councils/ii_vatican_council/documents/vat-ii _const_19651118_dei-verbum_en.html. ◆ When practicing the prayerful reading of Scripture called lectio divina, people are transformed by God's Word so that they may faithfully live it. Take time to savor the words of Scripture as you use this online resource for lectio divina: www.contempla tiveoutreach.org/category/category/lectio-divina.

Download more questions and activities for families, Christian initiation groups, and other adult groups at http://www.ltp.org/ahw.

Scripture Insights

Today's Scripture readings invite us to hear God's Word spoken in our midst and respond with confidence despite fears or concerns, because it is Good News.

In the First Reading, the scribe Ezra, newly returned from exile in Babylon, proclaims the Torah, the laws of the covenant that God made with Moses at Mount Sinai, at the entrance of Jerusalem. As the people begin to weep, Ezra and the others who had been instructing the people urge them to celebrate and be merry because this day is holy to God.

The Responsorial Psalm fleshes out Ezra's words of praise for God's law with a host of images that show that obedience to this covenant will bring great reward. May the psalmist's prayer become ours—that our words and thoughts are acceptable to God, our rock in times of doubt and fear.

Today's Gospel offers a story about Jesus at the beginning of his ministry. Already, crowds are chasing after him. When he gets to his hometown, he attends the synagogue as he had done many times before and stands to read from the prophet Isaiah. All await his words: "Today this Scripture passage is fulfilled in your hearing!" What does he mean? Jesus is telling his listeners that he is the fulfillment of the prophecy made to Israel that God would bring good news to the afflicted (Isaiah 61:1–2; 58:6).

◆ What do the descriptions of God's law in the Responsorial Psalm suggest about the nature of God's covenant and how we ought to relate to the law?

◆ What does the image of the Body of Christ that the Second Reading provides mean to you?

◆ Imagine yourself as a character in the Gospel. What do you see and hear as you wait for Jesus to speak?

READING I *Jeremiah 1:4–5, 17–19*

The word of the LORD came to me, saying:
  Before I formed you in the womb I knew you,
    before you were born I dedicated you,
    a prophet to the nations I appointed you.

  But do you gird your loins;
    stand up and tell them
    all that I command you.
  Be not crushed on their account,
    as though I would leave you crushed
        before them;
  for it is I this day
    who have made you a fortified city,
  a pillar of iron, a wall of brass,
    against the whole land:
  against Judah's kings and princes,
    against its priests and people.
  They will fight against you but not prevail
        over you,
    for I am with you to deliver you, says the LORD.

RESPONSORIAL PSALM *Psalm 71:1–2, 3–4, 5–6, 15, 17 (see 15ab)*

R. I will sing of your salvation.

In you, O LORD, I take refuge;
  let me never be put to shame.
In your justice rescue me, and deliver me;
  incline your ear to me, and save me.   R.

Be my rock of refuge,
  a stronghold to give me safety,
  for you are my rock and my fortress.
O my God, rescue me from the hand of
        the wicked.   R.

For you are my hope, O Lord;
  my trust, O God, from my youth.
On you I depend from birth;
  from my mother's womb you are
        my strength.   R.

My mouth shall declare your justice,
  day by day your salvation.
O God, you have taught me from my youth,
  and till the present I proclaim your
        wondrous deeds.   R.

READING II *1 Corinthians 12:31—13:13*

Shorter: 1 Corinthians 13:4–13

Brothers and sisters: Strive eagerly for the greatest spiritual gifts. But I shall show you a still more excellent way.

If I speak in human and angelic tongues, but do not have love, I am a resounding gong or a clashing cymbal. And if I have the gift of prophecy, and comprehend all mysteries and all knowledge; if I have all faith so as to move mountains, but do not have love, I am nothing. If I give away everything I own, and if I hand my body over so that I may boast, but do not have love, I gain nothing.

Love is patient, love is kind. It is not jealous, it is not pompous, it is not inflated, it is not rude, it does not seek its own interests, it is not quick-tempered, it does not brood over injury, it does not rejoice over wrongdoing but rejoices with the truth. It bears all things, believes all things, hopes all things, endures all things.

Love never fails. If there are prophecies, they will be brought to nothing; if tongues, they will cease; if knowledge, it will be brought to nothing. For we know partially and we prophesy partially, but when the perfect comes, the partial will pass away. When I was a child, I used to talk as a child, think as a child, reason as a child; when I became a man, I put aside childish things. At present we see indistinctly, as in a mirror, but then face to face. At present I know partially; then I shall know fully, as I am fully known. So faith, hope, love remain, these three; but the greatest of these is love.

GOSPEL *Luke 4:21–30*

Jesus began speaking in the synagogue, saying: "Today this Scripture passage is fulfilled in your hearing." And all spoke highly of him and were amazed at the gracious words that came from his mouth. They also asked, "Isn't this the son of Joseph?" He said to them, "Surely you will quote me this proverb, 'Physician, cure yourself,' and say, 'Do here in your native place the things that we heard were done in Capernaum.'" And he said, "Amen, I say to you, no prophet is accepted in his own native place. Indeed, I tell you, there were many widows in Israel in the days of Elijah when the sky was closed for three and a half years and a severe famine spread over the entire land. It was to none of these that Elijah was sent, but only to a widow in Zarephath in the land of Sidon. Again, there were many lepers in Israel during the time of Elisha the prophet; yet not one of them was cleansed, but only Naaman the Syrian." When the people in the synagogue heard this, they were all filled with fury. They rose up, drove him out of the town, and led him to the brow of the hill on which their town had been built, to hurl him down headlong. But Jesus passed through the midst of them and went away.

Practice of Charity

The prophets God sends to call his people back to faith are rarely welcomed. Each of us, as members of the Church, is called to share in the prophetic office of Christ, to give witness to God's love and faithfulness in the circumstances of our life. ◆ As you read or listen to the news this week, look for evidence of prophets among us. Choose a work for justice or way to advocate for another to share in the work of the prophets leading us to love beyond words. ◆ Use this resource from Catholic Relief Services to reflect on the prophetic example of St. Oscar Romero and discover ways you might follow his example: http://www.crs.org/sites /default/files/usops-resources/us15129-romero -advocacy-final.pdf. ◆ Ask God to strengthen your call to share in the prophetic office of Christ as you pray these words written by Bishop Kenneth Untener: www.usccb.org/prayer-and-worship /prayers-and-devotions/prayers/archbishop _romero_prayer.cfm.

Download more questions and activities for families, Christian initiation groups, and other adult groups at http://www.ltp.org/ahw.

Scripture Insights

All of us, because of our Baptism in Christ, are called to do the work of God. Today's readings help us to reflect on what it takes to respond to God's calling.

The First Reading recounts Jeremiah's call to be God's prophet. We are told that it is a vocation for which he was destined even before he was born, and it is not an easy one. He must make the leaders of Jerusalem recognize their wicked ways, but Jeremiah need not be afraid, because God will make him strong and give him the right words to speak.

Today's Gospel picks up where last week's Gospel ended, with Jesus identifying himself as the fulfillment of Isaiah's prophecy about bringing Good News to the afflicted. At first, the crowds clamor after him, until some realize that he grew up among them and begin to question, "Isn't this the son of Joseph?" Jesus responds by comparing himself to two prophets of old who, likewise, were rejected by their people. The tone is accusatory and the situation quickly escalates to the point that they try to throw him off a cliff.

In the Second Reading, Paul offers a teaching that is patterned after the Greek literary form, "praise of the greatest virtue." He writes of a love that surpasses all other spiritual gifts, is unfailing and totally self-giving. This is what it takes to respond to the call to do God's work. Without it, we are nothing.

◆ What message about love do you take away from the Second Reading?

◆ Ask Christ to speak with you about the attitude necessary to continue doing God's work in the face of opposition.

◆ When you have encountered obstacles when seeking to do what is right, how have you proceeded?

READING I *Isaiah 6:1–2a, 3–8*

In the year King Uzziah died, I saw the Lord seated on a high and lofty throne, with the train of his garment filling the temple. Seraphim were stationed above.

They cried one to the other, "Holy, holy, holy is the LORD of hosts! All the earth is filled with his glory!" At the sound of that cry, the frame of the door shook and the house was filled with smoke.

Then I said, "Woe is me, I am doomed! For I am a man of unclean lips, living among a people of unclean lips; yet my eyes have seen the King, the LORD of hosts!" Then one of the seraphim flew to me, holding an ember that he had taken with tongs from the altar.

He touched my mouth with it, and said, "See, now that this has touched your lips, your wickedness is removed, your sin purged."

Then I heard the voice of the Lord saying, "Whom shall I send? Who will go for us?" "Here I am," I said; "send me!"

RESPONSORIAL PSALM
Psalm 138:1–2, 2–3, 4–5, 7–8 (1c)

R. In the sight of the angels I will sing your
    praises, Lord.

I will give thanks to you, O LORD, with all
        my heart,
    for you have heard the words of my mouth;
    in the presence of the angels I will sing
        your praise;
I will worship at your holy temple
    and give thanks to your name. R.

Because of your kindness and your truth;
    for you have made great above all things
    your name and your promise.
When I called, you answered me;
    you built up strength within me. R.

All the kings of the earth shall give thanks to
        you, O LORD,
    when they hear the words of your mouth;
and they shall sing of the ways of the LORD:
    "Great is the glory of the LORD." R.

Your right hand saves me.
    The LORD will complete what he has done
        for me;
your kindness, O LORD, endures forever;
    forsake not the work of your hands. R.

READING II *1 Corinthians 15:1–11*

Shorter: 1 Corinthians 15:3–8, 11

I am reminding you, brothers and sisters, of the gospel I preached to you, which you indeed received and in which you also stand. Through it you are also being saved, if you hold fast to the word I preached to you, unless you believed in vain. For I handed on to you as of first importance what I also received: that Christ died for our sins in accordance with the Scriptures; that he was buried; that he was raised on the third day in accordance with the Scriptures; that he appeared to Cephas, then to the Twelve. After that, he appeared to more than five hundred brothers at once, most of whom are still living, though some have fallen asleep. After that he appeared to James, then to all the apostles. Last of all, as to one born abnormally, he appeared to me. For I am the least of the apostles, not fit to be called an apostle, because I persecuted the church of God. But by the grace of God I am what I am, and his grace to me has not been ineffective. Indeed, I have toiled harder than all of them; not I, however, but the grace of God that is with me. Therefore, whether it be I or they, so we preach and so you believed.

GOSPEL *Luke 5:1–11*

While the crowd was pressing in on Jesus and listening to the word of God, he was standing by the Lake of Gennesaret. He saw two boats there alongside the lake; the fishermen had disembarked and were washing their nets. Getting into one of the boats, the one belonging to Simon, he asked him to put out a short distance from the shore. Then he sat down and taught the crowds from the boat. After he had finished speaking, he said to Simon, "Put out into deep water and lower your nets for a catch." Simon said in reply, "Master, we have worked hard all night and have caught nothing, but at your command I will lower the nets." When they had done this, they caught a great number of fish and their nets were tearing. They signaled to their partners in the other boat to come to help them. They came and filled both boats so that the boats were in danger of sinking. When Simon Peter saw this, he fell at the knees of Jesus and said, "Depart from me, Lord, for I am a sinful man." For astonishment at the catch of fish they had made seized him and all those with him, and likewise James and John, the sons of Zebedee, who were partners of Simon. Jesus said to Simon, "Do not be afraid; from now on you will be catching men." When they brought their boats to the shore, they left everything and followed him.

Practice of Faith

In today's Second Reading, St. Paul summarizes the key elements of his preaching. In these words, we find expression of the faith that we still profess today as we pray the Creed. As Christ's disciples, we repeat these words often in hopes that they will find expression in our actions. ◆ Take opportunities this week to observe how your actions flow from what you believe. As you finish each day, offer a prayer of thanks to God for this sign of grace. ◆ Learn more about the profession of faith we make when we pray the Creed by reading paragraphs 185 to 197 of the Catechism of the Catholic Church: http://www.vatican.va/archive/ENG0015/_P14.HTM. ◆ Meditate on the words of the Creed that we pray at Mass. Consider writing in your own words what we profess in the Creed.

Download more questions and activities for families, Christian initiation groups, and other adult groups at http://www.ltp.org/ahw.

Scripture Insights

Today's Scripture readings invite us to reflect on our sense of inadequacy in answering God's call. This reality reminds us that we do not need to be fearful, because we are called to do God's work and not ours.

The First Reading is an account of Isaiah's vision of God seated on his throne in the Holy of Holies of the Jerusalem temple. When Isaiah realizes that he is in the presence of God, he laments, "Woe is me, I am doomed!" He thinks he will die, because ancients believed that no one could see the face of God and live, but the Hebrew root of the word translated here as "doomed" also means "brought to silence." Thus, the seraph responds by bringing a coal from God's altar to purify Isaiah's lips. Only then can he respond to God's call.

In today's Gospel, we also hear of Simon Peter's call. A fisherman by trade, he complains when Jesus tells him to take his boat into deep water and prepare for a catch. But before they know it, the nets are bursting and the boats so full that they are in danger of sinking. When Peter gets to shore, he is overcome with emotion, asking Jesus to leave him, because he feels he is not worthy of his presence. Instead, Jesus tells him, "Do not be afraid," and invites Peter to be a fisher of people on Jesus' behalf.

In the Second Reading, Paul assures the Corinthian community that they will be saved by believing in what he preaches. What follows is a creed and a list of witnesses to Jesus' post-Resurrection appearances. Paul identifies himself as the last to witness the resurrected Jesus and the least of his Apostles. To what does he attribute the honor of being an apostle? God's grace.

◆ In the First Reading, what do the descriptions of God's presence suggest about the nature of God?

◆ What is the source of Peter's fear? How is his fear alleviated?

◆ How do you experience God's grace?

Reading I *Jeremiah 17:5–8*

Thus says the LORD:
Cursed is the one who trusts in human beings,
　　who seeks his strength in flesh,
　　whose heart turns away from the LORD.
He is like a barren bush in the desert
　　that enjoys no change of season,
but stands in a lava waste,
　　a salt and empty earth.
Blessed is the one who trusts in the LORD,
　　whose hope is the LORD.
He is like a tree planted beside the waters
　　that stretches out its roots to the stream:
It fears not the heat when it comes;
　　its leaves stay green;
in the year of drought it shows no distress,
　　but still bears fruit.

Responsorial Psalm
Psalm 1:1–2, 3, 4, 6 (40:5a)

R. Blessed are they who hope in the Lord.

Blessed the man who follows not
　　the counsel of the wicked,
nor walks in the way of sinners,
　　nor sits in the company of the insolent,
but delights in the law of the LORD
　　and meditates on his law day and night.　R.

He is like a tree
　　planted near running water,
that yields its fruit in due season,
　　and whose leaves never fade.
Whatever he does, prospers.　R.

Not so the wicked, not so;
　　they are like chaff which the wind
　　　　drives away.
For the LORD watches over the way of the just,
　　but the way of the wicked vanishes.　R.

Reading II *1 Corinthians 15:12, 16–20*

Brothers and sisters: If Christ is preached as raised from the dead, how can some among you say there is no resurrection of the dead? If the dead are not raised, neither has Christ been raised, and if Christ has not been raised, your faith is vain; you are still in your sins. Then those who have fallen asleep in Christ have perished. If for this life only we have hoped in Christ, we are the most pitiable people of all.

But now Christ has been raised from the dead, the firstfruits of those who have fallen asleep.

Gospel *Luke 6:17, 20–26*

Jesus came down with the Twelve and stood on a stretch of level ground with a great crowd of his disciples and a large number of the people from all Judea and Jerusalem and the coastal region of Tyre and Sidon. And raising his eyes toward his disciples he said:
　"Blessed are you who are poor,
　　for the kingdom of God is yours.
　Blessed are you who are now hungry,
　　for you will be satisfied.
　Blessed are you who are now weeping,
　　for you will laugh.
　Blessed are you when people hate you,
　　and when they exclude and insult you,
　　and denounce your name as evil
　　on account of the Son of Man.

Rejoice and leap for joy on that day! Behold, your reward will be great in heaven. For their ancestors treated the prophets in the same way.

　But woe to you who are rich,
　　for you have received your consolation.
　Woe to you who are filled now,
　　for you will be hungry.
　Woe to you who laugh now,
　　for you will grieve and weep.
　Woe to you when all speak well of you,
　　for their ancestors treated
　　　　the false prophets in this way."

Practice of Hope

In the Beatitudes, Jesus teaches us that the path to true happiness lies in the understanding of the connection between heaven and earth. Those who are truly happy recognize their complete dependence on God in all circumstances of daily life and exhibit full trust in the fulfillment of the promised Kingdom of God. ◆ Consider how many of our daily actions are taken to obtain a specific result. Choose to offer an anonymous act of charity, one that you know cannot be rewarded now. ◆ Read Pope Francis' Message for World Youth Day, 2014, reflecting on the Beatitudes: http://w2.vatican.va /content/francesco/en/messages/youth/documents /papa-francesco_20140121_messaggio-giovani _2014.html. ◆ In the spirit of the Beatitudes, pray one or both of these prayers of surrender to God: the Suscipe of St. Ignatius of Loyola, founder of the Jesuits (http://jesuitprayer.org/wp-content /uploads/2014/11/st-ignatius.pdf), or the Suscipe prayer of Venerable Mother Catherine McAuley, founder of the Sisters of Mercy (http://www.mercy world.org/spirituality/index.cfm?loadref=55).

Download more questions and activities for families, Christian initiation groups, and other adult groups at http://www.ltp.org/ahw.

Scripture Insights

Trust is not easy to define in the abstract, but we know it when we see it. We also know that we must "take the leap," before something can be experienced. Today's readings invite us to take the leap and trust in the Lord who gives life.

The First Reading consists of a collection of wisdom sayings centered on the importance of trusting in God and the foolishness of turning away and trusting in human values. The imagery of a tree with deep roots (Psalm 1:3; 52:10; Proverbs 3:18; 11:13; Sirach 24:13–22) is frequently used to describe those who trust in God, because even in times of trouble they will survive.

In today's Gospel, we encounter Jesus and a large crowd of Jews and non-Jews gathered on a plain in Galilee to hear him speak. He goes on to deliver the Beatitudes, which are, in fact, about trust in God who cares for those who suffer. Jesus also includes a matching series of "woes" that focus on those who have turned away from God by refusing to do their part in alleviating these sufferings. Where will you stand?

The Second Reading is a small part of a longer teaching on the doctrine of bodily resurrection. In this section, Paul explains the consequences of not accepting this teaching. In effect, he says, we would have to declare that Christ was not raised and that our faith is in vain. We know Christ was raised. Paul says, and, with him, all who trust in his name will be raised to new life.

◆ What does the First Reading say about where to put your trust?

◆ If you are experiencing difficulties, how does today's Gospel comfort you?

◆ What might the image of a tree with roots that extend deep into the earth portray about God's love?

February 24, 2019 Seventh Sunday in Ordinary Time

Reading I
1 Samuel 26:2, 7–9, 12–13, 22–23

In those days, Saul went down to the desert of Ziph with three thousand picked men of Israel, to search for David in the desert of Ziph. So David and Abishai went among Saul's soldiers by night and found Saul lying asleep within the barricade, with his spear thrust into the ground at his head and Abner and his men sleeping around him.

Abishai whispered to David: "God has delivered your enemy into your grasp this day. Let me nail him to the ground with one throust on the spear; I will not need a second thrust!" But David said to Abishai, "Do not harm him, for who can lay hands on the Lord's anointed and remain unpunished?" So David took the spear and the water jug from their place at Saul's head, and they got awasy without anyone's seeing or knowing or awakening. All remained asleep, because the Lord had put them into a deep slumber.

Going across to an opposite slope, David stood on a remote hilltop at a great distance from Abner, son of Ner, and the troops.

He said: "Here is the king's spear. Let an attendant come over to get it. The Lord will reward each man for his justice and faithfulneess. Today, though the Lord delivered you into my grasp, I would not harm the Lord's anointed."

Responsorial Psalm
Psalm 103:1–2, 3–4, 8, 10, 12–13 (8a)

R. The Lord is kind and merciful.

Bless the Lord, O my soul;
    all my being, bless his holy name.
Bless the Lord, O my soul,
    forget not all his benefits. R.

He pardons all your iniquities,
    heals all your ills.
He redeems your life from destruction,
    crowns you with kindness
            and compassion. R.

Merciful and gracious is the Lord,
    slow to anger, and abounding in kindness.
Not according to our sins does he deal with us,
    nor does he requite us according to
            our crimes. R.

As far as the east is from the west,
    so far has he put our transgressions from us.
As a father has compassion on his children,
    so the Lord has compassion on those who
            fear him. R.

Reading II *1 Corinthians 15:45–49*

Brothers and sisters: It is written, *The first man, Adam, became a living being,* the last Adam a life-giving spirit. But the spiritual was not first; rather the natural and then the spiritual. The first man was from the earth, earthly; the second man, from heaven. As was the earthly one, so also are the earthly, and as is the heavenly one, so also are the heavenly. Just as we have borne the image of the earthly one, we shall also bear the image of the heavenly one.

Gospel *Luke 6:27–38*

Jesus said to his disciples: "To you who hear I say, love your enemies, do good to those who hate you, bless those who curse you, pray for those who mistreat you. To the person who strikes you on one cheek, offer the other one as well, and from the person who takes your cloak, do not withold even your tunic. Give to everyone who asks of you, and from the one who takes what is yours do not demand it back. Do to others as you would have them do to you. For if you love those who love you, what credit is that to you? Even sinners love those who love them. And if you do good to those who do good to you, what credit is that to you? Even sinners do the same. If you lend money to those from whom you expect repayment, what credit is that to you? Even sinners lend to sinners and get back the same amount. But rather, love your enemies and do good to them, and lend expecting nothing back; then your reward will be great and you will be children of the Most High, for he himself is kind to the ungrateful and the wicked. Be merciful, just as your Father is merciful.

"Stop judging and you will not be judged. Stop condemning and you will not be condemned. Forgive and you will be forgiven. Give and gifts will be given to you; a good measure, packed together, shaken down, and overflowing will be poured into your lap. For the measure with which you measure will in return be measured out to you."

Practice of Charity

In today's Gospel, Jesus instructs us to "be merciful, just as your Father is merciful." By the many examples given, it is clear that living mercy is a challenge that calls us beyond our comfort zone. Thankfully, so that we might be merciful, God has already gifted us with grace. ◆ As you move through your week, ask God to show you where you are being called to show mercy to others. Choose to act on a work of mercy that stretches you beyond your comfort zone. ◆ "The works of mercy are charitable actions by which we come to the aid of our neighbor in his spiritual and bodily necessities" (*Catechism of the Catholic Church*, 2447). Consider these suggestions for practicing the corporal and spiritual works of mercy: http:// www.usccb.org/beliefs-and-teachings/how-we -teach/new-evangelization/jubilee-of-mercy/the -spiritual-works-of-mercy.cfm. ◆ Reflect on the call to be merciful as you pray St. Faustina's Prayer to Be Merciful to Others: www.thedivinemercy.org /message/spirituality/prayer.php or this prayer of mercy www.crs.org/sites/default/files/usops -resources/vessels-of-mercy-2.pdf.

Download more questions and activities for families, Christian initiation groups, and other adult groups at http://www.ltp.org/ahw.

Scripture Insights

Many consider mercy to be the same as pity and that being merciful can make one feel superior to the offender. Today's Scripture readings, though, invite us to a more nuanced understanding of mercy that we must aspire to, if our lives are to be holy.

In the First Reading, we hear a story about King Saul, who with his army was seeking to kill David, because Saul was jealous of David's popularity among the people. In a strange turn of events, Saul and his commanders make camp very near where David and his troops are hiding. Thus, David and Abishai enter Saul's camp and even his tent in the middle of the night. Abishai suggests that they should kill Saul on the spot, but they choose not to do so, because, as David says, Saul is God's anointed. Only God can raise a hand against him.

Today's Gospel, which is part of Luke's sermon on the plain, is a teaching on loving one's enemies. From a practical point of view, we are told that we should treat others as we would want to be treated. More importantly, from a God-centered point of view, we are told to be merciful like our heavenly Father, who is kind to everyone, even the ungrateful and the wicked. The Greek word translated here as "kind" is *chréstos*, meaning "useful" or "kindly." Ironically, it was a common name for slaves in the ancient world.

◆ By not killing Saul, how does David perceive God's mercy?

◆ The Gospel provides examples of how we should behave. What do these tell us of God's mercy?

◆ If we are to bear the image "of the heavenly one" (Second Reading), how are we to act?

READING I *Sirach 27:4–7*

When a sieve is shaken, the husks appear;
    so do one's faults when one speaks.
As the test of what the potter molds is
        in the furnace,
    so in tribulation is the test of the just.
The fruit of a tree shows the care it has had;
    so too does one's speech disclose the bent
        of one's mind.
Praise no one before he speaks,
    for it is then that people are tested.

RESPONSORIAL PSALM
Psalm 92:2–3, 13–14, 15–16 (see 2a)

R. Lord, it is good to give thanks to you.

It is good to give thanks to the LORD,
    to sing praise to your name, Most High,
to proclaim your kindness at dawn
    and your faithfulness throughout
        the night.   R.

The just one shall flourish like the palm tree,
    like a cedar of Lebanon shall he grow.
They that are planted in the house of the LORD
    shall flourish in the courts of our God.   R.

They shall bear fruit even in old age;
    vigorous and sturdy shall they be,
declaring how just is the LORD,
    my rock, in whom there is no wrong.   R.

READING II *1 Corinthians 15:54–58*

Brothers and sisters: When this which is corruptible clothes itself with incorruptibility and this which is mortal clothes itself with immortality, then the word that is written shall come about:

    Death is swallowed up in victory.
    Where, O death, is your victory?
    Where, O death, is your sting?

The sting of death is sin, and the power of sin is the law. But thanks be to God who gives us the victory through our Lord Jesus Christ.

Therefore, my beloved brothers and sisters, be firm, steadfast, always fully devoted to the work of the Lord, knowing that in the Lord your labor is not in vain.

GOSPEL *Luke 6:39–45*

Jesus told his disciples a parable, "Can a blind person guide a blind person? Will not both fall into a pit? No disciple is superior to the teacher; but when fully trained, every disciple will be like his teacher. Why do you notice the splinter in your brother's eye, but do not perceive the wooden beam in your own? How can you say to your brother, 'Brother, let me remove that splinter in your eye,' when you do not even notice the wooden beam in your own eye? You hypocrite! Remove the wooden beam from your eye first; then you will see clearly to remove the splinter in your brother's eye.

A good tree does not bear rotten fruit, nor does a rotten tree bear good fruit. For every tree is known by its own fruit. For people do not pick figs from thornbushes, nor do they gather grapes from brambles. A good person out of the store of goodness in his heart produces good, but an evil person out of a store of evil produces evil; for from the fullness of the heart the mouth speaks."

Practice of Hope

Challenged to live as the Just One, we take steps to ensure that our speech and actions consistently show forth Christ, who seeks to bear fruit in us. This resolve is strengthened through daily reflection and attention to how we engage others and God's creation. ◆ When tempted to judge others, pause to consider your words and actions and take extra care that both consistently show forth the goodness of Christ at work in you. ◆ Learn more about Salesian spirituality, which offers wisdom for integrating faith and daily life: www.oblates. us/our-charism/salesian-spirituality/. ◆ As you examine in prayer your words and actions, hold fast to these words of encouragement: "Have patience with everyone, but especially with yourself. I mean, do not be over-troubled about your imperfections, but always have courage enough at once to rise up again when you fall into any of them" ("Upon Discouragement" in *The Spirit of Saint Francis de Sales*, by Jean-Pierre Camus).

Download more questions and activities for families, Christian initiation groups, and other adult groups at http://www.ltp.org/ahw.

Scripture Insights

The integrity and credibility of a person is evident in the words that he or she speaks. Today's readings help us reflect on our tendency to overlook our faults but judge others. These Scriptures provide an opportunity to examine our need to act harshly toward others while kindly to ourselves. As we are only a few days before entering the season of Lent, this is an apt time for such reflection.

In today's First Reading, we hear several wise sayings of Ben Sira, the author of the Book of Sirach. Each is a metaphor to help us recognize that our secret motives and intentions will be revealed in our words. Whether good or bad, we cannot keep them hidden.

In the Second Reading, Paul recalls the words of the prophet Hosea and exclaims, "Where, O death, is your victory?" This question is rhetorical insofar as it is designed not to elicit an answer but to emphasize a point. He knows without a doubt that death will never be victorious, because God gave us victory over sin and death through the crucified Christ. Earlier in this letter, Paul describes Christ as God's wisdom (1 Corinthians 1:22–24).

The Gospel presents Jesus as introducing a parable with the rhetorical query, "Can a blind person lead a blind person?" What follows is a collection of wise sayings about not judging others lest you come under judgment yourself. The teaching follows upon promises that the poor and disenfranchised will be blessed in God's kingdom and that one's enemies should be loved.

◆ The reading from Sirach states that no one should be praised before speaking. What is revealed in a person's words?

◆ Daily upon awaking and before sleeping, pray "Lord, it is good to give thanks to you."

◆ Ask Jesus to help you remove the "wooden beam" from your eye so that you can see clearly and not judge others.

Lent

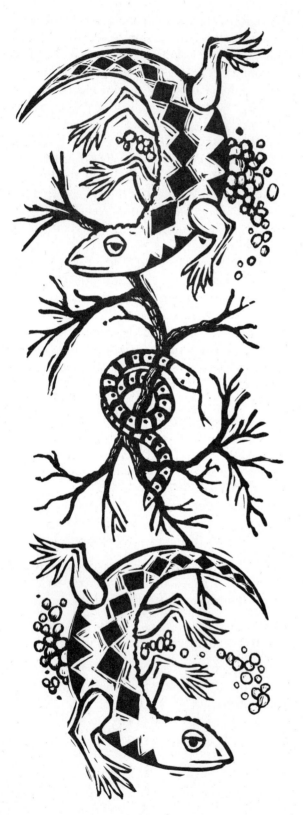

Prayer before Reading the Word

O Lord, great and faithful God,
it is good for us to be here!
Let us listen to your Son, your chosen One.

Shatter the hardness of our hearts
and open our minds to the wisdom of the Gospel,
that we may grasp the lessons you teach us daily
and bring forth the fruit of true
and continual conversion.

We ask this through the One
into whom we have been baptized,
our Lord Jesus Christ, your Son,
who lives and reigns with you
in the unity of the Holy Spirit,
one God, for ever and ever. Amen.

Prayer after Reading the Word

Infinite is your compassion, O God,
and gracious the pardon
that Jesus, the Teacher, offers
to every sinner who stands before him.

Gladden our hearts
at the Word that sends us on our way in peace;
and grant that we who have been found
    by your grace
may gladly welcome to the table of your family
all who long to find their way home.

We ask this through Christ,
our peace and reconciliation,
the Lord who lives and reigns with you
in the unity of the Holy Spirit,
one God, for ever and ever. Amen.

Weekday Readings

March 6: Ash Wednesday
Joel 2:12–18; 2 Corinthians 5:20—6:2;
Matthew 6:1–6, 16–18
March 7: *Deuteronomy 30:15–20; Luke 9:22–25*
March 8: *Isaiah 58:1–9a; Matthew 9:14–15*
March 9: *Isaiah 58:9b–14; Luke 5:27–32*

March 11: *Leviticus 19:1–2, 11–18; Matthew 25:31–46*
March 12: *Isaiah 55:10–11; Matthew 6:7–15*
March 13: *Jonah 3:1–10; Luke 11:29–32*
March 14: *Esther C:12, 14–16, 23–25; Matthew 7:7–12*
March 15: *Ezekiel 18:21–28; Matthew 5:20–26*
March 16: *Deuteronomy 26:16–19; Matthew 5:43–48*

March 18: *Daniel 9:4b–10; Luke 6:36-38*
March 19: Solemnity of St, Joseph, Spouse of the Blessed
Virgin Mary
2 Samuel 7:4-5a, 12-14a, 16; Romans 4:13, 16-18, 22;
Matthew 1:16, 18-21, 24a or Luke 2:41-51a
March 20: *Jeremiah 18:18–20; Matthew 20:17–28*
March 21: *Jeremiah 17:5–10; Luke 16:19–31*
March 22: *Genesis 37:3–4, 12–13a, 17b–28a;*
Matthew 21:33–43, 45–46
March 23: *Micah 7:14–15, 18–20; Luke 15:1–3, 11–32*

March 25: Solemnity of the Annunciation of the Lord
Isaiah 7:10-14; 8:10; Hebrews 10:4-10/Luke 1:26-38
March 26: *Daniel 3:25, 34–43; Matthew 18:21–35*
March 27: *Deuteronomy 4:1, 5–9; Matthew 5:17–19*
March 28: *Jeremiah 7:23-28; Luke 11:14–23*
March 29: *Hosea 14:2–10; Mark 12:28–34*
March 30: *Hos 6:1-6; Luke 18:9–14*

April 1: *Isaiah 65:17–21; John 4:43–54*
April 2: *Ezekiel 47:1–9, 12; John 5:1–16*
April 3: *Isaiah 49:8–15; John 5:17–30*
April 4: *Exodus 32:7–14; John 5:31–47*
April 5: *Wisdom 2:1a, 12–22; John 7:1–2, 10, 25–30*
April 6: *Jeremiah 11:18–20; John 7:40–53*

April 8: *Daniel 13:1–9, 15–17, 19–30, 33–62 or 13:41c–62;*
John 8:12–20, or, if Year A readings are used on the Fifth
Sunday of Lent, John 8:1–11
April 9: *Numbers 21:4–9; John 8:21–30*
April 10: *Daniel 3:14–20, 91–92, 95; John 8:31–42*
April 11: *Genesis 17:3–9; John 8:51–59*
April 12: *Jeremiah 20:10–13; John 10:31–42*
April 13: *Ezekiel 37:21–28; John 11:45-56*

April 15: *Isaiah 42:1–7; John 12:1–11*
April 16: *Isaiah 49:1–6; John 13:21–33, 36–38*
April 17: *Isaiah 50:4–9a; Matthew 26:14–25*

READING I *Deuteronomy 26:4–10*

Moses spoke to the people, saying: "The priest shall receive the basket from you and shall set it in front of the altar of the LORD, your God. Then you shall declare before the LORD, your God, 'My father was a wandering Aramean who went down to Egypt with a small household and lived there as an alien. But there he became a nation great, strong, and numerous. When the Egyptians maltreated and oppressed us, imposing hard labor upon us, we cried to the LORD, the God of our fathers, and he heard our cry and saw our affliction, our toil and our oppression. He brought us out of Egypt with his strong hand and outstretched arm, with terrifying power, with signs and wonders; and bringing us into this country, he gave us this land flowing with milk and honey. Therefore, I have now brought you the firstfruits of the products of the soil which you, O LORD, have given me.' And having set them before the LORD, your God, you shall bow down in his presence."

RESPONSORIAL PSALM *Psalm 91:1–2, 10–11, 12–13, 14–15 (see 15b)*

R. Be with me, Lord, when I am in trouble.

You who dwell in the shelter of the Most High,
    who abide in the shadow of the Almighty,
say to the LORD, "My refuge and fortress,
    my God, in whom I trust."   R.

No evil shall befall you,
    nor affliction come near your tent,
for to his angels he has given command
        about you,
    that they guard you in all your ways.   R.

Upon their hands they shall bear you up,
    lest you dash your foot against a stone.
You shall tread upon the asp and the viper;
    you shall trample down the lion and
        the dragon.   R.

Because he clings to me, I will deliver him;
    I will set him on high because he
        acknowledges my name.

He shall call upon me, and I will answer him;
    I will be with him in distress;
I will deliver him and glorify him.   R.

READING II *Romans 10:8–13*

Brothers and sisters: What does Scripture say? / *The word is near you, / in your mouth and in your heart /* —that is, the word of faith that we preach —, for, if you confess with your mouth that Jesus is Lord and believe in your heart that God raised him from the dead, you will be saved. For one believes with the heart and so is justified, and one confesses with the mouth and so is saved. For the Scripture says, *No one who believes in him will be put to shame.* For there is no distinction between Jew and Greek; the same Lord is Lord of all, enriching all who call upon him. For "everyone who calls on the name of the Lord will be saved."

GOSPEL *Luke 4:1–13*

Filled with the Holy Spirit, Jesus returned from the Jordan and was led by the Spirit into the desert for forty days, to be tempted by the devil. He ate nothing during those days, and when they were over he was hungry. The devil said to him, "If you are the Son of God, command this stone to become bread." Jesus answered him, "It is written, *One does not live on bread alone.*" Then he took him up and showed him all the kingdoms of the world in a single instant. The devil said to him, "I shall give to you all this power and glory; for it has been handed over to me, and I may give it to whomever I wish. All this will be yours, if you worship me." Jesus said to him in reply, "It is written:
    *You shall worship the Lord,
        your God,
    and him alone shall you serve.*"

Then he led him to Jerusalem, made him stand on the parapet of the temple, and said to him, "If you are the Son of God, throw yourself down from here, for it is written:
    *He will command his angels concerning you,
        to guard you,*

and:

> With their hands they will support you,
> lest you dash your foot against a stone."

Jesus said to him in reply, "It also says, *You shall not put the Lord, your God, to the test.*" When the devil had finished every temptation, he departed from him for a time.

Practice of Faith

On this First Sunday of Lent, we consider what we might offer to God throughout these forty days. Moses and the Israelites make an offering of "firstfruits," produce received from the land God has given to them. Similarly, Jesus offers resistance to each temptation, showing us that God alone is the source of existence. In Lent, we seek to make our prayer, fasting, and almsgiving an offering of "firstfruits," recognition of our total dependence on God. ◆ As you begin this season of Lent, take care to choose practices that will be reminders of your dependence on God. Consider focusing on prayers of thanksgiving and praise as well as sacrifices that acknowledge God's abundant gifts. ◆ Prayerfully reflect on this translation of "Nada te turbe", a poem written by St. Teresa of Avila: www.carmelitesistersbythesea.org/meditations/. ◆ Reread the Gospel as an examination of conscience. What keeps you from acknowledging your total dependence on God?

Download more questions and activities for families, Christian initiation groups, and other adult groups at http://www.ltp.org/ahw.

Scripture Insights

The readings for this First Sunday of Lent remind us of the giving of the Law to God's people on Mount Sinai and the covenant relationship that we share in Christ.

In today's First Reading, we hear about a ritual called the Offering of First Fruits. It was traditionally done in the Jerusalem Temple on the first day of Shavuot, also known as the Feast of Weeks or Pentecost, in thanksgiving for the spring wheat harvest. Even today, it is a celebration in remembrance of the giving of the Law on Mount Sinai.

In the Second Reading, however, Paul contrasts Israel's relationship with God that comes through Jewish Law with the relationship that comes through faith in the Christ whom God raised from the dead. This is not to say that the Law is useless or obsolete. It continues to be the obligation of Jews for all time, but Paul's point is that, in Jesus who was a faithful Jew and God's chosen, Jews and Gentiles can now worship the same God.

The Gospel also references Jewish Law but in a vastly different way. Here we are given the opportunity to witness a verbal wrestling match between Jesus and the devil, a spirit with malicious intent. Notice that the devil quotes Psalm 91 as he tests the limits of Jesus' allegiance to God, but Jesus holds strong and responds with quotations from Deuteronomy, which represents Moses' restatement of the Law before God's Chosen People returned to the Promised Land. But this story is not over. We are told that the devil left Jesus for a time.

◆ How does it feel to overcome temptation and know that the tempter has left you?

◆ In the First Reading, the story of God's presence is told. Why is this important?

◆ What is the meaning of the phrase "the word is near you, in your mouth and in your heart" for you?

March 17, 2019 SECOND SUNDAY OF LENT

READING I *Genesis 15:5–12, 17–18*

The Lord God took Abram outside and said, "Look up at the sky and count the stars, if you can. Just so," he added, "shall your descendants be." Abram put his faith in the LORD, who credited it to him as an act of righteousness.

He then said to him, "I am the LORD who brought you from Ur of the Chaldeans to give you this land as a possession." "O Lord GOD," he asked, "how am I to know that I shall possess it?" He answered him, "Bring me a three-year-old heifer, a three-year-old she-goat, a three-year-old ram, a turtledove, and a young pigeon." Abram brought him all these, split them in two, and placed each half opposite the other; but the birds he did not cut up. Birds of prey swooped down on the carcasses, but Abram stayed with them. As the sun was about to set, a trance fell upon Abram, and a deep, terrifying darkness enveloped him.

When the sun had set and it was dark, there appeared a smoking fire pot and a flaming torch, which passed between those pieces. It was on that occasion that the LORD made a covenant with Abram, saying: "To your descendants I give this land, from the Wadi of Egypt to the Great River, the Euphrates."

RESPONSORIAL PSALM
Psalm 27:1, 7–8, 8–9, 13–14 (see 1a)

R. The Lord is my light and my salvation.

The LORD is my light and my salvation;
  whom should I fear?
The LORD is my life's refuge;
  of whom should I be afraid? R.

Hear, O LORD, the sound of my call;
  have pity on me, and answer me.
Of you my heart speaks; you my glance seeks. R.

Your presence, O LORD, I seek.
  Hide not your face from me;
do not in anger repel your servant.
  You are my helper: cast me not off. R.

I believe that I shall see the bounty of the LORD
  in the land of the living.

Wait for the LORD with courage;
  be stouthearted, and wait for the LORD. R.

READING II *Philippians 3:17—4:1*

Shorter: Philippians 3:20—4:1

Join with others in being imitators of me, brothers and sisters, and observe those who thus conduct themselves according to the model you have in us. For many, as I have often told you and now tell you even in tears, conduct themselves as enemies of the cross of Christ. Their end is destruction. Their God is their stomach; their glory is in their "shame." Their minds are occupied with earthly things. But our citizenship is in heaven, and from it we also await a savior, the Lord Jesus Christ. He will change our lowly body to conform with his glorified body by the power that enables him also to bring all things into subjection to himself.

Therefore, my brothers and sisters, whom I love and long for, my joy and crown, in this way stand firm in the Lord.

GOSPEL *Luke 9:28b–36*

Jesus took Peter, John, and James and went up the mountain to pray. While he was praying, his face changed in appearance and his clothing became dazzling white. And behold, two men were conversing with him, Moses and Elijah, who appeared in glory and spoke of his exodus that he was going to accomplish in Jerusalem. Peter and his companions had been overcome by sleep, but becoming fully awake, they saw his glory and the two men standing with him. As they were about to part from him, Peter said to Jesus, "Master, it is good that we are here; let us make three tents, one for you, one for Moses, and one for Elijah." But he did not know what he was saying. While he was still speaking, a cloud came and cast a shadow over them, and they became frightened when they entered the cloud. Then from the cloud came a voice that said, "This is my chosen Son; listen to him." After the voice had spoken, Jesus was found alone. They fell silent and did not at that time tell anyone what they had seen.

Practice of Hope

In the Transfiguration, Peter, James, and John are granted a vision of Christ's glory, a foretaste of the Resurrection. In our lives, we sometimes find signs that give us hope in the promise of eternal life. In these, we find encouragement to take up our cross and follow in the footsteps of Jesus. ◆ Already in our Lenten journey, we seek signs of Easter joy. As you proceed through your week, look for signs of spring emerging in nature and give thanks to God for the promise of new life. ◆ Consider how the spiritual practices of prayer, fasting, and almsgiving, can draw us closer to God and enable us to be signs of hope for others: http://www.crsricebowl .org/about/how-to-practice-lent. ◆ Imagine yourself at the Transfiguration as you contemplate the scene as shown in this piece of sacred art: www .wikiart.org/en/raphael/the-transfiguration-1520.

Download more questions and activities for families, Christian initiation groups, and other adult groups at http://www.ltp.org/ahw.

Scripture Insights

Glory will come our way, if we but stand firm in the Lord! This is the theme of today's Scripture readings.

The First Reading is the second of three accounts of God's covenant with Abram, who is later known as Abraham (cf. Genesis 12:1–9; 17:1–27). This covenant is what scholars call a royal grant treaty, because God blessed Abram with this promise of land and descendants with no strings attached. Abram did not earn this honor but only believed God and, for that, God credited it to him as righteousness, meaning "right relationship" with God.

Today's Gospel is suggestive of the Sinai covenant. As the story unfolds we learn that Moses (representing the Law) and Elijah (representing the prophets) appeared alongside of Jesus, and the three of them converse about Jesus' "exodus" that will take place in Jerusalem. The evangelist uses this scene to prefigure Jesus' death and Resurrection, but the disciples do not understand. The three tents are perhaps a reminder of the pilgrimage during the Feast of Tabernacles, which commemorates the Israelites' desert wandering during the Exodus.

In the Second Reading, Paul urges the Philippian Christian community to imitate him, humbly following God's calling to be "perfectly mature" in their conduct. Why? So that they may one day be transformed and conformed to the risen Christ's glorious body. This is our inheritance, as well, if we but stand firm in the Lord.

◆ What might Peter have wanted to to ask Jesus on their way down the mountain.

◆ The First Reading highlights the value of ritual. When does ritual help you commemorate an event?

◆ What does Paul mean when he says, "Our citizenship is in heaven?"

READING I *Exodus 3:1–8a, 13–15*

Shorter: Exodus 1–3, 7–8, 12–17

Moses was tending the flock of his father-in-law Jethro, the priest of Midian. Leading the flock across the desert, he came to Horeb, the mountain of God. There an angel of the LORD appeared to Moses in fire flaming out of a bush. As he looked on, he was surprised to see that the bush, though on fire, was not consumed. So Moses decided, "I must go over to look at this remarkable sight, and see why the bush is not burned."

When the LORD saw him coming over to look at it more closely, God called out to him from the bush, "Moses! Moses!" He answered, "Here I am." God said, "Come no nearer! Remove the sandals from your feet, for the place where you stand is holy ground. I am the God of your fathers," he continued, "the God of Abraham, the God of Isaac, the God of Jacob." Moses hid his face, for he was afraid to look at God. But the LORD said, "I have witnessed the affliction of my people in Egypt and have heard their cry of complaint against their slave drivers, so I know well what they are suffering. Therefore I have come down to rescue them from the hands of the Egyptians and lead them out of that land into a good and spacious land, a land flowing with milk and honey."

Moses said to God, "But when I go to the Israelites and say to them, 'The God of your fathers has sent me to you,' if they ask me, 'What is his name?' what am I to tell them?" God replied, "I am who am." Then he added, "This is what you shall tell the Israelites: I AM sent me to you."

God spoke further to Moses, "Thus shall you say to the Israelites: The LORD, the God of your fathers, the God of Abraham, the God of Isaac, the God of Jacob, has sent me to you.

"This is my name forever; / thus am I to be remembered through all generations."

RESPONSORIAL PSALM
Psalm 103:1–2, 3–4, 6–7, 8, 11 (8a)

R. The Lord is kind and merciful.

Bless the LORD, O my soul;
    and all my being, bless his holy name.
Bless the LORD, O my soul,
    and forget not all his benefits.   R.

He pardons all your iniquities,
    he heals all your ills,
He redeems your life from destruction,
    he crowns you with kindness
        and compassion.   R.

The LORD secures justice
    and the rights of all the oppressed.
He has made known his ways to Moses,
    and his deeds to the children of Israel.   R.

Merciful and gracious is the LORD,
    slow to anger and abounding in kindness.
For as the heavens are high above the earth,
    so surpassing is his kindness toward those
        who fear him.   R.

READING II *1 Corinthians 10:1–6, 10–12*

I do not want you to be unaware, brothers and sisters, that our ancestors were all under the cloud and all passed through the sea, and all of them were baptized into Moses in the cloud and in the sea. All ate the same spiritual food, and all drank the same spiritual drink, for they drank from a spiritual rock that followed them, and the rock was the Christ. Yet God was not pleased with most of them, for they were struck down in the desert.

These things happened as examples for us, so that we might not desire evil things, as they did. Do not grumble as some of them did, and suffered death by the destroyer. These things happened to them as an example, and they have been written down as a warning to us, upon whom the end of the ages has come. Therefore, whoever thinks he is standing secure should take care not to fall.

GOSPEL *Luke 13:1–9*

Some people told Jesus about the Galileans whose blood Pilate had mingled with the blood of their sacrifices. Jesus said to them in reply, "Do you think that because these Galileans suffered in this way they were greater sinners than all other Galileans? By no means! But I tell you, if you do not repent, you will all perish as they did! Or those eighteen people who were killed when the tower at Siloam fell on them—do you think they were more guilty than everyone else who lived in Jerusalem? By no means! But I tell you, if you do not repent, you will all perish as they did!"

And he told them this parable: "There once was a person who had a fig tree planted in his orchard, and when he came in search of fruit on it but found none, he said to the gardener, 'For three years now I have come in search of fruit on this fig tree but have found none. So cut it down. Why should it exhaust the soil?' He said to him in reply, 'Sir, leave it for this year also, and I shall cultivate the ground around it and fertilize it; it may bear fruit in the future. If not you can cut it down.'"

Practice of Charity

Our encounter with God is to lead to a conversion of heart that bears fruit. As in Moses' encounter with God in the burning bush, each of us is called to make known God's justice and mercy for those who are suffering. ◆ Seek out the Sacrament of Penance this Lent. As you encounter God in this sacrament, you are being strengthened to bring God's mercy to those who suffer. How might you contribute to the work of your local Catholic Charities or St. Vincent de Paul Society? ◆ Read this reflection on the social dimensions of the Sacrament of Penance: www.usccb.org/about /justice-peace-and-human-development/upload /Penance-handout.pdf. ◆ As you seek God's forgiveness in you daily prayer, ask to be strengthened to work toward justice, peace, and reconciliation in situations of conflict and oppression.

Download more questions and activities for families, Christian initiation groups, and other adult groups at http://www.ltp.org/ahw.

Scripture Insights

The demands of daily life can be so great that we sometimes find it easy to rationalize bad behavior. But then something happens that makes us aware of our failures and limitations. We acknowledge our behaviors and move forward a changed person.

The First Reading tells the story of Moses' encounter with God in the burning bush. Distracted from herding sheep, Moses checks out a curious sight—a bush that burns without burning up. In that moment, God directs him to step out of his mundane world into a holy space. Moses responds in terror, afraid to see God's face. He is given a mission and again he cowers, saying something to the effect, "Who am I to do this thing?" and "I don't even know who you are!" He owns his inadequacies, but he goes forward in trust of God's care.

Sometimes we change our ways out of fear of punishment. In the Second Reading, Paul alludes to a later part of the Exodus story to remind the Corinthian community not to follow the Israelites' example. They had experienced God's presence in the parting of the sea, the manna, and the water from the rock, and still they grumbled against God and committed evil deeds, resulting in punishment by poisonous serpents (cf. Numbers 21:4–9).

People sometimes try to make sense of horrific tragedies by saying that it is God's punishment for wrongdoing. In today's Gospel, Jesus says that is not necessarily the case, but he uses the image of the slaughter and defilement of innocent Galileans to emphasize the necessity of repentance.

◆ What does the gardener's promise to tend the fig tree say about God's mercy?

◆ What does it mean to you that God is the God of Abraham, Isaac, and Jacob?

◆ Using the antiphon, "The Lord is kind and merciful," write a psalm of repentance patterned after today's Responsorial Psalm.

READING I *Exodus 17:3–7*

In those days, in their thirst for water, the people grumbled against Moses, saying, "Why did you ever make us leave Egypt? Was it just to have us die here of thirst with our children and our livestock?" So Moses cried out to the LORD, "What shall I do with this people? A little more and they will stone me!" The LORD answered Moses, "Go over there in front of the people, along with some of the elders of Israel, holding in your hand, as you go, the staff with which you struck the river. I will be standing there in front of you on the rock in Horeb. Strike the rock, and the water will flow from it for the people to drink." This Moses did, in the presence of the elders of Israel. The place was called Massah and Meribah, because the Israelites quarreled there and tested the LORD, saying, "Is the LORD in our midst or not?"

RESPONSORIAL PSALM
Psalm 95:1–2, 6–7, 8–9 (8)

R. If today you hear his voice, harden not
      your hearts.

Come, let us sing joyfully to the LORD;
    let us acclaim the Rock of our salvation.
Let us come into his presence with thanksgiving;
    let us joyfully sing psalms to him.

Come, let us bow down in worship;
    let us kneel before the LORD who made us.
For he is our God,
      and we are the people he shepherds, the flock
      he guides.

Oh, that today you would hear his voice:
    "Harden not your hearts as at Meribah,
    as in the day of Massah in the desert,
where your fathers tempted me;
    they tested me though they had seen my works."

READING II *Romans 5:1–2, 5–8*

Brothers and sisters: Since we have been justified by faith, we have peace with God through our Lord Jesus Christ, through whom we have gained access by faith to this grace in which we stand, and we boast in hope of the glory of God.

And hope does not disappoint, because the love of God has been poured out into our hearts through the Holy Spirit who has been given to us. For Christ, while we were still helpless, died at the appointed time for the ungodly. Indeed, only with difficulty does one die for a just person, though perhaps for a good person one might even find courage to die. But God proves his love for us in that while we were still sinners Christ died for us.

GOSPEL
John 4:5–15, 19b–26, 39a, 40–42

Longer: John 4:5–42

Jesus came to a town of Samaria called Sychar, near the plot of land that Jacob had given to his son Joseph. Jacob's well was there. Jesus, tired from his journey, sat down there at the well. It was about noon.

A woman of Samaria came to draw water. Jesus said to her, "Give me a drink." His disciples had gone into the town to buy food. The Samaritan woman said to him, "How can you, a Jew, ask me, a Samaritan woman, for a drink?"—For Jews use nothing in common with Samaritans.—Jesus answered and said to her, "If you knew the gift of God and who is saying to you, 'Give me a drink,' you would have asked him and he would have given you living water." The woman said to him, "Sir, you do not even have a bucket and the cistern is deep; where then can you get this living water? Are you greater than our father Jacob, who gave us this cistern and drank from it himself with his children and his flocks?" Jesus answered and said to her, "Everyone who drinks this water will be thirsty again; but whoever drinks the water I shall give will never thirst; the water I shall give will become in him a spring of water welling up to eternal life." The woman said to him, "Sir, give me this water, so that I may not be thirsty or have to keep coming here to draw water.

"I can see that you are a prophet. Our ancestors worshiped on this mountain; but you people say that the place to worship is in Jerusalem." Jesus said to her, "Believe me, woman, the hour is coming when you will worship the Father neither on this mountain nor in Jerusalem. You people worship what you do not understand; we worship what we understand, because salvation is from the Jews. But the hour is coming, and is now here, when true worshipers will worship the Father in Spirit and truth; and indeed the Father seeks such people to worship him. God is Spirit, and those who worship him must worship in Spirit and truth." The woman said to him, "I know that the Messiah is coming, the one called the Christ; when he comes, he will tell us everything." Jesus said to her, "I am he, the one speaking with you."

Many of the Samaritans of that town began to believe in him. When the Samaritans came to him, they invited him to stay with them; and he stayed there two days. Many more began to believe in him because of his word, and they said to the woman, "We no longer believe because of your word; for we have heard for ourselves, and we know that this is truly the savior of the world."

Practice of Hope

Today's readings point out that water is a natural and a spiritual gift. As Moses strikes the rock, God gives life to the Israelites by providing water for them to drink. In the encounter with the Samaritan woman at the well, Jesus promises life-giving water, the gift of eternal life. At Easter, we celebrate the life received in the waters of Baptism. ◆ Considering the availability of water in your daily life, pray these words from St. Francis of Assisi's Canticle of Creation: "Praised be you, my Lord, through Sister Water, who is very useful and humble and precious and chaste." ◆ Learn about Catholic Relief Services' clean water initiatives and choose an action to support these efforts: education.crs.org/issues/water. ◆

Download more questions and activities for families, Christian initiation groups, and other adult groups at http://www.ltp.org/ahw.

Scripture Insights

"Give us water to drink!" is a demand that provides meaningful reflection for the first of three scrutinies in the Rite of Christian Initiation of Adults and for all who need to experience healing of what hinders their relationship with God.

Today's First Reading recounts a story of God's people grumbling against Moses as they traveled from the desert of Sin (Hebrew *cyin*, probably meaning "clay"), near a place called Massah (Hebrew for "a place of testing") and Meribah (Hebrew for "a place of strife"). This is the third of three tests that God puts to the Israelites during the Exodus. God's people fail the test, as they cry out, "Give us water to drink." Still, God provides abundantly from a rock.

In the Second Reading, Paul captures the disposition of gratitude that we should have, in recognition of God's love that has been "poured out into our hearts" (Romans 5:5).

As today's Gospel begins, Jesus is seated at Jacob's well in the village of Sychar. In the Bible, wells have significance as places of encounter. Both Isaac and his son Jacob met their wives at a well. Jesus asks for a drink from a woman who came to draw water, and he receives a sarcastic response. Jews and Samaritans were not on good terms in the first century. Jesus suggests that the woman should ask him for water and he would give her living water. Though she fails to understand at first, her quest for water leads her to recognize Jesus as the messiah.

◆ Why did the Samaritan woman believe Jesus when he called himself the messiah?

◆ Compare the water in the First Reading to that in the Gospel. How does each satisfy?

◆ Pray in gratitude for the love "poured out" for you.

March 31, 2019 FOURTH SUNDAY OF LENT

READING I *Joshua 5:9a, 10–12*

The LORD said to Joshua, "Today I have removed the reproach of Egypt from you."

While the Israelites were encamped at Gilgal on the plains of Jericho, they celebrated the Passover on the evening of the fourteenth of the month. On the day after the Passover, they ate of the produce of the land in the form of unleavened cakes and parched grain. On that same day after the Passover, on which they ate of the produce of the land, the manna ceased. No longer was there manna for the Israelites, who that year ate of the yield of the land of Canaan.

RESPONSORIAL PSALM
Psalm 34:2–3, 4–5, 6–7 (9a)

R. Taste and see the goodness of the Lord.

I will bless the LORD at all times;
    his praise shall be ever in my mouth.
Let my soul glory in the LORD;
    the lowly will hear me and be glad.   R.

Glorify the LORD with me,
    let us together extol his name.
I sought the LORD, and he answered me
    and delivered me from all my fears.   R.

Look to him that you may be radiant with joy,
    and your faces may not blush with shame.
When the poor one called out, the LORD heard,
    and from all his distress he saved him.   R.

READING II *2 Corinthians 5:17–21*

Brothers and sisters: Whoever is in Christ is a new creation: the old things have passed away; behold, new things have come. And all this is from God, who has reconciled us to himself through Christ and given us the ministry of reconciliation, namely, God was reconciling the world to himself in Christ, not counting their trespasses against them and entrusting to us the message of reconciliation. So we are ambassadors for Christ, as if God were appealing through us. We implore you on behalf of Christ, be reconciled to God. For our sake he made him to be sin who did not know sin, so that we might become the righteousness of God in him.

GOSPEL *Luke 15:1–3, 11–32*

Tax collectors and sinners were all drawing near to listen to Jesus, but the Pharisees and scribes began to complain, saying, "This man welcomes sinners and eats with them." So to them Jesus addressed this parable: "A man had two sons, and the younger son said to his father, 'Father give me the share of your estate that should come to me.' So the father divided the property between them. After a few days, the younger son collected all his belongings and set off to a distant country where he squandered his inheritance on a life of dissipation. When he had freely spent everything, a severe famine struck that country, and he found himself in dire need. So he hired himself out to one of the local citizens who sent him to his farm to tend the swine. And he longed to eat his fill of the pods on which the swine fed, but nobody gave him any. Coming to his senses he thought, 'How many of my father's hired workers have more than enough food to eat, but here am I, dying from hunger. I shall get up and go to my father and I shall say to him, "Father, I have sinned against heaven and against you. I no longer deserve to be called your son; treat me as you would treat one of your hired workers."' So he got up and went back to his father. While he was still a long way off, his father caught sight of him, and was filled with compassion. He ran to his son, embraced him and kissed him. His son said to him, 'Father, I have sinned against heaven and against you; I no longer deserve to be called your son.' But his father ordered his servants, 'Quickly bring the finest robe and put it on him; put a ring on his finger and sandals on his feet. Take the fattened calf and slaughter it. Then let us celebrate with a feast, because this son of mine was dead, and has come to life again; he was lost, and has been found.' Then the celebration began. Now the older son had been out in the field and, on his way back, as he neared the house, he heard the sound of music and dancing. He called one of the servants and asked what this might mean. The servant said to him, 'Your brother has returned and your father has slaughtered the fattened calf because he has him back safe and sound.' He became angry, and when he refused to enter the house, his father came out and pleaded with him. He said to his father in reply, 'Look, all these years I served you and not once did I disobey your orders; yet you never gave me even a young goat to feast on with my friends. But when your son returns who swallowed up your property with prostitutes, for him you slaughter the fattened calf.' He said to him, 'My son, you are here with me always; everything I have is yours. But now we must celebrate and rejoice, because your brother was dead and has come to life again; he was lost and has been found.'"

Practice of Hope

The familiar parable of the prodigal son is Jesus' response to the Pharisees and scribes who are scandalized that Jesus shares meals with tax collectors and sinners. Their complaints seem to parallel the older son's objection to the feast offered by the Father upon the younger son's return. As the Father welcomes both of his sons to the feast, God draws us together, saints and sinners in need of mercy, in the Eucharist we share. ◆ As you share meals with others this week, consider how these meals are opportunities to strengthen relationships. Take extra time this week to offer hospitality and strengthen your sense of community. ◆ Reflect on the Eucharist as communion as you read paragraph 27 of the apostolic letter *Mane Nobiscum Domine*: w2.vatican.va/content/john-paul-ii/en/apost _letters/2004/documents/hf_jp-ii_apl_20041008 _mane-nobiscum-domine.html. ◆ Give thanks for the communion we share with God and one another in the Eucharist.

Download more questions and activities for families, Christian initiation groups, and other adult groups at http://www.ltp.org/ahw.

Scripture Insights

The Fourth Sunday of Lent is traditionally known as Laetare (Latin, "rejoice") Sunday or Rose Sunday. It represents a respite from the long Lenten season, and a glimpse at the wonderful new beginnings that come with Easter resurrection. It will be, in a sense, our homecoming.

Today's First Reading invites us to celebrate with the Israelites their entrance into the Promised Land. Those who had sinned against God had passed away, and a new generation was born during their desert wanderings. To re-consecrate the people to God, Joshua circumcised the males—a sign of the covenant God made with Abraham (Genesis 17:1–27)—and everyone observed Passover, a reminder of God's benevolent care during the Exodus. Then the manna was no more— they had come home.

Likewise, in the Second Reading, Paul invites us to celebrate the way in which God has reconciled all things to himself in Christ so that we can become a new creation in Christ. The Greek *katallassó* means "to reconcile" or "to decisively change," especially when used to refer to the redemption of sinners.

Today's Gospel provides us with another story of homecoming and new beginnings. In the parable, the father completely overlooks the young man's sin and restores him to his family status with a great celebration. How is this like our relationship with God?

◆ By whose power was the relationship between father and son restored in the Gospel?

◆ What does it mean to become a new creation in Christ?

◆ When have you tasted and seen "the goodness of the Lord"?

READING I
1 Samuel 16:1b, 6–7, 10–13a

The LORD said to Samuel: "Fill your horn with oil, and be on your way. I am sending you to Jesse of Bethlehem, for I have chosen my king from among his sons."

As Jesse and his sons came to the sacrifice, Samuel looked at Eliab and thought, "Surely the LORD's anointed is here before him." But the LORD said to Samuel: "Do not judge from his appearance or from his lofty stature, because I have rejected him. Not as man sees does God see, because man sees the appearance but the LORD looks into the heart." In the same way Jesse presented seven sons before Samuel, but Samuel said to Jesse, "The LORD has not chosen any one of these." Then Samuel asked Jesse, "Are these all the sons you have?" Jesse replied, "There is still the youngest, who is tending the sheep." Samuel said to Jesse, "Send for him; we will not begin the sacrificial banquet until he arrives here." Jesse sent and had the young man brought to them. He was ruddy, a youth handsome to behold and making a splendid appearance. The LORD said, "There—anoint him, for this is the one!" Then Samuel, with the horn of oil in hand, anointed David in the presence of his brothers; and from that day on, the spirit of the LORD rushed upon David.

READING II Ephesians 5:8–14

Brothers and sisters: You were once darkness, but now you are light in the Lord. Live as children of light, for light produces every kind of goodness and righteousness and truth. Try to learn what is pleasing to the Lord. Take no part in the fruitless works of darkness; rather expose them, for it is shameful even to mention the things done by them in secret; but everything exposed by the light becomes visible, for everything that becomes visible is light. Therefore, it says:

"Awake, O sleeper,
and arise from the dead,
and Christ will give you light."

GOSPEL John 9:1–41

Shorter: John 9:1, 6–9, 13–17, 34–38

As Jesus passed by he saw a man blind from birth. His disciples asked him, "Rabbi, who sinned, this man or his parents, that he was born blind?" Jesus answered, "Neither he nor his parents sinned; it is so that the works of God might be made visible through him. We have to do the works of the one who sent me while it is day. Night is coming when no one can work. While I am in the world, I am the light of the world." When he had said this, he spat on the ground and made clay with the saliva, and smeared the clay on his eyes, and said to him, "Go wash in the Pool of Siloam"—which means Sent—. So he went and washed, and came back able to see.

His neighbors and those who had seen him earlier as a beggar said, "Isn't this the one who used to sit and beg?" Some said, "It is," but others said, "No, he just looks like him." He said, "I am." So they said to him, "How were your eyes opened?" He replied, "The man called Jesus made clay and anointed my eyes and told me, 'Go to Siloam and wash.' So I went there and washed and was able to see." And they said to him, "Where is he?" He said, "I don't know."

They brought the one who was once blind to the Pharisees. Now Jesus had made clay and opened his eyes on a sabbath. So then the Pharisees also asked him how he was able to see. He said to them, "He put clay on my eyes, and I washed, and now I can see." So some of the Pharisees said, "This man is not from God, because he does not keep the sabbath." But others said, "How can a sinful man do such signs?" And there was a division among them. So they said to the blind man again, "What do you have to say about him, since he opened your eyes?" He said, "He is a prophet."

Now the Jews did not believe that he had been blind and gained his sight until they summoned the parents of the one who had gained his sight. They asked them, "Is this your son, who you say was born blind? How does he now see?" His parents answered and said, "We know that this is our son and that he was born blind. We do not know how he sees now, nor do we know who opened his eyes. Ask him, he is of age; he can speak for himself." His parents said this because they were afraid of the Jews, for the Jews had already agreed that if anyone acknowledged him as the Christ, he would be expelled from the synagogue. For this reason his parents said, "He is of age; question him."

So a second time they called the man who had been blind and said to him, "Give God the praise! We know that this man is a sinner." He replied, "If he is a sinner, I do not know. One thing I do know is that I was blind and now I see." So they said to him, "What did he do to you? How did he open your eyes?" He answered them, "I told you already and you did not listen. Why do you want to hear it again? Do you want to become his disciples, too?" They ridiculed him and said, "You are that man's disciple; we are disciples of Moses! We know that God spoke to Moses, but we do not know where this one is from." The man answered and said to them, "This is what is so amazing, that you do not know where he is from, yet he opened my eyes. We know that God does not listen to sinners, but if one is devout and does his will, he listens to him. It is unheard of that anyone ever opened the eyes of a person born blind. If this man were not from God, he would not be able to do anything." They answered and said to him, "You were born totally in sin, and are you trying to teach us?" Then they threw him out.

When Jesus heard that they had thrown him out, he found him and said, "Do you believe in the Son of Man?" He answered and said, "Who is he, sir, that I may believe in him?" Jesus said to him, "You have seen him, and the one speaking with you is he." He said, "I do believe, Lord," and he worshiped him. Then Jesus said, "I came into this world for judgment, so that those who do not see might see, and those who do see might become blind."

Some of the Pharisees who were with him heard this and said to him, "Surely we are not also blind, are we?" Jesus said to them, "If you were blind, you would have no sin; but now you are saying, 'We see,' so your sin remains."

Scripture Insights

Today's readings consider light and sight. Ancient peoples believed that humans could see because of the light that emanated from within them. Thus, the blind were shunned because they were thought to be full of darkness. Though biologically incorrect, the religious insight of this view is especially appropriate for the second scrutiny of the Lenten period: one needs the "light" to see with eyes of faith.

Today's First Reading tells the story of David's anointing. Samuel, a prophet and the last pre-monarchical leader of the Israelites, is sent by God to Jesse in Bethlehem. When he first arrives, he thinks he knows whom he should anoint, but he judges only based on physical appearances. God will choose based on what is in the person's heart. The one chosen would be David, a small boy of such low status that he had to be brought in from the pasture to participate in the feast.

The Second Reading is both a celebration and an exhortation. We no longer live in darkness, Paul says, because Christ is our light. Therefore, we must live as children of light.

Today's Gospel continues the idea that Christ is our light in the story of the formerly blind man. Twice we hear that Jesus made clay and put it on the blind man's eyes—a detail reminiscent of the creation story in which God took clay to create Adam (Genesis 2:4b–7). Likewise, the command to wash suggests Christian Baptism. Although the man's eyes are healed immediately, his spiritual eyes are gradually opened, when he comes to recognize Jesus as the messiah.

♦ How does Samuel know to continue seeking a person to anoint?

♦ Put yourself in the place of the blind man. What is he thinking as the story unfolds?

♦ What does it mean to you to be a child of the light?

READING I *Isaiah 43:16–21*

Thus says the LORD,
>who opens a way in the sea
>and a path in the mighty waters,
who leads out chariots and horsemen,
>a powerful army,
till they lie prostrate together, never to rise,
>snuffed out and quenched like a wick.
Remember not the events of the past,
>the things of long ago consider not;
see, I am doing something new!
>Now it springs forth, do you not perceive it?
In the desert I make a way;
>in the wasteland, rivers.
Wild beasts honor me,
>jackals and ostriches,
for I put water in the desert
>and rivers in the wasteland
>for my chosen people to drink,
the people whom I formed for myself,
>that they might announce my praise.

RESPONSORIAL PSALM
Psalm 126:1–2, 2–3, 4–5, 6 (3)

R. The Lord has done great things for us;
>we are filled with joy.

When the LORD brought back the captives
>of Zion,
>we were like men dreaming.
Then our mouth was filled with laughter,
>and our tongue with rejoicing. R.

Then they said among the nations,
>"The LORD has done great things for them."
The LORD has done great things for us;
>we are glad indeed. R.

Restore our fortunes, O LORD,
>like the torrents in the southern desert.
Those that sow in tears
>shall reap rejoicing. R.

Although they go forth weeping,
>carrying the seed to be sown,
they shall come back rejoicing,
>carrying their sheaves. R.

READING II *Philippians 3:8–14*

Brothers and sisters: I consider everything as a loss because of the supreme good of knowing Christ Jesus my Lord. For his sake I have accepted the loss of all things and I consider them so much rubbish, that I may gain Christ and be found in him, not having any righteousness of my own based on the law but that which comes through faith in Christ, the righteousness from God, depending on faith to know him and the power of his resurrection and the sharing of his sufferings by being conformed to his death, if somehow I may attain the resurrection from the dead.

It is not that I have already taken hold of it or have already attained perfect maturity, but I continue my pursuit in hope that I may possess it, since I have indeed been taken possession of by Christ Jesus. Brothers and sisters, I for my part do not consider myself to have taken possession. Just one thing: forgetting what lies behind but straining forward to what lies ahead, I continue my pursuit toward the goal, the prize of God's upward calling, in Christ Jesus.

GOSPEL *John 8:1–11*

Jesus went to the Mount of Olives. But early in the morning he arrived again in the temple area, and all the people started coming to him, and he sat down and taught them. Then the scribes and the Pharisees brought a woman who had been caught in adultery and made her stand in the middle. They said to him, "Teacher, this woman was caught in the very act of committing adultery. Now in the law, Moses commanded us to stone such women. So what do you say?" They said this to test him, so that they could have some charge to bring against him. Jesus bent down and began to write on the ground with his finger. But when they continued asking him, he straightened up and said to them, "Let the one among you who is without sin be the first to throw a stone at her." Again he bent down and wrote on the ground. And in response, they went away one by one, beginning with the elders. So he was left alone with the woman before him. Then Jesus straightened up and said to her,

"Woman, where are they? Has no one condemned you?" She replied, "No one, sir." Then Jesus said, "Neither do I condemn you. Go, and from now on do not sin any more."

Practice of Charity

The prophet Isaiah observes the ways in which God acts in the world, doing the unexpected and bringing forth something new. In today's Gospel, Jesus, indeed, acts in a new and unexpected way, refusing to condemn the woman caught in adultery and proposing a new future free from sin. We, too, are invited to share in this new way of life. ◆ This week, notice what holds you back from doing the good you want to do. Consider if acting in a new or unexpected way might make God's love more fully known. ◆ Reflect on the new life we share in Christ as you read paragraph 654 of the Catechism of the Catholic Church: www .vatican.va/archive/ENG0015/__P1S.HTM. ◆ In a time of prayer, imagine Jesus speaking these words to you: "Go, and . . . do not sin any more." Seek to open your heart to the life of grace given in the sacraments.

Download more questions and activities for families, Christian initiation groups, and other adult groups at http://www.ltp.org/ahw.

Scripture Insights

Today's readings invite us to reflect on our need for redemption and to open our eyes to the new things that God wants to do in us.

The First Reading is addressed to the exiles in Babylon. They are told that God is about to destroy the Babylonian empire. What a marvelous thing! God will buy back the exiles in the same way that he destroyed the pharaoh's army at the Red Sea. Moreover, this new Exodus will be so great that they will forget the first one. God makes all things new.

In the Second Reading, Paul tells the community at Philippi about his former life as a persecutor of the followers of Jesus and about how everything he once had is now considered rubbish in light of knowing Christ and his Resurrection. Here, "knowing" means experiencing Christ in faith.

In the Gospel's powerful story about Jesus and a woman charged with adultery, the scribes and Pharisees force Jesus to be a judge so that they might entrap him. But what about the woman? She is shamed at least twice. The men who brought charges against her would have witnessed the act, and now she is made to stand before these men while she awaits judgment. It is likely that she had been raped because most women in the ancient world were not given enough freedom to voluntarily engage in sexual relations. Jesus saves her by saying that the one who has no sin can cast the first stone.

◆ From the First Reading, what can you conclude about God's relationship to humanity?

◆ What would you have wanted to say to the woman accused of adultery?

◆ What phrases in Paul's testimony of faith resonate with you?

READING I *Ezekiel 37:12–14*

Thus says the LORD God: O my people, I will open your graves and have you rise from them, and bring you back to the land of Israel. Then you shall know that I am the LORD, when I open your graves and have you rise from them, O my people! I will put my spirit in you that you may live, and I will settle you upon your land; thus you shall know that I am the LORD. I have promised, and I will do it, says the LORD.

RESPONSORIAL PSALM
Psalm 130:1–2, 3–4, 5–6, 7–8 (7)

R. With the Lord there is mercy, and fullness
      of redemption.

Out of the depths I cry to you, O LORD;
   LORD, hear my voice!
Let your ears be attentive
   to my voice in supplication. R.

If you, O LORD, mark iniquities,
   LORD, who can stand?
But with you is forgiveness
   that you may be revered. R.

I trust in the LORD;
   my soul trusts in his word.
More than sentinels wait for the dawn,
   let Israel wait for the LORD. R.

For with the LORD is kindness
   and with him is plenteous redemption;
and he will redeem Israel
   from all their iniquities. R.

READING II *Romans 8:8–11*

Brothers and sisters: Those who are in the flesh cannot please God. But you are not in the flesh; on the contrary, you are in the spirit, if only the Spirit of God dwells in you. Whoever does not have the Spirit of Christ does not belong to him. But if Christ is in you, although the body is dead because of sin, the spirit is alive because of righteousness. If the Spirit of the One who raised Jesus from the dead dwells in you, the One who raised Christ from the dead will give life to your mortal bodies also, through his Spirit dwelling in you.

GOSPEL
John 11:3–7, 17, 20–27, 33b–45

Longer: John 11:1–45

The sisters of Lazarus sent word to Jesus, saying, "Master, the one you love is ill." When Jesus heard this he said, "This illness is not to end in death, but is for the glory of God, that the Son of God may be glorified through it." Now Jesus loved Martha and her sister and Lazarus. So when he heard that he was ill, he remained for two days in the place where he was. Then after this he said to his disciples, "Let us go back to Judea."

When Jesus arrived, he found that Lazarus had already been in the tomb for four days. When Martha heard that Jesus was coming, she went to meet him; but Mary sat at home. Martha said to Jesus, "Lord, if you had been here, my brother would not have died. But even now I know that whatever you ask of God, God will give you." Jesus said to her, "Your brother will rise." Martha said, "I know he will rise, in the resurrection on the last day." Jesus told her, "I am the resurrection and the life; whoever believes in me, even if he dies, will live, and everyone who lives and believes in me will never die. Do you believe this?" She said to him, "Yes, Lord. I have come to believe that you are the Christ, the Son of God, the one who is coming into the world."

He became perturbed and deeply troubled, and said, "Where have you laid him?" They said to him, "Sir, come and see." And Jesus wept. So the Jews said, "See how he loved him." But some of them said, "Could not the one who opened the eyes of the blind man have done something so that this man would not have died?"

So Jesus, perturbed again, came to the tomb. It was a cave, and a stone lay across it. Jesus said, "Take away the stone." Martha, the dead man's sister, said to him, "Lord, by now there will be a stench; he has been dead for four days." Jesus said to her, "Did I not tell you that if you believe you will see the glory of God?" So they took away the stone. And Jesus raised his eyes and said, "Father, I thank you for hearing me. I know that you always hear me; but because of the crowd here I have said this, that they may believe that you sent me." And when he had said this, he cried out in a loud voice, "Lazarus, come out!" The dead man came out, tied hand and foot with burial bands, and his face was wrapped in a cloth. So Jesus said to them, "Untie him and let him go."

Now many of the Jews who had come to Mary and seen what he had done began to believe in him.

Practice of Faith

Today's readings invite reflection on the new life given to us by the power of the Holy Spirit in the sacraments. As we die and rise with Christ in Baptism, we are given a share of the divine life and the Holy Spirit comes to dwell in us. In Confirmation, the grace of Baptism is strengthened as we receive the outpouring of the gifts of the Holy Spirit, enabling us to live as Christ's witnesses today. ◆ When facing a difficult situation, call to mind the gifts of the Holy Spirit and seek to utilize one or more of them. ◆ Reflect on the help given in the seven gifts of the Holy Spirit as described in the *United States Catholic Catechism for Adults*: ccc.usccb.org/flipbooks/uscca/files/assets/basic -html/page-236.html. ◆ Call on the Holy Spirit in your prayer. Consider using the Prayer to the Holy Spirit or the Prayer for the Indwelling of the Holy Spirit, attributed to St. Augustine: www1.villanova.edu/villanova/mission/campus ministry/RegularSpiritualPractices/resources /spirituality/restlesshearts/prayers.html.

Download more questions and activities for families, Christian initiation groups, and other adult groups at http://www.ltp.org/ahw.

Scripture Insights

On the Sunday of the third scrutiny of the elect, the readings proclaim that God can raise the dead and bring life to the lifeless.

The First Reading is the culmination of Ezekiel's vision of a valley of dry bones. The bones are a metaphor for the exiles in Babylon, broken and destroyed by their deportation, but God does not abandon his chosen. God will bring them out of their grave—Babylon—and put his spirit (ruah, also meaning "breath") in them so that they can come home alive. Then, they will know that he is YHWH. Usually translated as "Lord," YHWH is the name that God revealed to Moses when they met at the burning bush, but it means something like "I am who I am" or "being-ness itself."

In the Gospel, Jesus responds to the message that Lazarus is ill, saying, "This illness . . . is for the glory of God." Here, "glory" and its cognates refer to something that Jesus and the Father share as Jesus does the work that the Father has given him to do. Paradoxically, by doing the Father's work in raising Lazarus, the stage is set for Jesus' glorification on the Cross.

In the Second Reading, Paul writes about how humanity was once dead because of sin but is now alive, because of righteousness. For Paul, "righteousness" means acquittal in God's court of law. This is not something that humans can achieve through merit. Rather, it is God's gift to those who trust in God's power to save.

◆ What does the Gospel tell you about Martha? Did she expect Jesus to raise Lazarus?

◆ When has the Spirit of God changed "death" to life for you? What did those experiences teach you about the nature of God?

◆ Add a stanza praising God to the Responsorial Psalm.

READING I *Isaiah 50:4–7*

The Lord GOD has given me
  a well-trained tongue,
that I might know how to speak to the weary
  a word that will rouse them.
Morning after morning
  he opens my ear that I may hear;
and I have not rebelled,
  have not turned back.
I gave my back to those who beat me,
  my cheeks to those who plucked my beard;
my face I did not shield
  from buffets and spitting.

The Lord GOD is my help,
  therefore I am not disgraced;
I have set my face like flint,
  knowing that I shall not be put to shame.

READING II *Philippians 2:6–11*

Christ Jesus, though he was in the form of God,
  did not regard equality with God
  something to be grasped.
Rather, he emptied himself,
  taking the form of a slave,
  coming in human likeness;
  and found human in appearance,
  he humbled himself,
  becoming obedient to the point of death,
  even death on a cross.
Because of this, God greatly exalted him
  and bestowed on him the name
  which is above every name,
  that at the name of Jesus
  every knee should bend,
  of those in heaven and on earth and
      under the earth,
  and every tongue confess that
  Jesus Christ is Lord,
  to the glory of God the Father.

GOSPEL *Luke 22:14—23:56*

Shorter: Luke 23:1–49

When the hour came, Jesus took his place at table with the apostles. He said to them, "I have eagerly desired to eat this Passover with you before I suffer, for, I tell you, I shall not eat it again until there is fulfillment in the kingdom of God." Then he took a cup, gave thanks, and said, "Take this and share it among yourselves; for I tell you that from this time on I shall not drink of the fruit of the vine until the kingdom of God comes." Then he took the bread, said the blessing, broke it, and gave it to them, saying, "This is my body, which will be given for you; do this in memory of me." And likewise the cup after they had eaten, saying, "This cup is the new covenant in my blood, which will be shed for you.

"And yet behold, the hand of the one who is to betray me is with me on the table; for the Son of Man indeed goes as it has been determined; but woe to that man by whom he is betrayed." And they began to debate among themselves who among them would do such a deed.

Then an argument broke out among them about which of them should be regarded as the greatest. He said to them, "The kings of the Gentiles lord it over them and those in authority over them are addressed as 'Benefactors'; but among you it shall not be so. Rather, let the greatest among you be as the youngest, and the leader as the servant. For who is greater: the one seated at table or the one who serves? Is it not the one seated at table? I am among you as the one who serves. It is you who have stood by me in my trials; and I confer a kingdom on you, just as my Father has conferred one on me, that you may eat and drink at my table in my kingdom; and you will sit on thrones judging the twelve tribes of Israel.

"Simon, Simon, behold Satan has demanded to sift all of you like wheat, but I have prayed that your own faith may not fail; and once you have turned back, you must strengthen your brothers." He said to him, "Lord, I am prepared to go to prison and to die with you." But he replied, "I tell you, Peter, before the cock crows this day, you will deny three times that you know me."

He said to them, "When I sent you forth without a money bag or a sack or sandals, were you in need of anything?" "No, nothing," they replied. He said to them, "But now one who has a money bag should take it, and likewise a sack, and one who does not have a sword should sell his cloak and buy one. For I tell you that this Scripture must be fulfilled in me, namely, *He was counted among the wicked*; and indeed what is written about me is coming to fulfillment." Then they said, "Lord, look, there are two swords here." But he replied, "It is enough!"

Then going out, he went, as was his custom, to the Mount of Olives, and the disciples followed him. When he arrived at the place he said to them, "Pray that you may not undergo the test." After withdrawing about a stone's throw from them and kneeling, he prayed, saying, "Father, if you are willing, take this cup away from me; still, not my will but yours be done." And to strengthen him an angel from heaven appeared to him. He was in such agony and he prayed so fervently that his sweat became like drops of blood falling on the ground. When he rose from prayer and returned to his disciples, he found them sleeping from grief. He said to them, "Why are you sleeping? Get up and pray that you may not undergo the test."

While he was still speaking, a crowd approached and in front was one of the Twelve, a man named Judas. He went up to Jesus to kiss him. Jesus said to him, "Judas, are you betraying the Son of Man with a kiss?" His disciples realized what was about to happen, and they asked, "Lord, shall we strike with a sword?" And one of them struck the high priest's servant and cut off his right ear. But Jesus said in reply, "Stop, no more of this!" Then he touched the servant's ear and healed him. And Jesus said to the chief priests and temple guards and elders who had come for him, "Have you come out as against a robber, with swords and clubs? Day after day I was with you in the temple area, and you did not seize me; but this is your hour, the time for the power of darkness."

After arresting him they led him away and took him into the house of the high priest; Peter was following at a distance. They lit a fire in the middle of the courtyard and sat around it, and Peter sat down with them. When a maid saw him seated in the light, she looked intently at him and said, "This man too was with him." But he denied it saying, "Woman, I do not know him." A short while later someone else saw him and said, "You too are one of them"; but Peter answered, "My friend, I am not." About an hour later, still another insisted, "Assuredly, this man too was with him, for he also is a Galilean." But Peter said, "My friend, I do not know what you are talking about." Just as he was saying this, the cock crowed, and the Lord turned and looked at Peter; and Peter remembered the word of the Lord, how he had said to him, "Before the cock crows today, you will deny me three times." He went out and began to weep bitterly. The men who held Jesus in custody were ridiculing and beating him. They blindfolded him and questioned him, saying, "Prophesy! Who is it that struck you?" And they reviled him in saying many other things against him.

When day came the council of elders of the people met, both chief priests and scribes, and they brought him before their Sanhedrin. They said, "If you are the Christ, tell us," but he replied to them, "If I tell you, you will not believe, and if I question, you will not respond. But from this time on the Son of Man will be seated at the right hand of the power of God." They all asked, "Are you then the Son of God?" He replied to them, "You say that I am." Then they said, "What further need have we for testimony? We have heard it from his own mouth."

Then the whole assembly of them arose and brought him before Pilate. They brought charges against him, saying, "We found this man misleading our people; he opposes the payment of taxes to Caesar and maintains that he is the Christ, a king." Pilate asked him, "Are you the king of the Jews?" He said to him in reply, "You say so." Pilate then addressed the chief priests and the crowds, "I find this man not guilty." But they were adamant and said, "He is inciting the people with his teaching throughout all Judea, from Galilee where he began even to here."

On hearing this Pilate asked if the man was a Galilean; and upon learning that he was under Herod's jurisdiction, he sent him to Herod, who was in Jerusalem at that time. Herod was very glad to see Jesus; he had been wanting to see him for a long time, for he had heard about him and had been hoping to see him perform some sign. He questioned him at length, but he gave him no answer. The chief priests and scribes, meanwhile, stood by accusing him harshly. Herod and his soldiers treated him contemptuously and mocked him, and after clothing him in resplendent garb, he sent him back to Pilate. Herod and Pilate became friends that very day, even though they had been enemies formerly. Pilate then summoned the chief priests, the rulers, and the people and said to them, "You brought this man to me and accused him of inciting the people to revolt. I have conducted my investigation in your presence and have not found this man guilty of the charges you have brought against him, nor did Herod, for he sent him back to us. So no capital crime has been committed by him. Therefore I shall have him flogged and then release him."

But all together they shouted out, "Away with this man! Release Barabbas to us." — Now Barabbas had been imprisoned for a rebellion that had taken place in the city and for murder. — Again Pilate addressed them, still wishing to release Jesus, but they continued their shouting, "Crucify him! Crucify him!" Pilate addressed them a third time, "What evil has this man done? I found him guilty of no capital crime. Therefore I shall have him flogged and then release him." With loud shouts, however, they persisted in calling for his crucifixion, and their voices prevailed. The verdict of Pilate was that their demand should be granted. So he released the man who had been imprisoned for rebellion and murder, for whom they asked, and he handed Jesus over to them to deal with as they wished.

As they led him away they took hold of a certain Simon, a Cyrenian, who was coming in from the country; and after laying the cross on him, they made him carry it behind Jesus. A large crowd of people followed Jesus, including many women who mourned and lamented him. Jesus turned to them and said, "Daughters of Jerusalem, do not weep for me; weep instead for yourselves and for your children for indeed, the days are coming when people will say, 'Blessed are the bar-

ren, the wombs that never bore and the breasts that never nursed.' At that time people will say to the mountains, 'Fall upon us!' and to the hills, 'Cover us!' for if these things are done when the wood is green what will happen when it is dry?" Now two others, both criminals, were led away with him to be executed.

When they came to the place called the Skull, they crucified him and the criminals there, one on his right, the other on his left. Then Jesus said, "Father, forgive them, they know not what they do." They divided his garments by casting lots. The people stood by and watched; the rulers, meanwhile, sneered at him and said, "He saved others, let him save himself if he is the chosen one, the Christ of God." Even the soldiers jeered at him. As they approached to offer him wine they called out, "If you are King of the Jews, save yourself." Above him there was an inscription that read, "This is the King of the Jews."

Now one of the criminals hanging there reviled Jesus, saying, "Are you not the Christ? Save yourself and us." The other, however, rebuking him, said in reply, "Have you no fear of God, for you are subject to the same condemnation? And indeed, we have been condemned justly, for the sentence we received corresponds to our crimes, but this man has done nothing criminal." Then he said, "Jesus, remember me when you come into your kingdom." He replied to him, "Amen, I say to you, today you will be with me in Paradise."

It was now about noon and darkness came over the whole land until three in the afternoon because of an eclipse of the sun. Then the veil of the temple was torn down the middle. Jesus cried out in a loud voice, "Father, into your hands I commend my spirit"; and when he had said this he breathed his last.

[Here all kneel and pause for a short time.]

The centurion who witnessed what had happened glorified God and said, "This man was innocent beyond doubt." When all the people who had gathered for this spectacle saw what had happened, they returned home beating their breasts; but all his acquaintances stood at a distance, including the women who had followed him from Galilee and saw these events.

Now there was a virtuous and righteous man named Joseph, who, though he was a member of the council, had not consented to their plan of action. He came from the Jewish town of Arimathea and was awaiting the kingdom of God. He went to Pilate and asked for the body of Jesus. After he had taken the body down, he wrapped it in a linen cloth and laid him in a rock-hewn tomb in which no one had yet been buried. It was the day of preparation, and the sabbath was about to begin. The women who had come from Galilee with him followed behind, and when they had seen the tomb and the way in which his body was laid in it, they returned and prepared spices and perfumed oils. Then they rested on the sabbath according to the commandment.

Practice of Charity

During Holy Week, we walk with Christ through his passion, death, and Resurrection. As we do so, we seek to recognize the face of Christ in all who suffer injustice and recommit ourselves to serve the suffering Christ in our brothers and sisters. ◆ Carry a cross in your pocket this week as a reminder to pray for those who bear the burdens of violence and suffering. ◆ Learn more about the Church's response to torture and take action: http://www.usccb.org/issues-and-action/human-life-and-dignity/torture/torture-is-a-moral-issue.cfm. ◆ Pray that the Church will stand strong in defending the dignity of the human person as you prayerfully reflect on these words of St. Oscar Romero: "The church . . . believes that in each person is the Creator's image and that everyone who tramples it offends God. As holy defender of God's rights and of his images, the church must cry out. It takes as spittle in its face, as lashes on its back, as the cross in its passion, all that human beings suffer" (Homily, December 31, 1977).

Download more questions and activities for families, Christian initiation groups, and other adult groups at http://www.ltp.org/ahw.

Scripture Insights

Today's readings for Palm Sunday highlight the resolve of God's servant to fulfill his will.

In the First Reading, the "servant" speaks. This is the third of four servant oracles in the Book of Isaiah. The servant goes unnamed, but he is depicted as freely giving over his will to God. Here we are told that he did not refuse when God opened his ear to hear what a disciple needs to know, and he set his face like flint to do God's will, knowing that God would not allow him to be put to shame.

The Second Reading invites us to join our voices in praise of the Christ who emptied himself to take on the form of a slave and accept death on a cross. Because of his openness to God's will, he is exalted above every other name in the universe, but Paul situates the hymn in an admonition, "Have among yourselves the same attitude that is also yours in Christ Jesus." Thus, we are called to join our lives to the self-emptying of Christ.

Today's Gospel recounts the story of Jesus' passion and death as told by Luke, beginning with the Passover meal that he shared with his disciples to his burial by Joseph of Arimathea. But this journey to death began much earlier in Luke's Gospel account. In Luke 9:51, we are told, "When the days for his being taken up were fulfilled, he resolutely determined to journey to Jerusalem." Indeed, Jesus' entire life was oriented to the Paschal Mystery, the process of dying and rising to new life. As his disciples, we are called to do the same.

◆ In the Gospel, how do we see Jesus' resolve to accomplish what God called him to do?

◆ When have you needed to set your face like flint (First Reading)? Why?

◆ Ask God to open your heart to more deeply ponder and give thanks for Christ's self-emptying.

Holy Thursday brings to an end the forty days of Lent, which make up the season of anticipation of the great Three Days. Composed of prayer, alms-giving, fasting, and the preparation of the cate-chumens for Baptism, the season of Lent is now brought to a close, and the Three Days begin as we approach the liturgy of Holy Thursday evening. As those to be initiated into the Church have pre-pared themselves for their entrance into the fullness of life, so have we been awakening in our hearts, minds, and bodies our own entrances into the life of Christ, experienced in the life of the Church.

Easter Triduum (Latin for "three days") is the center, the core, of the entire year for Christians. These Three Days mark the mystery around which our entire lives are played out. Adults in the com-munity are invited to plan ahead so that the whole time from Thursday night until Easter Sunday is free of social engagements, free of entertainment, and free of meals except for the most basic nour-ishment. We measure these days—indeed, our very salvation in the life of God—in step with the catechumens themselves; we are revitalized as we support them along the way and participate in their initiation rites.

We are asked to fast on Good Friday and to continue fasting, if possible, all through Holy Saturday as strictly as we can so that we come to the Easter Vigil hungry and full of excitement, parched and longing to feel the sacred water of the font on our skin. We pare down distractions on Good Friday and Holy Saturday so that we may be free for prayer and anticipation, for reflection, preparation, and silence. The Church is getting ready for the great night of the Easter Vigil.

As one who has been initiated into the Church, as one whose life has been wedded to this community gathered at the table, you should anticipate the Triduum with concentration and vigor. With you, the whole Church knows that our presence for the liturgies of the Triduum is not just an invitation. Everyone is needed. We pull out all the stops for these days. As humans, wedded to humanity by the joys and travails of life and grafted onto the body of the Church by the sanctifying waters of Baptism, we lead the new members into new life in this community of faith.

To this end, the Three Days are seen not as three distinct liturgies, but as one movement. These days have been connected liturgically from the early days of the Christian Church. As mem-bers of this community, we should be personally committed to preparing for and attending the Triduum and its culmination in the Easter Vigil of Holy Saturday.

The Church proclaims the direction of the Triduum with the opening antiphon of Holy Thursday, which comes from Paul's Letter to the Galatians (6:14). With this verse the Church sets a spiritual environment into which we as committed Christians enter the Triduum:

> *We should glory in the cross*
> *of our Lord Jesus Christ, for he*
> *is our salvation, our life and*
> *resurrection; through him we*
> *are saved and made free.*

HOLY THURSDAY

On Thursday evening we enter into this Triduum together. Whether presider, lector, preacher, greeter, altar server, minister of the Eucharist, decorator, or person in the remote corner in the last pew of the church, we begin, as always, by hearkening to the Word of God. These are the Scriptures for the liturgy of Holy Thursday:

Exodus 12:1–8, 11–14
Ancient instructions for the meal of the Passover.

1 Corinthians 11:23–26
Eat the bread and drink the cup until the return of the Lord.

John 13:1–15
Jesus washes the feet of the disciples.

Then the priest, like Jesus, does something strange: he washes feet. Jesus gave us this image of what the Church is supposed to look like, feel like, act like. Our position—whether as observer, washer or washed, servant or served—may be difficult. Yet we learn from the discomfort, from the awkwardness.

Then we celebrate the Eucharist. Because it is connected to the other liturgies of the Triduum on Good Friday and Holy Saturday night, the evening liturgy of Holy Thursday has no ending. Whether we stay to pray awhile or leave, we are now in the quiet, peace, and glory of the Triduum.

GOOD FRIDAY

We gather quietly in community on Friday and again listen to the Word of God:

Isaiah 52:13—53:12
The servant of the Lord was crushed for our sins.

Hebrews 4:14–16; 5:7–9
The Son of God learned obedience through his suffering.

John 18:1—19:42
The Passion of Jesus Christ.

After the sermon, we pray at length for all the world's needs: for the Church; for the pope, the clergy and all the baptized; for those preparing for initiation; for the unity of Christians; for Jews; for non-Christians; for atheists; for all in public office; and for those in special need.

Then there is another once-a-year event: the holy cross is held up in our midst, and we come forward one by one to do reverence with a kiss, bow, or genuflection. This communal reverence of an instrument of torture recalls the painful price, in the past and today, of salvation, the way in which our redemption is wrought, the scourging and humiliation of Jesus Christ that bring direction and life back to a humanity that is lost and dead. During the adoration of the cross, we sing not only of the sorrow, but of the glory of the Cross by which we have been saved.

Again, we bring to mind the words of Paul (Galatians 6:14), on which last night's entrance antiphon is loosely based: "May I never boast except in the cross of our Lord Jesus Christ, through which the world has been crucified to me, and I to the world."

We continue in fasting and prayer and vigil, in rest and quiet, through Saturday. This Saturday for us is God's rest at the end of creation. It is Christ's repose in the tomb. It is Christ's visit with the dead.

EASTER VIGIL

Hungry now, pared down to basics, lightheaded from vigilance and full of excitement, we, the already baptized, gather in darkness and light a new fire. From this blaze we light a great candle that will make this night bright for us and will burn throughout Easter Time.

We hearken again to the Word of God with some of the most powerful narratives and proclamations of our tradition:

Genesis 1:1—2:2
The creation of the world.

Genesis 22:1–18
The sacrifice of Isaac.

Exodus 14:15—15:1
The crossing of the Red Sea.

Isaiah 54:5–14
You will not be afraid.

Isaiah 55:1–11
Come, come to the water.

Baruch 3:9–15, 32—4:4
Walk by the light of wisdom.

Ezekiel 36:16–17a, 18–28
The Lord says: I will sprinkle water.

Romans 6:3–11
United with him in death.

Year A: Matthew 28:1–10, Year B: Mark 16:1–7, Year C: Luke 24:1–12
Jesus has been raised.

After the readings, we call on our saints to stand with us as we go to the font and the priest celebrant blesses the waters. The chosen of all times and all places attend to what is about to take place. The elect renounce evil, profess the faith of the Church, and are baptized and anointed.

All of us renew our Baptism. These are the moments when death and life meet, when we reject evil and make our promises to God. All of this is in the communion of the Church. So together we go to the table and celebrate the Easter Eucharist.

Prayer before Reading the Word

God of our ancestors,
you have raised up Jesus
and exalted him at your right hand
as Leader and Savior.

Open our minds to understand the Scriptures,
and, as with great joy we bless you in your temple,
make us witnesses who can proclaim
the repentance and forgiveness
you extend to all the nations
in the name of Jesus,
the Messiah, our great high priest,
who intercedes before you on our behalf,
living and reigning with you
in the unity of the Holy Spirit,
one God, for ever and ever. Amen.

Prayer after Reading the Word

O God, the fountain of joy and of peace,
into the hands of your risen Son
you have entrusted the destinies
of peoples and of nations.

Keep us safe in those arms
from which no one can snatch us,
that we may proclaim your Word
in peace and in persecution,
until at last we stand before the Lamb
with songs of praise on our lips.

We ask this through the Lord Jesus,
our Passover and our Peace,
who lives and reigns with you
in the unity of the Holy Spirit,
one God, for ever and ever. Amen.

Weekday Readings

April 22: Monday within the Octave of Easter
    Acts 2:14, 22–33; Matthew 28:8–15
April 23: Tuesday within the Octave of Easter
    Acts 2:36–41; John 20:11–18
April 24: Wednesday within the Octave of Easter
    Acts 3:1–10; Luke 24:13–35
April 25: Thursday within the Octave of Easter
    Acts 3:11–26; Luke 24:35–48
April 26: Friday within the Octave of Easter
    Acts 4:1–12; John 21:1–14
April 27: Saturday within the Octave of Easter
    Acts 4:13–21; Mark 16:9–15

April 29: *Acts 4:23–31; John 3:1–8*
April 30: *Acts 4:32–37; John 3:7b–15*
May 1: *Acts 5:17–26; John 3:16–21*
May 2: *Acts 5:27–33; John 3:31–36*
May 3: Feast of Sts. Philip and James, Apostles
    1 Corinthians 15:1–8; John 14:6–14
May 4: *Acts 6:1–7; John 6:16–21*

May 6: *Acts 6:8–15; John 6:22–29*
May 7: *Acts 7:51—8:1a; John 6:30–35*
May 8: *Acts 8:1b–8; John 6:35–40*
May 9: *Acts 8:26–40; John 6:44–51*
May 10: *Acts 9:1–20; John 6:52–59*
May 11: *Acts 9:31–42; John 6:60–69*

May 13: *Acts 11:1–18; John 10:1–10*
May 14: Feast of St. Matthias, Apostle
    Acts 1:15–17, 20–26; John 15:9–17
May 15: *Acts 12:24—13:5a; John 12:44–50*
May 16: *Acts 13:13–25; John 13:16–20*
May 17: *Acts 13:26–33; John 14:1–6*
May 18: *Acts 13:44–52; John 14:7–14*

May 20: *Acts 14:5–18; John 14:21–26*
May 21: *Acts 14:19–28; John 14:27–31a*
May 22: *Acts 15:1–6; John 15:1–8*
May 23: *Acts 15:7–21; John 15:9–11*
May 24: *Acts 15:22–31; John 15:12–17*
May 25: *Acts 16:1–10; John 15:18–21*

May 27: *Acts 16:11–15; John 15:26—16:4a*
May 28: *Acts 16:22-34; John 16:5–11*
May 29: *Acts 17:15, 22—18:1; John 16:12–15*
May 30: Solemnity of the Ascension of the Lord [In some
    regions, transferred to Seventh Sunday of Easter]
    Acts 1:1–11; Ephesians 1:17–23 or Hebrews 9:24–28;
    10:19–23; Luke 24:46–53
May 31: Feast of the Visitation of the
    Blessed Virgin Mary
    Zephaniah 3:14–18a or Romans 12:9–16/
    Luke 1:39–56
June 1: *Acts 18:23–28; John 16:23b–28*

June 3: *Acts 19:1–8; John 16:29–33*
June 4: *Acts 20:17–27; John 17:1–11a*
June 5: *Acts 20:28–38; John 17:11b–19*
June 6: *Acts 22:30; 23:6–11; John 17:20–26*
June 7: *Acts 25:13b–21; John 21:15–19*
June 8: *Morning: Acts 28:16-20, 30–31; John 21:20–25*

READING I *Acts 10:34a; 37–43*

Peter proceeded to speak and said: "You know what has happened all over Judea, beginning in Galilee after the baptism that John preached, how God anointed Jesus of Nazareth with the Holy Spirit and power. He went about doing good and healing all those oppressed by the devil, for God was with him. We are witnesses of all that he did both in the country of the Jews and in Jerusalem. They put him to death by hanging him on a tree. This man God raised on the third day and granted that he be visible, not to all the people, but to us, the witnesses chosen by God in advance, who ate and drank with him after he rose from the dead. He commissioned us to preach to the people and testify that he is the one appointed by God as judge of the living and the dead. To him all the prophets bear witness, that everyone who believes in him will receive forgiveness of sins through his name."

RESPONSORIAL PSALM
Psalm 118:1–2, 16–17, 22–23 (24)

R. This is the day the Lord has made; let us
       rejoice and be glad.
or: Alleluia.

Give thanks to the LORD, for he is good,
  for his mercy endures forever.
Let the house of Israel say,
  "His mercy endures forever." R.

"The right hand of the LORD has struck
     with power;
  the right hand of the LORD is exalted.
I shall not die, but live,
  and declare the works of the LORD." R.

The stone which the builders rejected
  has become the cornerstone.
By the LORD has this been done;
  it is wonderful in our eyes. R.

READING II *Colossians 3:1–4*

Alternate: 1 Corinthians 5:6b–8

Brothers and sisters: If then you were raised with Christ, seek what is above, where Christ is seated at the right hand of God. Think of what is above, not of what is on earth. For you have died, and your life is hidden with Christ in God. When Christ your life appears, then you too will appear with him in glory.

GOSPEL *John 20:1–9*

Alternate readings: Luke 24:1–12; or at an afternoon or evening Mass: Luke 24:13–35

On the first day of the week, Mary of Magdala came to the tomb early in the morning, while it was still dark, and saw the stone removed from the tomb. So she ran and went to Simon Peter and to the other disciple whom Jesus loved, and told them, "They have taken the Lord from the tomb, and we don't know where they put him." So Peter and the other disciple went out and came to the tomb. They both ran, but the other disciple ran faster than Peter and arrived at the tomb first; he bent down and saw the burial cloths there, but did not go in. When Simon Peter arrived after him, he went into the tomb and saw the burial cloths there, and the cloth that had covered his head, not with the burial cloths but rolled up in a separate place. Then the other disciple also went in, the one who had arrived at the tomb first, and he saw and believed. For they did not yet understand the Scripture that he had to rise from the dead.

Practice of Faith

Throughout the fifty-day Easter season, we marvel at the empty tomb as we seek to renew and strengthen our faith in Christ. ♦ This week, savor the joy of Easter, knowing that Christ is truly raised from the dead, bringing the promise of new life. Hold fast to all that strengthens your faith in God's power at work in your life. ♦ Consider the message of hope that Bishop Douglas Crosby, OMI, president of the Canadian Catholic Conference of Bishops, offered in 2017: "This Easter, with our hearts lit by the unquenchable fire of God's love, we are asked to entrust ourselves to Christ's care as we hope in the divine power that 'dispels wickedness, washes faults away, restores innocence to the fallen, and joy to mourners, drives out hatred, fosters concord, and brings down the mighty'" (*Roman Missal*, Longer Form of the Easter Proclamation: https://www.cwl.ca/wp-content/uploads/2017/04/Message-Easter-2017-EN.pdf). ♦ Pray the Easter Sequence, Victimae Paschali Laudes: https://www.youtube.com/watch?v=3zbd46jANDU.

Download more questions and activities for families, Christian initiation groups, and other adult groups at http://www.ltp.org/ahw.

Scripture Insights

Alleluia! Christ is risen from the dead! Today's readings remind us that this acclamation is about more than looking back. They also anticipate the time when our lives will be united with Christ in glory.

In today's First Reading, Peter gives a speech at the home of Cornelius, a Roman centurion and proselyte to Judaism who had been prompted in a vision to call Peter to his household. When Peter arrives, he testifies about Jesus' deeds and about how he died and was raised by God. The phrase "hanging him on a tree" refers to the Crucifixion, and likely reminds its readers of Deuteronomy 21:22, which says the crucified one is cursed by God. Yet this is not the end. Peter declares, "Everyone who believes in him will receive forgiveness of sins in his name."

The Gospel's recounting of Mary Magdalene coming upon the empty tomb is interrupted by the story of Peter and the Beloved Disciple arriving at the tomb. The men entered and saw the burial cloths and go home. The verses after the conclusion of today's Gospel show that only Mary remains at the tomb. Twice she hears, "Woman, why are you weeping?" Twice she laments that she cannot find Jesus' body, but then the Risen Lord calls her by name and she recognizes him. He commissions her to go to the disciples as an apostle of the Resurrection.

The Second Reading addresses the impact of Christ's Resurrection for all of us. Our life is hidden now in Christ, but when he returns we, too, will appear with him in glory. Alleluia!

♦ What did it mean to Peter to be a witness of the Resurrection? What does it mean to you?

♦ Imagine yourself as Mary searching for the Lord. What do you do?

♦ Compose a stanza to the Responsorial Psalm that tells what the Lord's Resurrection means to you.

READING I   *Acts 5:12–16*

Many signs and wonders were done among the people at the hands of the apostles. They were all together in Solomon's portico. None of the others dared to join them, but the people esteemed them. Yet more than ever, believers in the Lord, great numbers of men and women, were added to them. Thus they even carried the sick out into the streets and laid them on cots and mats so that when Peter came by, at least his shadow might fall on one or another of them. A large number of people from the towns in the vicinity of Jerusalem also gathered, bringing the sick and those disturbed by unclean spirits, and they were all cured.

RESPONSORIAL PSALM
Psalm 118:2–4, 13–15, 22–24 (1)

R. Give thanks to the Lord, for he is good, his
       love is everlasting.
or: Alleluia.

Let the house of Israel say,
   "His mercy endures forever."
Let the house of Aaron say,
   "His mercy endures forever."
Let those who fear the LORD say,
   "His mercy endures forever."   R.

I was hard pressed and was falling,
   but the LORD helped me.
My strength and my courage is the LORD,
   and he has been my savior.
The joyful shout of victory
   in the tents of the just.   R.

The stone which the builders rejected
   has become the cornerstone.
By the LORD has this been done;
   it is wonderful in our eyes.
This is the day the LORD has made;
   let us be glad and rejoice in it.   R.

READING II
Revelation 1:9–11a, 12–13, 17–19

I, John, your brother, who share with you the distress, the kingdom, and the endurance we have in Jesus, found myself on the island called Patmos because I proclaimed God's word and gave testimony to Jesus. I was caught up in spirit on the Lord's day and heard behind me a voice as loud as a trumpet, which said, "Write on a scroll what you see." Then I turned to see whose voice it was that spoke to me, and when I turned, I saw seven gold lampstands and in the midst of the lampstands one like a son of man, wearing an ankle-length robe, with a gold sash around his chest.

When I caught sight of him, I fell down at his feet as though dead. He touched me with his right hand and said, "Do not be afraid. I am the first and the last, the one who lives. Once I was dead, but now I am alive forever and ever. I hold the keys to death and the netherworld. Write down, therefore, what you have seen, and what is happening, and what will happen afterwards."

GOSPEL   *John 20:19–31*

On the evening of that first day of the week, when the doors were locked, where the disciples were, for fear of the Jews, Jesus came and stood in their midst and said to them, "Peace be with you." When he had said this, he showed them his hands and his side. The disciples rejoiced when they saw the Lord. Jesus said to them again, "Peace be with you. As the Father has sent me, so I send you." And when he had said this, he breathed on them and said to them, "Receive the Holy Spirit. Whose sins you forgive are forgiven them, and whose sins you retain are retained."

Thomas, called Didymus, one of the Twelve, was not with them when Jesus came. So the other disciples said to him, "We have seen the Lord." But he said to them, "Unless I see the mark of the nails in his hands and put my finger into the nailmarks and put my hand into his side, I will not believe."

Now a week later his disciples were again inside and Thomas was with them. Jesus came, although the doors were locked, and stood in their midst and said, "Peace be with you." Then he said to Thomas, "Put your finger here and see my hands, and bring your hand and put it into my side, and do not be unbelieving, but believe." Thomas answered and said to him, "My Lord and my God!" Jesus said to him, "Have you come to believe because you have seen me? Blessed are those who have not seen and have believed."

Now Jesus did many other signs in the presence of his disciples that are not written in this book. But these are written that you may come to believe that Jesus is the Christ, the Son of God, and that through this belief you may have life in his name.

Practice of Charity

Again and again, Jesus says, "Peace be with you." As in today's Gospel, this gift of peace is connected with the power of the Holy Spirit and the mandate that God's mercy be shared with others. ◆ Share the gift of peace with someone who is expressing doubt about God's love and mercy by offering your presence and words of reassurance. ◆ Learn more about Catholic peacemaking efforts, such as Pax Christi USA: https://paxchristiusa.org/about/our-history/. Consider how you might contribute to peacemaking efforts locally. ◆ Place a symbol of peace in a prominent place and pray for peace throughout the day. Consider this prayer attributed to St. John of the Cross: O blessed Jesus, give me stillness of soul in You. Let your mighty calmness reign in me. Rule me, O King of Gentleness, King of Peace.

Scripture Insights

Today's readings call us to open our eyes and experience the many ways that God's mercy touches us.

The First Reading notes the growing Christian community that assembles under Solomon's Portico, on the eastern side of the outer court of the Jerusalem Temple. People come from the nearby villages to receive God's mercy in the form of healing. They even resort to putting their sick into the streets in the hope that Peter's shadow might pass over them when he walks by.

The Second Reading recounts a vision of "one like a son of man" dressed as priest and king. We soon learn that he is the Risen Christ. The seer is afraid, because he thinks (correctly) that he is encountering a divine being, but the Risen Christ offers him consolation, saying, "Do not be afraid." We should be consoled, as well, since seven is a symbol of fullness. The seven lampstands that stand in the presence of the divine symbolize all of us. We are not alone.

In today's Gospel, ten of Jesus' disciples are hiding behind locked doors on the night of the Resurrection, because they are afraid. Jesus appears in their midst with a greeting of peace, giving them evidence that he was, in fact, alive. Thomas, who was not with them that evening, provides a powerful profession of faith when he exclaims, "My Lord and my God."

◆ In what ways did a time of doubting strengthen your belief?

◆ Why did the people in the First Reading come to believe?

◆ How is the message that Christ is the first and last, the one who lives, a consolation for you?

READING I *Acts 5:27–32, 40b–41*

When the captain and the court officers had brought the apostles in and made them stand before the Sanhedrin, the high priest questioned them, "We gave you strict orders, did we not, to stop teaching in that name? Yet you have filled Jerusalem with your teaching and want to bring this man's blood upon us." But Peter and the apostles said in reply, "We must obey God rather than men. The God of our ancestors raised Jesus, though you had him killed by hanging him on a tree. God exalted him at his right hand as leader and savior to grant Israel repentance and forgiveness of sins. We are witnesses of these things, as is the Holy Spirit whom God has given to those who obey him."

The Sanhedrin ordered the apostles to stop speaking in the name of Jesus, and dismissed them. So they left the presence of the Sanhedrin, rejoicing that they had been found worthy to suffer dishonor for the sake of the name.

RESPONSORIAL PSALM
Psalm 30:2, 4, 5–6, 11–12, 13 (2a)

R. I will praise you, Lord, for you have rescued me.
or: Alleluia.

I will extol you, O LORD, for you drew me clear
   and did not let my enemies rejoice over me.
O LORD, you brought me up from the
      netherworld;
   you preserved me from among those going
      down into the pit. R.

Sing praise to the LORD, you his faithful ones,
   and give thanks to his holy name.
For his anger lasts but a moment;
   a lifetime, his good will.
At nightfall, weeping enters in,
   but with the dawn, rejoicing. R.

Hear, O LORD, and have pity on me;
   O LORD, be my helper.
You changed my mourning into dancing;
   O LORD, my God, forever will I give
      you thanks. R.

READING II *Revelation 5:11–14*

I, John, looked and heard the voices of many angels who surrounded the throne and the living creatures and the elders. They were countless in number, and they cried out in a loud voice:
  "Worthy is the Lamb that was slain
    to receive power and riches, wisdom
        and strength,
    honor and glory and blessing."
Then I heard every creature in heaven and on earth and under the earth and in the sea, everything in the universe, cry out:
  "To the one who sits on the
        throne and to the Lamb
    be blessing and honor, glory and might,
    forever and ever."
The four living creatures answered, "Amen," and the elders fell down and worshiped.

GOSPEL *John 21:1–19*

Shorter: John 21:1–14

At that time, Jesus revealed himself again to his disciples at the Sea of Tiberias. He revealed himself in this way. Together were Simon Peter, Thomas called Didymus, Nathanael from Cana in Galilee, Zebedee's sons, and two others of his disciples. Simon Peter said to them, "I am going fishing." They said to him, "We also will come with you." So they went out and got into the boat, but that night they caught nothing. When it was already dawn, Jesus was standing on the shore; but the disciples did not realize that it was Jesus. Jesus said to them, "Children, have you caught anything to eat?" They answered him, "No." So he said to them, "Cast the net over the right side of the boat and you will find something." So they cast it, and were not able to pull it in because of the number of fish. So the disciple whom Jesus loved said to Peter, "It is the Lord." When Simon Peter heard that it was the Lord, he tucked in his garment, for he was lightly clad, and jumped into the sea. The other disciples came in the boat, for they were not far from shore, only about a hundred yards, dragging the net with the fish. When they climbed out on shore, they saw a charcoal fire with fish on it and bread. Jesus said to them, "Bring some of the fish you just caught." So Simon Peter went over and dragged the net ashore full of one hundred fifty-three large fish. Even though there were so many, the net was not torn. Jesus said to them, "Come, have breakfast." And none of the disciples dared to ask him, "Who are you?" because they realized it was the Lord. Jesus came over and took the bread and gave it to them, and in like manner the fish. This was now the third time Jesus was revealed to his disciples after being raised from the dead.

When they had finished breakfast, Jesus said to Simon Peter, "Simon, son of John, do you love me more than these?" Simon Peter answered him, "Yes, Lord, you know that I love you." Jesus said to him, "Feed my lambs." He then said to Simon Peter a second time, "Simon, son of John, do you love me?" Simon Peter answered him, "Yes, Lord, you know that I love you." Jesus said to him, "Tend my sheep." Jesus said to him the third time, "Simon, son of John, do you love me?" Peter was distressed that Jesus had said to him a third time, "Do you love me?" and he said to him, "Lord, you know everything; you know that I love you." Jesus said to him, "Feed my sheep. Amen, amen, I say to you, when you were younger, you used to dress yourself and go where you wanted; but when you grow old, you will stretch out your hands, and someone else will dress you and lead you where you do not want to go." He said this signifying by what kind of death he would glorify God. And when he had said this, he said to him, "Follow me."

Practice of Charity

The care we give to those entrusted to us flows from the Lord's love for us and is an expression of our love for the Lord. ◆ Give thanks for the privilege of caring for those entrusted to you. ◆ In your prayer, name those who care for you and give thanks for their example.

Download more questions and activities for families, Christian initiation groups, and other adult groups at http://www.ltp.org/ahw.

Scripture Insights

Today's readings portray the Good News of Jesus Christ overflowing and growing like leaven. It cannot be stifled or stamped out.

In the First Reading, we learn that the Apostles were arrested and put on trial before the Sanhedrin that had earlier condemned Jesus. The high priest of the Jerusalem Temple scolded them for continuing to speak about Jesus, even after they were told to keep silent. However, with all boldness, they persisted in their testimony. When they were flogged and released with strong warnings against teaching about Jesus, what did they do? They continued to proclaim Jesus as Messiah everywhere. Such is the power of the Good News.

The Second Reading contains a vision of a heavenly liturgy in honor of the Lamb (the Risen Christ) and the one seated on the throne (God). Notice how the place is crammed with myriads of angels and other beings, all singing their song of praise to the Lamb who was slain and is now exalted in glory.

In today's Gospel, the disciples seem not to know what to do with themselves without Jesus, until Peter announces that he is going fishing—back to his old way of life—and the others join in. Suddenly the Risen Lord appears on the shore, waiting to share breakfast with them. The bread and fish suggest that the meal has Eucharistic overtones. After breakfast, Jesus gives Peter a mission and foreshadows the manner in which he would die—all for the spread of the Good News.

◆ What does today's Gospel tell us about Peter?

◆ What was the source of the Apostles' boldness in spreading the Good News?

◆ Give praise to God as you imagine yourself as part of those honoring the Lord in the reading from Revelation.

READING I *Acts 13:14, 43–52*

Paul and Barnabas continued on from Perga and reached Antioch in Pisidia. On the sabbath they entered the synagogue and took their seats. Many Jews and worshipers who were converts to Judaism followed Paul and Barnabas, who spoke to them and urged them to remain faithful to the grace of God.

On the following sabbath almost the whole city gathered to hear the word of the Lord. When the Jews saw the crowds, they were filled with jealousy and with violent abuse contradicted what Paul said. Both Paul and Barnabas spoke out boldly and said, "It was necessary that the word of God be spoken to you first, but since you reject it and condemn yourselves as unworthy of eternal life, we now turn to the Gentiles. For so the Lord has commanded us, *I have made you a light to the Gentiles, that you may be an instrument of salvation to the ends of the earth.*"

The Gentiles were delighted when they heard this and glorified the word of the Lord. All who were destined for eternal life came to believe, and the word of the Lord continued to spread through the whole region. The Jews, however, incited the women of prominence who were worshipers and the leading men of the city, stirred up a persecution against Paul and Barnabas, and expelled them from their territory. So they shook the dust from their feet in protest against them, and went to Iconium. The disciples were filled with joy and the Holy Spirit.

RESPONSORIAL PSALM
Psalm 100:1–2, 3, 5 (3c)

R. We are his people, the sheep of his flock.
or: Alleluia.

Sing joyfully to the LORD, all you lands;
serve the LORD with gladness;
come before him with joyful song.   R.

Know that the LORD is God;
he made us, his we are,
his people, the flock he tends.   R.

The LORD is good:
his kindness endures forever,
and his faithfulness, to all generations.   R.

READING II *Revelation 7:9, 14b–17*

I, John, had a vision of a great multitude, which no one could count, from every nation, race, people, and tongue. They stood before the throne and before the Lamb, wearing white robes and holding palm branches in their hands.

Then one of the elders said to me, "These are the ones who have survived the time of great distress; they have washed their robes and made them white in the blood of the Lamb.

"For this reason they stand before God's throne
and worship him day and night in
his temple.
The one who sits on the throne
will shelter them.
They will not hunger or thirst anymore,
nor will the sun or any heat strike them.
For the Lamb who is in the center of the throne
will shepherd them
and lead them to springs
of life-giving water,
and God will wipe away every tear from
their eyes."

GOSPEL *John 10:27–30*

Jesus said: "My sheep hear my voice; I know them, and they follow me. I give them eternal life, and they shall never perish. No one can take them out of my hand. My Father, who has given them to me, is greater than all, and no one can take them out of the Father's hand. The Father and I are one."

Practice of Hope

The image of sheep and shepherd described in the Gospel remains a cherished image of God's care for us. It also describes the heart of the prayer of contemplation. This intimate encounter with the Lord in prayer is a glimpse of what we hope one day to obtain: to be at peace in the presence of the Good Shepherd. ◆ Share time this week with someone close to you, making sure to set aside distractions, recognizing that our relationships are gifts from God that need careful tending. ◆ Learn more about contemplative prayer, described in paragraphs 2709–2719 of the *Catechism of the Catholic Church*: http://www.vatican.va/archive/ccc_css/archive/catechism/p4s1c3a1.htm. ◆ Spend time in quiet prayer, listening to the voice of the Good Shepherd. Conclude with Psalm 23 or this prayer: http://www.crs.org/resource-center/prayer-good-shepherd.

Download more questions and activities for families, Christian initiation groups, and other adult groups at http://www.ltp.org/ahw.

Scripture Insights

Witnessing to the Good News of Jesus Christ can be fraught with danger, but we can be assured that we will be victorious if we heed the voice of the Good Shepherd.

In the First Reading, we hear of Paul and Barnabas' missionary work in Antioch of Pisidia. We see that their message is not well received by some of their Jewish brethren, which provides the context for their declaration that God has sent them to be a light to the Gentiles. Persecuted and expelled from the region, they move on in joyful confidence that their mission has been inspired by God. A word of caution: we should not take Luke's words as a condemnation of Judaism. Rather, he was simply trying to give a reason for why the Good News spread beyond its original boundaries to the rest of the world.

The Second Reading provides a commentary on John's vision of a great multitude of people in white robes—a symbol of victory—carrying palm branches, typically used to greet kings returning from battle. An elder informs him the people are the martyrs who endured the great persecution. God now shelters them and the Lamb shepherds them.

In today's Gospel, Jesus assures his followers and warns his detractors by saying that he knows his sheep and they know him. His sheep hear his voice and, because he gives them eternal life, no one can harm them ever.

◆ What do you think it means that Paul and Barnabas "shook the dust from their feet"?

◆ How does Jesus' unity with the Father affect us?

◆ Offer a prayer of gratitude to God for leading you to life-giving water.

READING I *Acts 14:21−27*

After Paul and Barnabas had proclaimed the good news to that city and made a considerable number of disciples, they returned to Lystra and to Iconium and to Antioch. They strengthened the spirits of the disciples and exhorted them to persevere in the faith, saying, "It is necessary for us to undergo many hardships to enter the kingdom of God." They appointed elders for them in each church and, with prayer and fasting, commended them to the Lord in whom they had put their faith. Then they traveled through Pisidia and reached Pamphylia. After proclaiming the word at Perga they went down to Attalia. From there they sailed to Antioch, where they had been commended to the grace of God for the work they had now accomplished. And when they arrived, they called the church together and reported what God had done with them and how he had opened the door of faith to the Gentiles.

RESPONSORIAL PSALM
Psalm 145:8−9, 10−11, 12−13 (see 1)

R. I will praise your name for ever, my king and
       my God.
or: Alleluia.

The LORD is gracious and merciful,
    slow to anger and of great kindness.
The LORD is good to all
    and compassionate toward all his works. R.

Let all your works give you thanks, O LORD,
    and let your faithful ones bless you.
Let them discourse of the glory of your kingdom
    and speak of your might. R.

Let them make known your might to the
       children of Adam,
    and the glorious splendor of your kingdom.
Your kingdom is a kingdom for all ages,
    and your dominion endures through
       all generations. R.

READING II *Revelation 21:1−5a*

Then I, John, saw a new heaven and a new earth. The former heaven and the former earth had passed away, and the sea was no more. I also saw the holy city, a new Jerusalem, coming down out of heaven from God, prepared as a bride adorned for her husband. I heard a loud voice from the throne saying, "Behold, God's dwelling is with the human race. He will dwell with them and they will be his people and God himself will always be with them as their God. He will wipe every tear from their eyes, and there shall be no more death or mourning, wailing or pain, for the old order has passed away."

The One who sat on the throne said, "Behold, I make all things new."

GOSPEL *John 13:31−33a, 34−35*

When Judas had left them, Jesus said, "Now is the Son of Man glorified, and God is glorified in him. If God is glorified in him, God will also glorify him in himself, and God will glorify him at once. My children, I will be with you only a little while longer. I give you a new commandment: love one another. As I have loved you, so you also should love one another. This is how all will know that you are my disciples, if you have love for one another."

Practice of Charity

Today's Gospel prompts the queries: Would others recognize us as disciples of Jesus by how we love? Do we reflect the love of our Creator in our charity? ◆ Take some time for quiet reflection. Ask God to reveal where or whom in your life you love well and where you fall short in how you love. Notice if there is a person or situation that challenges you and plan to consciously bring patience, love, and charity to that person or situation this week. ◆ If you recognize a pattern of sin in your life, free yourself to love well by receiving God's mercy through the sacrament of Reconciliation. ◆ Consider learning to pray the Examen, the central prayer of the Jesuits, as a way to grow in love. Resources on this prayer abound, but a good place to start is at www.bc.edu/content/dam/files/top /church21/pdf/C-%5Cfakepath%5CThe%20 Ignatian%20Examen_Scala.pdf.

Download more questions and activities for families, Christian initiation groups, and other adult groups at http://www.ltp.org/ahw.

Scripture Insights

In a few weeks, we will celebrate the Solemnity of Pentecost, which marks the beginning of the Church. Today's readings offer a sense of the spread of the Church and what the Lord calls each of us to do.

The reading from Acts shows Paul and Barnabas concluding their first missionary journey by returning to the church of Antioch that had authorized their mission. On their journey, they set up structures of leadership to empower and encourage their new communities "to persevere in the faith" in view of the inevitable hardships and persecutions to come.

The Book of Revelation reminds us of our future hopes, when creation is renewed and the old world of hardships gives way to a glorious future. "He [God] will dwell with them and they will be his people and God himself will always be with them as their God." The Resurrection offers us a foretaste of this promised union with God.

In bidding farewell to his disciples at the Last Supper, Jesus offers encouragement by summarizing for them his teaching during his three-year ministry. Jesus' central message is captured in these words: "I give you a new commandment: love one another. As I have loved you, so you also should love one another." His sacrificial death for humanity provides the model for how we are to love others. In this sense, it is a new commandment that challenges Christ's followers to embrace, at the heart of love, a sacrifice for others. Jesus left us this legacy of sacrificial love and calls on followers to live it out in their lives. Sacrificial love becomes the mark of disciples.

◆ Why do Paul and Barnabas return to Antioch at the end of their first missionary journey?

◆ In what way is the commandment to love one another a "new commandment"?

◆ How do you live out concretely Jesus' call to sacrificial love?

May 26, 2019 Sixth Sunday of Easter

Reading I *Acts 15:1–2, 22–29*

Some who had come down from Judea were instructing the brothers, "Unless you are circumcised according to the Mosaic practice, you cannot be saved." Because there arose no little dissension and debate by Paul and Barnabas with them, it was decided that Paul, Barnabas, and some of the others should go up to Jerusalem to the apostles and elders about this question.

The apostles and elders, in agreement with the whole church, decided to choose representatives and to send them to Antioch with Paul and Barnabas. The ones chosen were Judas, who was called Barsabbas, and Silas, leaders among the brothers. This is the letter delivered by them:

"The apostles and the elders, your brothers, to the brothers in Antioch, Syria, and Cilicia of Gentile origin: greetings. Since we have heard that some of our number who went out without any mandate from us have upset you with their teachings and disturbed your peace of mind, we have with one accord decided to choose representatives and to send them to you along with our beloved Barnabas and Paul, who have dedicated their lives to the name of our Lord Jesus Christ. So we are sending Judas and Silas who will also convey this same message by word of mouth: 'It is the decision of the Holy Spirit and of us not to place on you any burden beyond these necessities, namely, to abstain from meat sacrificed to idols, from blood, from meats of strangled animals, and from unlawful marriage. If you keep free of these, you will be doing what is right. Farewell.'"

Responsorial Psalm
Psalm 67:2–3, 5, 6, 8 (4)

R. O God, let all the nations praise you!
or: Alleluia.

May God have pity on us and bless us;
   may he let his face shine upon us.
So may your way be known upon earth;
   among all nations, your salvation. R.

May the nations be glad and exult
   because you rule the peoples in equity;
   the nations on the earth you guide. R.

May the peoples praise you, O God;
   may all the peoples praise you!
May God bless us,
   and may all the ends of the earth
      fear him! R.

Reading II *Revelation 21:10–14, 22–23*

The angel took me in spirit to a great, high mountain and showed me the holy city Jerusalem coming down out of heaven from God. It gleamed with the splendor of God. Its radiance was like that of a precious stone, like jasper, clear as crystal. It had a massive, high wall, with twelve gates where twelve angels were stationed and on which names were inscribed, the names of the twelve tribes of the Israelites. There were three gates facing east, three north, three south, and three west. The wall of the city had twelve courses of stones as its foundation, on which were inscribed the twelve names of the twelve apostles of the Lamb.

I saw no temple in the city for its temple is the Lord God almighty and the Lamb. The city had no need of sun or moon to shine on it, for the glory of God gave it light, and its lamp was the Lamb.

Gospel *John 14:23–29*

Jesus said to his disciples: "Whoever loves me will keep my word, and my Father will love him, and we will come to him and make our dwelling with him. Whoever does not love me does not keep my words; yet the word you hear is not mine but that of the Father who sent me.

"I have told you this while I am with you. The Advocate, the Holy Spirit, whom the Father will send in my name, will teach you everything and remind you of all that I told you. Peace I leave with you; my peace I give to you. Not as the world gives do I give it to you. Do not let your hearts be troubled or afraid. You heard me tell you, 'I am going away and I will come back to you.' If you loved me, you would rejoice that I am going to the Father;

for the Father is greater than I. And now I have told you this before it happens, so that when it happens you may believe."

Practice of Hope

At Mass each Sunday, we extend a sign of peace to those around us. In hope, we trust what Christ promises: that the Holy Spirit will bring peace to our hearts, families, parishes, communities, and world. ◆ Reflect on what you sometimes count on for peace and hope. Is it money, success, or another person? What steps can you take to return your hope to God? ◆ Is something troubling your heart and pulling you away from God's peace? Invite the Holy Spirit into the situation by taking a deep breath and praying, "Come, Holy Spirit." Do this whenever you notice yourself slipping into anxiety or fear. ◆ In 1873, Horatio Spafford, amid great personal tragedy, penned the hopeful hymn "All Is Well with My Soul." Learn his story and hear his song at www.youtube.com/watch?v=BX_50A ERr8M&index=1&list=RDBX_50AERr8M.

Download more questions and activities for families, Christian initiation groups, and other adult groups at http://www.ltp.org/ahw.

Scripture Insights

The Gospel reading shows Jesus preparing his disciples for his departure. He promises them the gift of peace, a peace the world cannot give, since Jesus' sacrifice of love on the cross brings about a reconciliation of humanity with God. Jesus reassures his followers that although he will not be physically present among them, he will continue to be present spiritually through the Holy Spirit. One of the Spirit's tasks is "to teach you everything and remind you of all that I told you." The Spirit's inspiration enables Jesus' followers to fathom more deeply the meaning of Jesus' teachings. This provides the foundation for our Catholic teaching on the sensus fidei ("sense of the faith"), also called sensus fidelium ("sense of the faithful"), that the *Catechism of the Catholic Church* defines as "the supernatural appreciation of faith on the part of the whole people, when, from the bishops to the last of the faithful, they manifest a universal consent in matters of faith and morals" (92).

The First Reading notes the early Church's dependence on the Holy Spirit. In their outreach to the pagan world, the early Christians encounter problems that bring disagreements. Of major concern was the question about whether the pagan converts were still subject to the Jewish laws. Today's reading gives insight on how to resolve similar issues: by prayer and open dialogue under the inspiration of the Holy Spirit: "It is the decision of the Holy Spirit and of us not to place on you any burden beyond these necessities." The Holy Spirit operates at the heart of the Christian community by guiding it toward wise decisions. This example shows that all plans and decisions must begin under the guidance of and in the name of the Holy Spirit.

◆ How was the disagreement among the first followers of Jesus in the Acts of the Apostles resolved?

◆ How does our Catholic concept of sensus fidei derive from the Gospel passage read today?

◆ How has the Holy Spirit guided you in the important decisions of your life?

READING I *Acts 1:1–11*

In the first book, Theophilus, I dealt with all that Jesus did and taught until the day he was taken up, after giving instructions through the Holy Spirit to the apostles whom he had chosen. He presented himself alive to them by many proofs after he had suffered, appearing to them during forty days and speaking about the kingdom of God. While meeting with them, he enjoined them not to depart from Jerusalem, but to wait for "the promise of the Father about which you have heard me speak; for John baptized with water, but in a few days you will be baptized with the Holy Spirit."

When they had gathered together they asked him, "Lord, are you at this time going to restore the kingdom to Israel?" He answered them, "It is not for you to know the times or seasons that the Father has established by his own authority. But you will receive power when the Holy Spirit comes upon you, and you will be my witnesses in Jerusalem, throughout Judea and Samaria, and to the ends of the earth." When he had said this, as they were looking on, he was lifted up, and a cloud took him from their sight. While they were looking intently at the sky as he was going, suddenly two men dressed in white garments stood beside them. They said, "Men of Galilee, why are you standing there looking at the sky? This Jesus who has been taken up from you into heaven will return in the same way as you have seen him going into heaven."

RESPONSORIAL PSALM
Psalm 47:2–3, 6–7, 8–9 (6)

R. God mounts his throne to shouts of joy:
    a blare of trumpets for the Lord.
or: Alleluia.

All you peoples, clap your hands,
    shout to God with cries of gladness,
for the LORD, the Most High, the awesome,
    is the great king over all the earth.   R.

God mounts his throne amid shouts of joy;
    the LORD, amid trumpet blasts.
Sing praise to God, sing praise;
    sing praise to our king, sing praise.   R.

For king of all the earth is God;
    sing hymns of praise.
God reigns over the nations,
    God sits upon his holy throne.   R.

READING II
Hebrews 9:24–28; 10:19–23

Alternate reading: Ephesians 1:17–23

Christ did not enter into a sanctuary made by hands, a copy of the true one, but heaven itself, that he might now appear before God on our behalf. Not that he might offer himself repeatedly, as the high priest enters each year into the sanctuary with blood that is not his own; if that were so, he would have had to suffer repeatedly from the foundation of the world. But now once for all he has appeared at the end of the ages to take away sin by his sacrifice. Just as it is appointed that men and women die once, and after this the judgment, so also Christ, offered once to take away the sins of many, will appear a second time, not to take away sin but to bring salvation to those who eagerly await him.

Therefore, brothers and sisters, since through the blood of Jesus we have confidence of entrance into the sanctuary by the new and living way he opened for us through the veil, that is, his flesh, and since we have "a great priest over the house of God," let us approach with a sincere heart and in absolute trust, with our hearts sprinkled clean from an evil conscience and our bodies washed in pure water. Let us hold unwaveringly to our confession that gives us hope, for he who made the promise is trustworthy.

GOSPEL *Luke 24:46–53*

Jesus said to his disciples: "Thus it is written that the Christ would suffer and rise from the dead on the third day and that repentance, for the forgiveness of sins, would be preached in his name to all the nations, beginning from Jerusalem. You are witnesses of these things. And behold I am sending the promise of my Father upon you; but stay in the city until you are clothed with power from on high."

Then he led them out as far as Bethany, raised his hands, and blessed them. As he blessed them he parted from them and was taken up to heaven. They did him homage and then returned to Jerusalem with great joy, and they were continually in the temple praising God.

Practice of Faith

Imagine you are one of Jesus' disciples. You have traveled with him for three years, witnessed miracles, mourned his death, and rejoiced in his Resurrection. Now you witness his ascension. What emotions do you feel? Today, how might your heart honor Jesus' return to heaven? ◆ At his ascension, Jesus charges us to witness to the ends of the earth, and the Holy Spirit gives each one of us gifts to spread the Good News. What gifts has the Holy Spirit given you? How is God calling you to spread gospel joy? ◆ Read paragraphs one through nine of Pope Francis' The Joy of the Gospel. Do the pope's words resonate with you? How might you respond? See https://w2.vatican .va/content/francesco/en/apost_exhortations/docu ments/papa-francesco_esortazione-ap_20131124 _evangelii-gaudium.html.

Download more questions and activities for families, Christian initiation groups, and other adult groups at http://www.ltp.org/ahw.

Scripture Insights

The spirit of joy permeates today's readings: joy for Jesus' return to his Father and joy for what this means for us who are united to Jesus in our humanity.

In comparing the priesthood of Jesus to that of the high priests of Israel, the Letter to the Hebrews shows the uniqueness of Jesus' priesthood. Through his ascension, Jesus enters the realm of God the Father to present his sacrifice for the forgiveness of the sins of humanity. Compared to the sacrifices of the high priests who performed this ritual annually, the sacrifice of Jesus is an eternal sacrifice that continues to be offered to the Father for the salvation of all humanity.

Today's readings from the Acts of the Apostles and the Gospel both come from St. Luke, who offers an account full of symbolism of Jesus' ascension and promise to his disciples of the gift of the Spirit.

As both man and God, human and divine, Jesus Christ, has ascended to heaven. Our humanity has entered with him into the realm of God. By returning to the Father, Jesus, divine and human, has taken our humanity into the godhead, giving us confident hope that where he is present we hope to follow. Included in this hope is the assurance that Jesus, who shared the same body as we, has conquered sin and death. United to him through Baptism, we will inherit with him the fullness of the resurrection in the life to come: "Let us hold unwaveringly to our confession that gives us hope for he who made the promise is trustworthy."

◆ What is the difference between the sacrifice of Jesus and that of the high priests?

◆ Why is the gift of the Spirit a necessary consequence of Christ's Ascension?

◆ What meaning does the Ascension hold for you?

READING I *Acts 7:55–60*

Stephen, filled with the Holy Spirit, looked up intently to heaven and saw the glory of God and Jesus standing at the right hand of God, and Stephen said, "Behold, I see the heavens opened and the Son of Man standing at the right hand of God." But they cried out in a loud voice, covered their ears, and rushed upon him together. They threw him out of the city, and began to stone him. The witnesses laid down their cloaks at the feet of a young man named Saul. As they were stoning Stephen, he called out, "Lord Jesus, receive my spirit." Then he fell to his knees and cried out in a loud voice, "Lord, do not hold this sin against them"; and when he said this, he fell asleep.

RESPONSORIAL PSALM
Psalm 97:1–2, 6–7, 9 (1a, 9a)

R. The Lord is king, the most high over all
             the earth.
or: Alleluia.

The LORD is king; let the earth rejoice;
    let the many islands be glad.
Justice and judgment are the foundation of
             his throne. R.

The heavens proclaim his justice,
    and all peoples see his glory.
All gods are prostrate before him. R.

You, O LORD, are the Most High over all
             the earth,
    exalted far above all gods. R.

READING II
Revelation 22:12–14, 16–17, 20

I, John, heard a voice saying to me: "Behold, I am coming soon. I bring with me the recompense I will give to each according to his deeds. I am the Alpha and the Omega, the first and the last, the beginning and the end."

Blessed are they who wash their robes so as to have the right to the tree of life and enter the city through its gates.

"I, Jesus, sent my angel to give you this testimony for the churches. I am the root and offspring of David, the bright morning star."

The Spirit and the bride say, "Come." Let the hearer say, "Come." Let the one who thirsts come forward, and the one who wants it receive the gift of life-giving water.

The one who gives this testimony says, "Yes, I am coming soon." Amen! Come, Lord Jesus!

GOSPEL *John 17:20–26*

Lifting up his eyes to heaven, Jesus prayed, saying: "Holy Father, I pray not only for them, but also for those who will believe in me through their word, so that they may all be one, as you, Father, are in me and I in you, that they also may be in us, that the world may believe that you sent me. And I have given them the glory you gave me, so that they may be one, as we are one, I in them and you in me, that they may be brought to perfection as one, that the world may know that you sent me, and that you loved them even as you loved me. Father, they are your gift to me. I wish that where I am they also may be with me, that they may see my glory that you gave me, because you loved me before the foundation of the world. Righteous Father, the world also does not know you, but I know you, and they know that you sent me. I made known to them your name and I will make it known, that the love with which you loved me may be in them and I in them."

Practice of Charity

In today's Gospel, Jesus prays for all who will come to faith through the word of the disciples, asking that we might be "brought to perfection as one," in charity with one another and with him. By this oneness, Christ says, the world will know God's love. ♦ Those baptized at the Easter Vigil, the neophytes, need to continue to be welcomed. Introduce yourself to one of the neophytes, offering to accompany him or her to a parish program or social event. ♦ Mystagogy, the revelation of God's mysteries, is a lifelong process for all who belong to Christ. Notice and record how God reveals his presence to you this week in your daily life, and especially in the Sunday liturgy. ♦ Is there division in your parish community? Think of ways you can contribute toward reconciliation and healing, then take steps to create "oneness."

Download more questions and activities for families, Christian initiation groups, and other adult groups at http://www.ltp.org/ahw.

Scripture Insights

Waiting in confident prayer is a theme in today's readings. In this Sunday between the Solemnities of the Ascension and Pentecost, we emulate the first disciples as they hoped for Jesus' promise of the outpouring of the Holy Spirit.

In the First Reading, taken from the Acts of the Apostles, we hear Stephen pray, "Lord Jesus, receive my prayer." Like Jesus, Stephen dies praying for forgiveness for his enemies: "Lord, do not hold this sin against them."

The Second Reading contains the final words of the Bible. John, who was entrusted with these visions, ends with a confident prayer by which he calls out: "Come, Lord Jesus." These words continue to echo as Christians pray with confidence the prayer the Lord taught us: "Thy Kingdom come."

On the eve of his death, Jesus prays with expectation for the unity of all his followers who are to come. He entrusts them, and we are included among them, to the care of his Father. The faith of future generations is transmitted through the witness of the lives of disciples. The unity for which Jesus prays is a unity with each other but more especially a unity with the Trinity: "So that they may all be one, as you Father, are in me and I in you, that they also may be in us." The final hope of our confident prayer is to be united with one another in the happiness of our union with the Father, Son, and Holy Spirit.

♦ How does Stephen's prayer echo that of Jesus' just before he died?

♦ What do these two images in the second reading refer to: "Blessed are they *who wash their robes* so as to have the right to *the tree of life*"?

♦ How has your life been enriched by the Spirit as you wait in confident prayer?

READING I *Acts 2:1–11*

When the time for Pentecost was fulfilled, they were all in one place together. And suddenly there came from the sky a noise like a strong driving wind, and it filled the entire house in which they were. Then there appeared to them tongues as of fire, which parted and came to rest on each one of them. And they were all filled with the Holy Spirit and began to speak in different tongues, as the Spirit enabled them to proclaim.

Now there were devout Jews from every nation under heaven staying in Jerusalem. At this sound, they gathered in a large crowd, but they were confused because each one heard them speaking in his own language. They were astounded, and in amazement they asked, "Are not all these people who are speaking Galileans? Then how does each of us hear them in his native language? We are Parthians, Medes, and Elamites, inhabitants of Mesopotamia, Judea and Cappadocia, Pontus and Asia, Phrygia and Pamphylia, Egypt and the districts of Libya near Cyrene, as well as travelers from Rome, both Jews and converts to Judaism, Cretans and Arabs, yet we hear them speaking in our own tongues of the mighty acts of God."

RESPONSORIAL PSALM *Psalm 104:1, 24, 29–30, 31, 34 (see 30)*

R. Lord, send out your Spirit, and renew the face
      of the earth.
or: Alleluia.

Bless the LORD, O my soul!
  O LORD, my God, you are great indeed!
How manifold are your works, O LORD!
  The earth is full of your creatures. R.

If you take away their breath, they perish
  and return to their dust.
When you send forth your spirit,
      they are created,
  and you renew the face of the earth. R.

May the glory of the LORD endure forever;
  may the LORD be glad in his works!
Pleasing to him be my theme;
  I will be glad in the LORD. R.

READING II *Romans 8:8–17*

Alternate reading: 1 Corinthians 12:3b–7, 12–13

Brothers and sisters: Those who are in the flesh cannot please God. But you are not in the flesh; on the contrary, you are in the spirit, if only the Spirit of God dwells in you. Whoever does not have the Spirit of Christ does not belong to him. But if Christ is in you, although the body is dead because of sin, the spirit is alive because of righteousness. If the Spirit of the one who raised Jesus from the dead dwells in you, the one who raised Christ from the dead will give life to your mortal bodies also, through his Spirit that dwells in you. Consequently, brothers and sisters, we are not debtors to the flesh, to live according to the flesh. For if you live according to the flesh, you will die, but if by the Spirit you put to death the deeds of the body, you will live.

For those who are led by the Spirit of God are sons of God. For you did not receive a spirit of slavery to fall back into fear, but you received a spirit of adoption, through whom we cry, "Abba, Father!" The Spirit himself bears witness with our spirit that we are children of God, and if children, then heirs, heirs of God and joint heirs with Christ, if only we suffer with him so that we may also be glorified with him.

GOSPEL *John 14:15–16, 23b–26*

Alternate reading: John 20:19–23

Jesus said to his disciples: "If you love me, you will keep my commandments. And I will ask the Father, and he will give you another Advocate to be with you always.

"Whoever loves me will keep my word, and my Father will love him, and we will come to him and make our dwelling with him. Those who do not love me do not keep my words; yet the word you hear is not mine but that of the Father who sent me.

"I have told you this while I am with you. The Advocate, the Holy Spirit whom the Father will send in my name, will teach you everything and remind you of all that I told you."

Practice of Faith

The Holy Spirit empowered the Apostles to share the "mighty acts of God" (Acts 2:11) with all nations, and gives us the faith and power to do the same. ◆ Have your family wear red this Sunday to celebrate Pentecost. Discuss with your family how the Spirit is at work in each of your lives and within your family unit. ◆ Throughout the centuries, beautiful icons have been written to celebrate Pentecost. Search "Pentecost icons" to view a host of images. For a concise explanation of Pentecost icons, see https://iconreader.wordpress.com/2011/06/14/pentecost-icon-as-an-icon-of-the-church/. ◆ Throughout this week, pray St. Augustine's prayer to the Holy Spirit: "Breathe in me, O Holy Spirit, / That my thoughts may all be holy / Act in me, O Holy Spirit, / That my work, too, may be holy. / Draw my heart, O Holy Spirit, / That I love but what is holy. / Strengthen me, O Holy Spirit, / To defend all that is holy. / Guard me, then, O Holy Spirit, / That I always may be holy."

Download more questions and activities for families, Christian initiation groups, and other adult groups at http://www.ltp.org/ahw.

Scripture Insights

The First Reading draws upon a long tradition in the Old Testament where God has been preparing for the outpouring of the gift of the Holy Spirit. In the creation account, God's Spirit hovers over the waters of the chaos and brings about the creation of the world. Now with the outpouring of the Spirit on the first Apostles, God brings to birth a new world. When God created the human person, God breathed on the clay he had formed and it became a living human being. In today's reading, the Apostles gathered as a strong wind rocks the room. This symbolizes God's breath transforming these scared followers into courageous missionaries. At the Tower of Babel, the quest to become equal with God resulted in disharmony. The numerous languages of humanity symbolize their inability to communicate with each other, resulting in alienation. With the appearance of the tongues of fire, a reversal takes place: God grants the Apostles the gift of speaking to enable all who hear to understand. What first divided humanity, now unites them. In this gift of the Spirit, God restores human beings to unity with one another and with God—what God had intended at the very beginning of creation.

In the Second Reading, Paul teaches that the gift of the Spirit makes us God's children, uniting us with one another and with Christ. We become Christ's heirs, called to embrace his life of suffering that will lead us to "be glorified with him."

Today's Gospel portrays Jesus promising to send the Holy Spirit to "teach you everything." Through the power of the Spirit, God dwells within us, enabling us to live anew.

◆ What do the images of wind and "tongues of fire" symbolize in the First Reading?

◆ Why is the gift of the Spirit God's greatest gift to us?

◆ On what occasions have you experienced the presence of God's Spirit in your life?

Ordinary Time, Summer

Prayer before Reading the Word

Wise and merciful God,
grant us a heart
thirsting for your truth,
longing for your presence,
and ready to hear you in the word of your Son.
Grant us the wisdom of your Spirit,
the understanding bestowed on
　　　　　the true disciples,
that we may carry the cross each day
and follow after your Son, our Lord Jesus Christ,
who lives and reigns with you
in the unity of the Holy Spirit,
one God, for ever and ever. Amen.

Prayer after Reading the Word

Your word resounds in your Church, O God,
as a fountain of wisdom and a rule of life;
make us, O God, faithful disciples of
　　　　　that wisdom,
whose Teacher and Master is Christ
and whose chair of learning is the Cross.
Schooled in this unique wisdom,
may we be prepared to conquer our fears
　　　　　and temptations,
to take up our cross daily
and to follow Jesus toward true life.
We ask this through our Lord Jesus Christ,
　　　　　your Son,
who lives and reigns with you
in the unity of the Holy Spirit,
one God, for ever and ever. Amen.

Weekday Readings

June 10: *2 Corinthians 1:1–7; Matthew 5:1–12*
June 11: *Acts 11:21b–26; 13:1–3; Matthew 5:13–16*
June 12: *2 Corinthians 3:4–11; Matthew 5:17–19*
June 13: *2 Corinthians 3:15—4:1, 3–6; Matthew 5:20–26*
June 14: *2 Corinthians 4:7–15; Matthew 5:27–32*
June 15: *2 Corinthians 5:14–21; Matthew 5:33–37*

June 17: *2 Corinthians 6:1–10; Matthew 5:38–42*
June 18: *2 Corinthians 8:1–9; Matthew 5:43–48*
June 19: *2 Corinthians 9:6–11; Matthew 6:1–6, 16–18*
June 20: *2 Corinthians 11:1–11; Matthew 6:7–15*
June 21: *2 Corinthians 11:18, 21–30; Matthew 6:19–23*
June 22: *2 Corinthians 12:1–10; Matthew 6:24–34*

June 24: Solemnity of the Nativity of St. John the Baptist
Isaiah 49:1-6; Acts 13:22–26; Luke 1:57–66, 80
June 25: *Genesis 13:2, 5–18; Matthew 7:6, 12–14*
June 26: *Genesis 15:1–12, 17–18; Matthew 7:15–20*
June 27: *Genesis 16:1–12, 15–16 or 16:6b–12, 15–16; Matthew 7:21–29*
June 28: Solemnity of the Most Sacred Heart of Jesus
Ezekiel 34:11–16; Romans 5:5b–11; Luke 15:3–7
June 29: Solemnity of Sts. Peter and Paul, Apostles
Acts 12:1–11/2 Timothy 4:6–8, 17–18; Matthew 16:13–19

July 1: *Genesis 18:16–33; Matthew 8:18–22*
July 2: *Genesis 19:15–29; Matthew 8:23–27*
July 3: Feast of St. Thomas, Apostle
Ephesians 2:19-22; John 20:24-29
July 4: *Genesis 22:1b–19; Matthew 9:1–8*
July 5: *Genesis 23:1–4, 19; 24:1–8, 62–67; Matthew 9:9–13*
July 6: *Genesis 27:1–5, 15–29; Matthew 9:14–17*

July 8: *Genesis 28:10–22a; Matthew 9:18–26*
July 9: *Genesis 32:23–33; Matthew 9:32–38*
July 10: *Genesis 41:55–57; 42:5–7a, 17–24a; Matthew 10:1–7*
July 11: *Genesis 44:18–21, 23b–29; 45:1–5; Matthew 10:7–15*
July 12: *Genesis 46:1–7, 28–30; Matthew 10:16–23*
July 13: *Genesis 49:29–32; 50:15–26a; Matthew 10:24–33*

July 15: *Exodus 1:8–14, 22; Matthew 10:34—11:1*
July 16: *Exodus 2:1–15a; Matthew 11:20–24*
July 17: *Exodus 3:1–6, 9–12; Matthew 11:25–27*
July 18: *Exodus 3:13–20; Matthew 11:28–30*
July 19: *Exodus 11:10—12:14; Matthew 12:1–8*
July 20: *Exodus 12:37–42; Matthew 12:14–21*

July 22: Feast of St. Mary Magdalene
Song of Songs 3:1–4b or 2 Corinthians 5:14–17;
John 20:1–2, 11–18
July 23: *Exodus 14:21—15:1; Matthew 12:46–50*
July 24: *Exodus 16:1–5, 9–15; Matthew 13:1–9*
July 25: Feast of St. James, Apostle
2 Corinthians 4:7–15; Matthew 20:20–28
July 26: *Exodus 20:1–17; Matthew 13:18–23*
July 27: *Exodus 24:3–8; Matthew 13:24–30*

July 29: *Exodus 32:15–24, 30–34; John 11:19–27 or Luke 10:38–42*
July 30: *Exodus 33:7–11; 34:5b–9, 28; Matthew 13:36–43*
July 31: *Exodus 34:29–35; Matthew 13:44–46*
August 1: *Exodus 40:16–21, 34–38; Matthew 13:47–53*
August 2: *Leviticus 23:1, 4–11, 15–16, 27, 34b–37; Matthew 13:54–58*
August 3: *Leviticus 25:1, 8–17; Matthew 14:1–12*

August 5: *Numbers 11:4b–15; Matthew 14:13–21*
August 6: Feast of the Transfiguration of the Lord
Daniel 7:9–10, 13–14; 2 Peter 1:16–19; Luke 9:28b–36
August 7: *Numbers 13:1–2, 25—14:1, 26–29a, 34–35; Matthew 15:21–28*
August 8: *Numbers 20:1–13; Matthew 16:13–23*
August 9: *Deuteronomy 4:32–40; Matthew 16:24–28*
August 10: Feast of St. Lawrence, Deacon and Martyr
2 Corinthians 9:6–10; John 12:24–26

August 12: *Deuteronomy 10:12–22; Matthew 17:22–27*
August 13: *Deuteronomy 31:1–8; Matthew 18:1–5, 10, 12–14*
August 14: *Deuteronomy 34:1–12; Matthew 18:15–20*
August 15: Solemnity of the Assumption of the Blessed Virgin Mary
Revelation 11:19a; 12:1–6a, 10ab;
1 Corinthians 15:20–27; Luke 1:39–56
August 16: *Joshua 24:1–13; Matthew 19:3–12*
August 17: *Joshua 24:14–29; Matthew 19:13–15*

August 19: *Judges 2:11–19; Matthew 19:16–22*
August 20: *Judges 6:11–24a; Matthew 19:23–30*
August 21: *Judges 9:6–15; Matthew 20:1–16*
August 22: *Judges 11:29–39a; Matthew 22:1–14*
August 23: *Ruth 1:1, 3–6, 14b–16, 22; Matthew 22:34–40*
August 24: Feast of St. Bartholomew, Apostle
Revelation 21:9b–14; John 1:45–51

August 26: *1 Thessalonians 1:1–5, 8b–10; Matthew 23:13–22*
August 27: *1 Thessalonians 2:1–8; Matthew 23:23–26*
August 28: *1 Thessalonians 2:9–13; Matthew 23:27–32*
August 29: *1 Thessalonians 3:7–13; Mark 6:17–29*
August 30: *1 Thessalonians 4:1–8; Matthew 25:1–13*
August 31: *1 Thessalonians 4:9–11; Matthew 25:14–30*

READING I *Proverbs 8:22–31*

Thus says the wisdom of God:
"The LORD possessed me, the beginning
of his ways,
the forerunner of his prodigies of long ago;
from of old I was poured forth,
at the first, before the earth.
When there were no depths I was
brought forth,
when there were no fountains or springs
of water;
before the mountains were settled into place,
before the hills, I was brought forth;
while as yet the earth and fields were not made,
nor the first clods of the world.

"When the Lord established the heavens
I was there,
when he marked out the vault over the face
of the deep;
when he made firm the skies above,
when he fixed fast the foundations of
the earth;
when he set for the sea its limit,
so that the waters should not transgress
his command;
then was I beside him as his craftsman,
and I was his delight day by day,
playing before him all the while,
playing on the surface of his earth;
and I found delight in the human race."

RESPONSORIAL PSALM
Psalm 8:4–5, 6–7, 8–9 (2a)

R. O Lord, our God, how wonderful your name
in all the earth!

When I behold your heavens, the work of
your fingers,
the moon and the stars which you set
in place—
what is man that you should be mindful of him,
or the son of man that you should care
for him? R.

You have made him little less than the angels,
and crowned him with glory and honor.
You have given him rule over the works of
your hands,
putting all things under his feet. R.

All sheep and oxen,
yes, and the beasts of the field,
the birds of the air, the fishes of the sea,
and whatever swims the paths
of the seas. R.

READING II *Romans 5:1–5*

Brothers and sisters: Therefore, since we have been justified by faith, we have peace with God through our Lord Jesus Christ, through whom we have gained access by faith to this grace in which we stand, and we boast in hope of the glory of God. Not only that, but we even boast of our afflictions, knowing that affliction produces endurance, and endurance, proven character, and proven character, hope, and hope does not disappoint, because the love of God has been poured out into our hearts through the Holy Spirit that has been given to us.

GOSPEL *John 16:12–15*

Jesus said to his disciples: "I have much more to tell you, but you cannot bear it now. But when he comes, the Spirit of truth, he will guide you to all truth. He will not speak on his own, but he will speak what he hears, and will declare to you the things that are coming. He will glorify me, because he will take from what is mine and declare it to you. Everything that the Father has is mine; for this reason I told you that he will take from what is mine and declare it to you."

Practice of Hope

Today we celebrate the Triune God in whose name we are baptized. What a gift that God reveals himself in the person of Jesus Christ and lives with us and within us through the Holy Spirit. ◆ Spend time in prayer meditating on the words or phrases that strike you in today's Collect: "Father, / you sent your Word / to bring us truth / and your Spirit to make us holy. / Through them we come to know the mystery of your life. / Help us to worship you, / one God in three Persons, / by proclaiming and living our faith in you. / We ask you this, Father, Son, and Holy Spirit, / one God, true and living, for ever and ever." ◆ If children are in your home, baking clover leaf, or "Trinity" rolls, can spark family discussion on the Trinity. Make them from scratch or from frozen bread dough. ◆ The hymn of praise "Holy, Holy, Holy" was written by Reginald Heber for Trinity Sunday nearly 200 years ago. Listen to it at https://www.youtube.com/watch?v=Vrg7jQ5Ic8c.

Download more questions and activities for families, Christian initiation groups, and other adult groups at http://www.ltp.org/ahw.

Scripture Insights

"The love of God has been poured out into our hearts through the Holy Spirit that has been given to us." With these words, St. Paul captures the essence of this solemnity and shows that the path to understand the Trinity is through the experience of love. At the heart of God is a bond of love among the Father, Son, and Spirit. God's love is communicated through the gift of the Holy Spirit.

Each of the readings today offers an insight into the life of the Trinity. While the precision of the Trinitarian language will only come to completion in later centuries, the foundation for this belief is evident in today's readings. In the Book of Proverbs, God the Creator brings all things into being through his wisdom like a master "craftsman." The imagery of wisdom "playing before God" conveys God's joy, excitement, and love over his creation.

Paul's Letter to the Romans captures the essence of our Catholic faith by stressing that it is through our Lord Jesus Christ that we have been justified and have been brought into a relationship of peace with God. God's love for us is poured into us through the Holy Spirit.

"Everything that the Father has is mine," Jesus says in the Gospel. "The Spirit of truth" will take from what is Jesus' and communicate it to his followers. The Trinity is a communion of love: God's love comes to us from the Father through his Son Jesus and is communicated to us in the Holy Spirit. The Church professed these New Testament thoughts at the Council of Constantinople II: "one God and Father from whom all things are, and one Lord Jesus Christ, through whom all things are, and one Holy Spirit in whom all things are" (DS, 421).

◆ If the Father, Son, and Spirit are in a communion of love, what is our relationship to be to all of humankind?

◆ How does the concept of love guide you toward understanding the mystery of the Holy Trinity?

◆ Which Person of the Trinity do you relate to the most often?

READING I *Genesis 14:18–20*

In those days, Melchizedek, king of Salem, brought out bread and wine, and being a priest of God Most High, he blessed Abram with these words: / "Blessed be Abram by God Most High, / the creator of heaven and earth; / and blessed be God Most High, / who delivered your foes into your hand." / Then Abram gave him a tenth of everything.

RESPONSORIAL PSALM
Psalm 110:1, 2, 3, 4 (4b)

R. You are a priest for ever, in the line
of Melchizedek.

The LORD said to my Lord: "Sit at my right hand
till I make your enemies your footstool."   R.

The scepter of your power the LORD will stretch
forth from Zion:
"Rule in the midst of your enemies."   R.

"Yours is princely power in the day of your birth,
in holy splendor;
before the daystar, like the dew,
I have begotten you."   R.

The LORD has sworn, and he will not repent:
"You are a priest forever, according to the
order of Melchizedek."   R.

READING II *1 Corinthians 11:23–26*

Brothers and sisters: I received from the Lord what I also handed on to you, that the Lord Jesus, on the night he was handed over, took bread, and, after he had given thanks, broke it and said, "This is my body that is for you. Do this in remembrance of me." In the same way also the cup, after supper, saying, "This cup is the new covenant in my blood. Do this, as often as you drink it, in remembrance of me." For as often as you eat this bread and drink the cup, you proclaim the death of the Lord until he comes.

GOSPEL *Luke 9:11b–17*

Jesus spoke to the crowds about the kingdom of God, and he healed those who needed to be cured. As the day was drawing to a close, the Twelve approached him and said, "Dismiss the crowd so that they can go to the surrounding villages and farms and find lodging and provisions; for we are in a deserted place here." He said to them, "Give them some food yourselves." They replied, "Five loaves and two fish are all we have, unless we ourselves go and buy food for all these people." Now the men there numbered about five thousand. Then he said to his disciples, "Have them sit down in groups of about fifty." They did so and made them all sit down. Then taking the five loaves and the two fish, and looking up to heaven, he said the blessing over them, broke them, and gave them to the disciples to set before the crowd. They all ate and were satisfied. And when the leftover fragments were picked up, they filled twelve wicker baskets.

Practice of Charity

The Church refers to the Eucharist as "the source and summit" of our Christian life. St. Catherine of Sienna calls it the "food of angels." The Eucharist is a gift of charity from God to us that allows us to commune with Christ in the most intimate of ways and helps us to become like the One we receive. ◆ In *The Joy of the Gospel*, Pope Francis say the Eucharist is "not a prize for the perfect, but a powerful medicine and nourishment for the weak." When you approach Communion next, ask God to heal the places in you that feel broken or weak. After receiving the Eucharist, kneel quietly with God, savoring this intimate moment, and allow God to strengthen you. ◆ Make time for adoration of the Eucharist. If your parish does not offer weekly adoration time, find a nearby church to visit. ◆ For other questions on the Eucharist, visit the United States Conference of Catholic Bishops website: www.usccb.org/prayer -and-worship/the-mass/order-of-mass/liturgy -of-the-eucharist/the-real-presence-of-jesus -christ-in-the-sacrament-of-the-eucharist-basic -questions-and-answers.cfm.

Download more questions and activities for families, Christian initiation groups, and other adult groups at http://www.ltp.org/ahw.

Scripture Insights

The First Reading shows the Eucharist being foreshadowed at the beginning of God's plan of salvation. Melchizedek, a king and a priest, brings bread and wine to celebrate Abram's victory over his enemies. This king of Salem (shalom, meaning "peace") acknowledges that "God the Most High" has blessed Abram. Chapter seven of the Letter to the Hebrews references this event, pointing out that Melchizedek foreshadows Jesus in his role as priest and king. Melchizedek's feast with bread and wine also points forward to the Last Supper that Jesus celebrates with his disciples and which we continue to celebrate in the Eucharist. Finally, Melchizedek's feast is a celebration over the forces of evil just as the Eucharist celebrates Jesus' victory over sin and death and brings peace.

In Corinthians, Paul's account of the institution of the Eucharist reminds the community that the Eucharist is a sacrament of unity. Reading this passage, we have an insight into how early Christians celebrated the Eucharist some twenty years after Jesus' death and Resurrection.

In describing the miracle of the multiplication of bread, Luke uses language that is contained in his account of the institution: "Then he [Jesus] took the bread, said the blessing, broke it, and gave it to them" (Luke 22:19). By describing the miracle with these words, Luke shows that this event foreshadows the gift of the Eucharist. Just as Jesus fed the crowds with an abundance of physical nourishment, so in the gift of his Body and Blood, Christ feeds us spiritually with an abundance of his life and love, uniting us to himself and to one another as the Body of Christ.

◆ What similarities can you identify between Luke's account of the multiplication of bread and that of the institution of the Eucharist (Luke 22:14–20)?

◆ How does Melchizedek foreshadow Jesus Christ and the Eucharist?

◆ Are there aspects of today's reading that enrich your understanding of the Eucharist?

June 30, 2019 THIRTEENTH SUNDAY IN ORDINARY TIME

READING I *1 Kings 19:16b, 19−21*

The LORD said to Elijah: "You shall anoint Elisha, son of Shaphat of Abel-meholah, as prophet to succeed you."

Elijah set out and came upon Elisha, son of Shaphat, as he was plowing with twelve yoke of oxen; he was following the twelfth. Elijah went over to him and threw his cloak over him. Elisha left the oxen, ran after Elijah, and said, "Please, let me kiss my father and mother goodbye, and I will follow you." Elijah answered, "Go back! Have I done anything to you?" Elisha left him, and taking the yoke of oxen, slaughtered them; he used the plowing equipment for fuel to boil their flesh, and gave it to his people to eat. Then Elisha left and followed Elijah as his attendant.

RESPONSORIAL PSALM *Psalm 16:1−2, 5, 7−8, 9−10, 11 (see 5a)*

R. You are my inheritance, O Lord.

Keep me, O God, for in you I take refuge;
   I say to the LORD, "My Lord are you."
O LORD, my allotted portion and my cup,
   you it is who hold fast my lot.   R.

I bless the LORD who counsels me;
   even in the night my heart exhorts me.
I set the LORD ever before me;
   with him at my right hand, I shall not be
      disturbed.   R.

Therefore my heart is glad and my soul rejoices;
   my body, too, abides in confidence,
because you will not abandon my soul to the
      netherworld,
   nor will you suffer your faithful one to
      undergo corruption.   R.

You will show me the path to life,
   fullness of joys in your presence,
   the delights at your right hand forever.   R.

READING II *Galatians 5:1, 13−18*

Brothers and sisters: For freedom Christ set us free; so stand firm and do not submit again to the yoke of slavery.

For you were called for freedom, brothers and sisters. But do not use this freedom as an opportunity for the flesh; rather, serve one another through love. For the whole law is fulfilled in one statement, namely, *You shall love your neighbor as yourself.* But if you go on biting and devouring one another, beware that you are not consumed by one another.

I say, then: live by the Spirit and you will certainly not gratify the desire of the flesh. For the flesh has desires against the Spirit, and the Spirit against the flesh; these are opposed to each other, so that you may not do what you want. But if you are guided by the Spirit, you are not under the law.

GOSPEL *Luke 9:51−62*

When the days for Jesus' being taken up were fulfilled, he resolutely determined to journey to Jerusalem, and he sent messengers ahead of him. On the way they entered a Samaritan village to prepare for his reception there, but they would not welcome him because the destination of his journey was Jerusalem. When the disciples James and John saw this they asked, "Lord, do you want us to call down fire from heaven to consume them?" Jesus turned and rebuked them, and they journeyed to another village.

As they were proceeding on their journey someone said to him, "I will follow you wherever you go." Jesus answered him, "Foxes have dens and birds of the sky have nests, but the Son of Man has nowhere to rest his head."

And to another he said, "Follow me." But he replied, "Lord, let me go first and bury my father." But he answered him, "Let the dead bury their dead. But you, go and proclaim the kingdom of God." And another said, "I will follow you, Lord, but first let me say farewell to my family at home." To him Jesus said, "No one who sets a hand to the plow and looks to what was left behind is fit for the kingdom of God."

Practice of Hope

For some people, conversion is as instantaneous and dramatic as it was for Elisha in today's reading. For most, however, it is a lifelong process of growing in trust and hope, and requires a supportive, compassionate community. Homeboy Industries, founded by Rev. Gregory Boyle, sj, trains and employs former gang members and prisoners in East Los Angeles, and offers them support in their steps toward a better life. "Gang violence is about a lethal absence of hope," Father Boyle has said. "Nobody has ever met a hopeful kid who joined a gang." ◆ Read *Tattoos on the Heart: The Power of Boundless Compassion,* Father Boyle's stories that reveal the redemptive power of bringing Christ's unconditional love to the streets. ◆ Listen to Father Boyle speak on growing compassionate kinship at https://www.youtube.com /watch?v=ipR0kWt1Fkc. ◆ Learn more about Homeboy Industries and how you can support them at www.homeboyindustries.org.

Download more questions and activities for families, Christian initiation groups, and other adult groups at http://www.ltp.org/ahw.

Scripture Insights

In our Sunday readings from Luke's Gospel account, Jesus has been preaching in Galilee. Now he turns his attention to Jerusalem, "When the days for Jesus being taken up were fulfilled, he resolutely determined to journey to Jerusalem." His decision will result in his death, yet he embraces this outcome.

Difficult challenges also face Jesus' potential followers. Three would-be followers ask to join Jesus. Before setting out, each has a request. One would like to return home to bury a father and another to bid farewell to family. Nothing could be more human than these requests, but Jesus rejects them. This shocks us until we realize that Jesus is exaggerating to get across his point. Jesus never opposes upholding family ties. After all, "Honor your father and your mother" is one of the Ten Commandments. Jesus had also criticized the Pharisees for their refusal to support their elderly parents by "dedicating their money to God" (Matthew 15:4–5).

Jesus highlights the foundational requirement for following him. Commitment to Jesus must be total. Even family bonds cannot take precedence over one's bond with God.

The same was true in Old Testament times. The people of Israel constantly turned away from following God wholeheartedly by worshipping other gods. In the First Reading, Elisha offered a similar excuse for delaying following Elijah.

Pope Francis expresses well the wholehearted demand of our relationship with Christ: "Being Christian is not just obeying orders but means being in Christ, thinking like him, acting like him, loving like him; it means letting him take possession of our life and change it, transform it" (General Audience, Wednesday, April 10, 2017).

◆ How might Pope Francis' statement on being a Christian change your views on your relationship with Christ?

◆ What does Jesus' response to the three would-be followers indicate about how you should follow Christ?

◆ Have you ever experienced your bonds with your family being in conflict with your relationship with Christ?

July 7, 2019   Fourteenth Sunday in Ordinary Time

Reading I   *Isaiah 66:10–14c*

Thus says the Lord:
Rejoice with Jerusalem and be glad because
    of her,
  all you who love her;
exult, exult with her,
  all you who were mourning over her!
Oh, that you may suck fully
  of the milk of her comfort,
that you may nurse with delight
  at her abundant breasts!
For thus says the Lord:
Lo, I will spread prosperity over Jerusalem
    like a river,
  and the wealth of the nations
    like an overflowing torrent.
As nurslings, you shall be carried in her arms,
  and fondled in her lap;
as a mother comforts her child,
  so will I comfort you;
  in Jerusalem you shall find your comfort.

When you see this, your heart shall rejoice
  and your bodies flourish like the grass;
the Lord's power shall be known to
    his servants.

Responsorial Psalm
Psalm 66:1–3, 4–5, 6–7, 16, 20 (1)

R. Let all the earth cry out to God with joy.

Shout joyfully to God, all the earth;
  sing praise to the glory of his name;
  proclaim his glorious praise.
Say to God, "How tremendous are
    your deeds!" R.

"Let all on earth worship and sing praise to you,
  sing praise to your name!"
Come and see the works of God,
  his tremendous deeds among the children
    of Adam. R.

He changed the sea into dry land;
  through the river they passed on foot;
  therefore let us rejoice in him.
He rules by his might forever. R.

Hear now, all you who fear God,
  while I declare what he has done for me.
Blessed be God, who refused me not
    my prayer or his kindness! R.

Reading II   *Galatians 6:14–18*

Brothers and sisters: May I never boast except in the cross of our Lord Jesus Christ, through which the world has been crucified to me, and I to the world. For neither does circumcision mean anything, nor does uncircumcision, but only a new creation. Peace and mercy be to all who follow this rule and to the Israel of God.

From now on, let no one make troubles for me; for I bear the marks of Jesus on my body.

The grace of our Lord Jesus Christ be with your spirit, brothers and sisters. Amen.

Gospel   *Luke 10:1–12, 17–20*

Shorter: Luke 10:1–9

At that time the Lord appointed seventy-two others whom he sent ahead of him in pairs to every town and place he intended to visit. He said to them, "The harvest is abundant but the laborers are few; so ask the master of the harvest to send out laborers for his harvest. Go on your way; behold, I am sending you like lambs among wolves. Carry no money bag, no sack, no sandals; and greet no one along the way. Into whatever house you enter, first say, 'Peace to this household.' If a peaceful person lives there, your peace will rest on him; but if not, it will return to you. Stay in the same house and eat and drink what is offered to you, for the laborer deserves his payment. Do not move about from one house to another. Whatever town you enter and they welcome you, eat what is set before you, cure the sick in it and say to them, 'The kingdom of God is at hand for you.' Whatever town you enter and they do not receive you, go out into the streets and say, 'The dust of your town that clings to our feet, even that we shake off against you.' Yet know this: the kingdom of God is at hand. I tell you, it will be more tolerable for Sodom on that day than for that town."

The seventy-two returned rejoicing, and said, "Lord, even the demons are subject to us because of your name." Jesus said, "I have observed Satan fall like lightning from the sky. Behold, I have given you the power to 'tread upon serpents' and scorpions and upon the full force of the enemy and nothing will harm you. Nevertheless, do not rejoice because the spirits are subject to you, but rejoice because your names are written in heaven."

Practice of Faith

Living in a place where we have freedom to worship, it can be hard to imagine being a "lamb among wolves." Yet, in many parts of the world, Christians still pay with their lives for their faith in Christ. In Pope Francis' April 21, 2015, homily focusing on today's martyrs, he reminded us that throughout history, Christians have been killed "for their faith and loyalty towards God's Word, God's Truth." In our time, thousands of martyrs have died and continue to die all over the world. ◆ To read a report of the pope's homily, see www.catholicnewsagency.com/news/pope-francis-and-his-growing-litany-of-modern-day-martyrs-50871/. ◆ Pope Francis speaks also of "hidden martyrs": Christians working to help others know Christ's love. In what ways are you a "hidden martyr"? What sacrifices in faith do you make of your time, talents, or resources to help others know the love of God? ◆ Include the martyrs of today in your prayers this week, or pray the Rosary in their honor.

Download more questions and activities for families, Christian initiation groups, and other adult groups at http://www.ltp.org/ahw.

Scripture Insights

True peace is a gift only God can give. The readings today convey this message strikingly. The prophet Isaiah offers a vision of God's care for the people. God compares the comfort and support he offers to that of a mother who nurses her child. "As nurslings, you shall be carried in her arms, and fondled in her lap; as a mother comforts her child, so will I comfort you."

In the Gospel, Jesus sends out seventy-two disciples to bring the gift of peace to whatever household they enter. As they enter households, they are to say, "Peace to this household." Of all messages, Jesus asks them to convey the message of peace.

The concept of peace (*shalom*) in the world of Judaism and of Christianity bears a wealth of meaning. Essentially peace means "being in a right relationship with God and with one another." Peace is a gift only God can communicate through the power of the Spirit. Peace brings God's blessings into every dimension of one's being. Jesus instructs us through this Gospel that we are his instruments in communicating his peace to others. This relationship of peace with God is extended to others through our actions.

In the Second Reading, St. Paul shows us that he suffered greatly as he carried Christ's peace to others. Paul always views his sufferings as sharing in the sufferings of the crucified Christ. Paul's relationship with Christ shows us that peace is attained not through our actions but through Christ's actions in changing us. As Paul says, what matters is that we become a totally "new creation" in Christ.

◆ How do you understand the biblical notion of peace?

◆ How do you see yourself as a fellow worker in bringing Christ's peace to our world?

◆ The First Reading likens God's comfort to that of a mother. Do you ever imagine God as a mother?

READING I *Deuteronomy 30:10–14*

Moses said to the people: "If only you would heed the voice of the LORD, your God, and keep his commandments and statutes that are written in this book of the law, when you return to the LORD, your God, with all your heart and all your soul.

"For this command that I enjoin on you today is not too mysterious and remote for you. It is not up in the sky, that you should say, 'Who will go up in the sky to get it for us and tell us of it, that we may carry it out?' Nor is it across the sea, that you should say, 'Who will cross the sea to get it for us and tell us of it, that we may carry it out?' No, it is something very near to you, already in your mouths and in your hearts; you have only to carry it out."

RESPONSORIAL PSALM *Psalm 69:14, 17, 30–31, 33–34, 36, 37 (see 33)*

Alternate reading: Psalm 19:8, 9, 10, 11 (9a)

R. Turn to the Lord in your need, and you
        will live.

I pray to you, O LORD,
    for the time of your favor, O God!
In your great kindness answer me
    with your constant help.
Answer me, O LORD, for bounteous is
        your kindness;
    in your great mercy turn toward me. R.

I am afflicted and in pain;
    let your saving help, O God, protect me.
I will praise the name of God in song,
    and I will glorify him
        with thanksgiving. R.

"See, you lowly ones, and be glad;
    you who seek God, may your hearts revive!
For the LORD hears the poor,
    and his own who are in bonds
        he spurns not." R.

For God will save Zion
    and rebuild the cities of Judah.
The descendants of his servants shall inherit it,
    and those who love his name shall inhabit it.

READING II *Colossians 1:15–20*

Christ Jesus is the image of the invisible God,
    the firstborn of all creation.
For in him were created all things
        in heaven and on earth,
    the visible and the invisible,
    whether thrones or dominions or
        principalities or powers;
    all things were created through him and
        for him.
He is before all things,
    and in him all things hold together.
He is the head of the body, the church.
He is the beginning, the firstborn from the dead,
    that in all things he himself might
        be preeminent.
For in him all the fullness was pleased to dwell,
    and through him to reconcile
        all things for him,
    making peace by the blood of his cross
    through him, whether those on earth or
        those in heaven.

GOSPEL *Luke 10:25–37*

There was a scholar of the law who stood up to test him and said, "Teacher, what must I do to inherit eternal life?" Jesus said to him, "What is written in the law? How do you read it?" He said in reply,
    "You shall love the Lord, your God,
    with all your heart,
    with all your being,
    with all your strength,
    and with all your mind,
    and your neighbor as yourself."
He replied to him, "You have answered correctly; do this and you will live."

But because he wished to justify himself, he said to Jesus, "And who is my neighbor?" Jesus replied, "A man fell victim to robbers as he went down from Jerusalem to Jericho. They stripped and beat him and went off leaving him half-dead. A priest happened to be going down that road, but when he saw him, he passed by on the opposite side. Likewise a Levite came to the place, and when he saw him, he passed by on the opposite side. But a Samaritan traveler who came upon him was moved with compassion at the sight. He approached the victim, poured oil and wine over his wounds and bandaged them. Then he lifted him up on his own animal, took him to an inn, and cared for him. The next day he took out two silver coins and gave them to the innkeeper with the instruction, 'Take care of him. If you spend more than what I have given you, I shall repay you on my way back.' Which of these three, in your opinion, was neighbor to the robbers' victim?" He answered, "The one who treated him with mercy." Jesus said to him, "Go and do likewise."

Practice of Charity

Christ offers today's parable in response to the question a scholar of the law asked: "But who is my neighbor?" In Christ's time, Samaritans were enemies, not only of the beaten man in the parable but of the scholar asking the question. Christ's words call us to extend charity to those we fear but also to understand that they have gifts to offer. In our wounded world, it is imperative that we come to know our religious neighbors, no matter how distant they are from us. ◆ If possible, join a Daughters of Abraham Book Club, where Muslim, Jewish, and Christian women gather monthly to discuss fiction and nonfiction books that promote interfaith dialogue. Find out more at daughtersofabraham.com/. ◆ Volunteer with your local Catholic Charities to assist a refugee or refugee family, helping them to navigate day-to-day life in their new home. ◆ Learn about Religions for Peace, a Vatican-supported organization in which diverse religious communities worldwide cooperate in working for peace through concrete, common action. Find them at http://www.religionsforpeace.org/.

Download more questions and activities for families, Christian initiation groups, and other adult groups at http://www.ltp.org/ahw.

Scripture Insights

In the First Reading, Moses challenges his people to heed the Lord's voice by keeping the Commandments. Their familiarity with the law is such that they can recite it with their mouths and are aware of it in their hearts. However, more is required: they need to carry it out in their actions.

The Gospel reading also gives attention to the carrying out of the Law. A scholar of the Law asks Jesus, "Teacher, what must I do to inherit eternal life?" Jesus elicits from him the essence of the Commandments, "Love the Lord your God with all your heart . . . and your neighbor as yourself" Demanding more precision, the lawyer asks, "And who is my neighbor?" Jesus answers with the story of the Good Samaritan.

In this parable, a Samaritan cares for a man who has been left for dead after a priest and Levite pass by the man. The Samaritan tends the man's wounds, finds lodging for him, and pays for it. With this act of compassion, the Samaritan loves the stranger as his neighbor. Jesus concludes his story by asking the lawyer, "Which of these three (the priest, the Levite, and the Samaritan) in your opinion was neighbor to the robbers' victim?" Now, Jesus' question to the lawyer draws attention to the fact that the Samaritan is the true neighbor! This poses a problem for the lawyer because Jews considered Samaritans as enemies. The lawyer finds it difficult to answer Jesus' question. He cannot say, "The Samaritan!" Instead he answers, "The one who treated him with mercy." Jesus leaves him and us with the challenge, "Go and do likewise."

◆ Does the Gospel parable challenge how you mete out mercy?

◆ How is the parable a challenge to every form of prejudice?

◆ How does the parable change your understanding of obeying the commandments?

July 21, 2019 SIXTEENTH SUNDAY IN ORDINARY TIME

READING I *Genesis 18:1–10a*

The LORD appeared to Abraham by the terebinth of Mamre, as he sat in the entrance of his tent, while the day was growing hot. Looking up, Abraham saw three men standing nearby. When he saw them, he ran from the entrance of the tent to greet them; and bowing to the ground, he said: "Sir, if I may ask you this favor, please do not go on past your servant. Let some water be brought, that you may bathe your feet, and then rest yourselves under the tree. Now that you have come this close to your servant, let me bring you a little food, that you may refresh yourselves; and afterward you may go on your way." The men replied, "Very well, do as you have said."

Abraham hastened into the tent and told Sarah, "Quick, three measures of fine flour! Knead it and make rolls." He ran to the herd, picked out a tender, choice steer, and gave it to a servant, who quickly prepared it. Then Abraham got some curds and milk, as well as the steer that had been prepared, and set these before the three men; and he waited on them under the tree while they ate.

They asked Abraham, "Where is your wife Sarah?" He replied, "There in the tent." One of them said, "I will surely return to you about this time next year, and Sarah will then have a son."

RESPONSORIAL PSALM
Psalm 15:2–3, 3–4, 5 (1a)

R. He who does justice will live in the presence
      of the Lord.

One who walks blamelessly and does justice;
   who thinks the truth in his heart
   and slanders not with his tongue. R.

Who harms not his fellow man,
   nor takes up a reproach against his neighbor;
by whom the reprobate is despised,
   while he honors those who fear the LORD. R.

Who lends not his money at usury
   and accepts no bribe against the innocent.
One who does these things
   shall never be disturbed. R.

READING II *Colossians 1:24–28*

Brothers and sisters: Now I rejoice in my sufferings for your sake, and in my flesh I am filling up what is lacking in the afflictions of Christ on behalf of his body, which is the church, of which I am a minister in accordance with God's stewardship given to me to bring to completion for you the word of God, the mystery hidden from ages and from generations past. But now it has been manifested to his holy ones, to whom God chose to make known the riches of the glory of this mystery among the Gentiles; it is Christ in you, the hope for glory. It is he whom we proclaim, admonishing everyone and teaching everyone with all wisdom, that we may present everyone perfect in Christ.

GOSPEL *Luke 10:38–42*

Jesus entered a village where a woman whose name was Martha welcomed him. She had a sister named Mary who sat beside the Lord at his feet listening to him speak. Martha, burdened with much serving, came to him and said, "Lord, do you not care that my sister has left me by myself to do the serving? Tell her to help me." The Lord said to her in reply, "Martha, Martha, you are anxious and worried about many things. There is need of only one thing. Mary has chosen the better part and it will not be taken from her."

Practice of Charity

Jesus notices that Martha feels distracted and burdened in her hospitality. Her service has become disconnected from love of God, while Mary has chosen to sit at Christ's feet. As Christians, we are called to charitable action in response to God's love for us. ◆ Jesus fueled his ministry by going away to pray. This week, commit to finding time alone to pray, even if it is just for five minutes each day. ◆ Volunteer to serve at your local soup kitchen this month. Reach out personally to one of the guests, to nurture spirit as well as body. ◆ Take time to pray this week with Catholic Relief Services, whose people are "putting our faith into action to help the world's poorest create lasting change." See www.crs.org/get-involved/prayer-resources.

Download more questions and activities for families, Christian initiation groups, and other adult groups at http://www.ltp.org/ahw.

Scripture Insights

Throughout the ancient world, hospitality was the most significant virtue practiced by every culture. In welcoming a guest, people believed that they may unknowingly be welcoming a divinity in disguise, as occurs in the First Reading today. From his tent, Abraham sees three men passing in the distance. He runs to offer hospitality. Unknowingly, they are angels (messengers) sent by God. They bless Abraham and Sarah with the news that Sarah will bear a son. "Do not neglect hospitality, for through it some have unknowingly entertained angels" (Hebrews 13:2).

Hospitality is also at the heart of today's Gospel as Jesus visits the home of Martha and Mary. Jesus uses this visit to teach something deeper about hospitality. While Mary sits at Jesus' feet, Martha complains to Jesus because Mary is not doing anything to help her. Instead of agreeing with Martha, Jesus chides her in a kindly way: "Martha, Martha, you are anxious and worried about many things." He goes on to say that "Mary has chosen the better part." While not rejecting Martha's cooking, Jesus wants to remind Martha, and through her us, that service must also be connected to listening. Service that does not embrace listening to Jesus' word misses the heart of everything. That is why Jesus says that Mary has chosen "the good portion." Mary has in fact chosen the best part of the meal. Christianity requires service, but the Word of the Lord needs to be heard first.

◆ What was your initial reaction to the interchange between Jesus and Martha in the Gospel reading?

◆ How do you understand Jesus' words to Martha, "Mary has chosen the good portion"?

◆ How would you treat strangers if you considered them a messenger from God?

READING I *Genesis 18:20–32*

In those days, the LORD said: "The outcry against Sodom and Gomorrah is so great, and their sin so grave, that I must go down and see whether or not their actions fully correspond to the cry against them that comes to me. I mean to find out."

While Abraham's visitors walked on farther toward Sodom, the LORD remained standing before Abraham. Then Abraham drew nearer and said: "Will you sweep away the innocent with the guilty? Suppose there were fifty innocent people in the city; would you wipe out the place, rather than spare it for the sake of the fifty innocent people within it? Far be it from you to do such a thing, to make the innocent die with the guilty so that the innocent and the guilty would be treated alike! Should not the judge of all the world act with justice?" The LORD replied, "If I find fifty innocent people in the city of Sodom, I will spare the whole place for their sake." Abraham spoke up again: "See how I am presuming to speak to my LORD, though I am but dust and ashes! What if there are five less than fifty innocent people? Will you destroy the whole city because of those five?" He answered, "I will not destroy it, if I find forty-five there." But Abraham persisted, saying "What if only forty are found there?" He replied, "I will forbear doing it for the sake of the forty." Then Abraham said, "Let not my Lord grow impatient if I go on. What if only thirty are found there?" He replied, "I will forbear doing it if I can find but thirty there." Still Abraham went on, "Since I have thus dared to speak to my Lord, what if there are no more than twenty?" The LORD answered, "I will not destroy it, for the sake of the twenty." But he still persisted: "Please, let not my Lord grow angry if I speak up this last time. What if there are at least ten there?" He replied, "For the sake of those ten, I will not destroy it."

RESPONSORIAL PSALM
Psalm 138:1–2, 2–3, 6–7, 7–8 (3a)

R. Lord, on the day I called for help, you
     answered me.

I will give thanks to you, O LORD,
          with all my heart,
     for you have heard the words of my mouth;
     in the presence of the angels
          I will sing your praise;
I will worship at your holy temple
     and give thanks to your name.   R.

Because of your kindness and your truth;
     for you have made great above all things
     your name and your promise.
When I called you answered me;
     you built up strength within me.   R.

The LORD is exalted, yet the lowly he sees,
     and the proud he knows from afar.
Though I walk amid distress, you preserve me;
     against the anger of my enemies you raise
          your hand.   R.

Your right hand saves me.
     The LORD will complete what he has done
          for me;
your kindness, O LORD, endures forever;
     forsake not the work of your hands.

READING II *Colossians 2:12–14*

Brothers and sisters: You were buried with him in baptism, in which you were also raised with him through faith in the power of God, who raised him from the dead. And even when you were dead in transgressions and the uncircumcision of your flesh, he brought you to life along with him, having forgiven us all our transgressions; obliterating the bond against us, with its legal claims, which was opposed to us, he also removed it from our midst, nailing it to the cross.

GOSPEL *Luke 11:1–13*

Jesus was praying in a certain place, and when he had finished, one of his disciples said to him, "Lord, teach us to pray just as John taught his disciples." He said to them, "When you pray, say:
     Father, hallowed be your name,
     your kingdom come.
     Give us each day our daily bread
     and forgive us our sins

for we ourselves forgive everyone in debt to us, and do not subject us to the final test."

And he said to them, "Suppose one of you has a friend to whom he goes at midnight and says, 'Friend, lend me three loaves of bread, for a friend of mine has arrived at my house from a journey and I have nothing to offer him,' and he says in reply from within, 'Do not bother me; the door has already been locked and my children and I are already in bed. I cannot get up to give you anything.' I tell you, if he does not get up to give the visitor the loaves because of their friendship, he will get up to give him whatever he needs because of his persistence.

"And I tell you, ask and you will receive; seek and you will find; knock and the door will be opened to you. For everyone who asks, receives; and the one who seeks, finds; and to the one who knocks, the door will be opened. What father among you would hand his son a snake when he asks for a fish? Or hand him a scorpion when he asks for an egg? If you then, who are wicked, know how to give good gifts to your children, how much more will the Father in heaven give the Holy Spirit to those who ask him?"

Practice of Faith

To form and sustain the relationships that give life meaning, people spend time together. This week's readings challenge us to spend time with God to build our relationship. ◆ Meditate on the mysteries of Christ while praying the Rosary. ◆ Pray each night with your children. A free daily Gospel reflection and daily prayer that is great for teens is available at faith.nd.edu/s/1210/faith/start.aspx ?gid=609&pgid=61. ◆ Practice *lectio divina*, or "divine reading," a Scripture-based contemplative prayer. James Martin, sj, offers instructions at https://wau.org/archives/article/read_think _pray_act/.

Download more questions and activities for families, Christian initiation groups, and other adult groups at http://www.ltp.org/ahw.

Scripture Insights

Today's readings provide the insight that our image of God influences how we pray. In the First Reading, Abraham bargains with God over the number of good people needed to save all the inhabitants in the city. God emerges as a kind and patient negotiator.

In Paul's Letter to the Colossians, God is kind and compassionate. God has "forgiven us all our transgressions; obliterating the bond against us, . . . nailing it to the cross." God's forgiveness is total. Both readings contain the foundational dimension of the Christian image of God as kind, generous, and completely forgiving.

Luke's Gospel account presents Jesus as a man of prayer. Inspired by Jesus' example, his disciples ask him to teach them how to pray. In the prayer he gives them (a shortened version of Matthew's account of the Lord's Prayer), Jesus deepens their image of God as generous and forgiving. Beginning with "Abba"/"Father," a small child's address to a Father ("Daddy"), Jesus issues an invitation to approach God with the trust and love a child has for parents. Jesus shows them that prayer is about forming a relationship with God.

In the rest of the Gospel passage, Jesus continues this intimate relationship between God and God's children. "Would a parent offer a child a snake when they asked for a fish? . . . How much more will the Father in heaven give the Holy Spirit to those who ask?" In prayer, God knows his children's needs better than they know themselves. Prayer will establish the most intimate of relationships between the believer and God through "the Holy Spirit" of love.

◆ How do today's readings reflect the image of a generous and compassionate God?

◆ What are the implications of Paul's statement that God brought us to life again even after we were "dead in transgressions"?

◆ What image of God appeals the most to you?

August 4, 2019

Reading I *Ecclesiastes 1:2; 2:21–23*

Vanity of vanities, says Qoheleth,
    vanity of vanities! All things are vanity!

    Here is one who has labored with wisdom and knowledge and skill, and yet to another who has not labored over it, he must leave property. This also is vanity and a great misfortune. For what profit comes to man from all the toil and anxiety of heart with which he has labored under the sun? All his days sorrow and grief are his occupation; even at night his mind is not at rest. This also is vanity.

Responsorial Psalm *Psalm 90:3–4, 5–6, 12–13, 14 and 17 (8)*

R. If today you hear his voice, harden not
        your hearts.

You turn man back to dust,
    saying, "Return, O children of men."
For a thousand years in your sight
    are as yesterday, now that it is past,
    or as a watch of the night.   R.

You make an end of them in their sleep;
    the next morning they are like
            the changing grass,
which at dawn springs up anew,
    but by evening wilts and fades.   R.

Teach us to number our days aright,
    that we may gain wisdom of heart.
Return, O Lord! How long?
    Have pity on your servants!   R.

Fill us at daybreak with your kindness,
    that we may shout for joy
            and gladness all our days.
And may the gracious care of the Lord our God
            be ours;
    prosper the work of our hands for us!
    Prosper the work of our hands!   R.

Reading II *Colossians 3:1–5, 9–11*

Brothers and sisters: If you were raised with Christ, seek what is above, where Christ is seated at the right hand of God. Think of what is above, not of what is on earth. For you have died, and your life is hidden with Christ in God. When Christ your life appears, then you too will appear with him in glory.

    Put to death, then, the parts of you that are earthly: immorality, impurity, passion, evil desire, and the greed that is idolatry. Stop lying to one another, since you have taken off the old self with its practices and have put on the new self, which is being renewed, for knowledge, in the image of its creator. Here there is not Greek and Jew, circumcision and uncircumcision, barbarian, Scythian, slave, free; but Christ is all and in all.

Gospel *Luke 12:13–21*

Someone in the crowd said to Jesus, "Teacher, tell my brother to share the inheritance with me." He replied to him, "Friend, who appointed me as your judge and arbitrator?" Then he said to the crowd, "Take care to guard against all greed, for though one may be rich, one's life does not consist of possessions."

    Then he told them a parable. "There was a rich man whose land produced a bountiful harvest. He asked himself, 'What shall I do, for I do not have space to store my harvest?' And he said, 'This is what I shall do: I shall tear down my barns and build larger ones. There I shall store all my grain and other goods and I shall say to myself, "Now as for you, you have so many good things stored up for many years, rest, eat, drink, be merry!"' But God said to him, 'You fool, this night your life will be demanded of you; and the things you have prepared, to whom will they belong?' Thus will it be for all who store up treasure for themselves but are not rich in what matters to God."

Practice of Faith

A poem attributed to Father Pedro Arrupe, SJ (1907–1991), reads: "Nothing is more practical than finding God, / than falling in Love / in a quite absolute, final way. / What you are in love with, / what seizes your imagination, will affect everything. / It will decide what will get you out of bed in the morning, / what you do with your evenings, / how you spend your weekends, / what you read, whom you know, / what breaks your heart, / and what amazes you with joy and gratitude. / Fall in Love, stay in love, / and it will decide everything." ◆ If someone were to look at your life, what or whom would they believe you are in love with, or have faith in? ◆ Consider your gifts. Can you volunteer for a service organization such as Habitat for Humanity or help fund education for a teenager in need? ◆ Volunteer in a liturgical ministry in your parish, as a member of the choir, a gift bearer, or on the art and environment team.

Download more questions and activities for families, Christian initiation groups, and other adult groups at http://www.ltp.org/ahw.

Scripture Insights

"If today you hear his voice, harden not your hearts." Today's readings contain God's challenge to reassess life's priorities and live accordingly. "Vanity of vanities. . . . All things are vanity," shouts the preacher who offers a sober evaluation of life and work. He questions the value of someone working so hard to acquire a fortune that on death will go to an idle, lazy person. Trust should be placed in what matters.

Paul answers the question raised by the First Reading. Ultimately, our priority should be set on "what is above, not what is on earth." In Baptism, we have died with Christ and have been raised to a new creation. We are called to a life with Christ in God for eternity.

Jesus' parable challenges a reassessment of true security. A rich man placed all his security in amassing an ever larger fortune. He dies suddenly and "the things you have prepared, to whom will they belong?" The lesson of the parable is that we should place our security in our relationship with God rather than on earthly wealth.

Another dimension to this parable emerges from its context. The parable is given in response to the question shouted from the crowd: "Teacher, tell my brother to share the inheritance with me." Jesus turns the query back on the questioner: "Is money more important than your relationship with your brother?" The parable provides a challenge to reassess our priorities in life. Our focus should not be on temporal wealth that soon disappears but on our spiritual relationship with God and one another.

◆ How does the parable in the Gospel challenge us to see our relationships with new eyes?

◆ What does Paul mean when he says that in Christ "there is not Greek and Jew, circumcision and uncircumcision, barbarian, Scythian, slave, free; but Christ is all in all"?

◆ How do you understand the words "Vanity of vanities. . . . All things are vanity"?

READING I   *Wisdom 18:6–9*

The night of the passover was known
      beforehand to our fathers,
   that, with sure knowledge of the oaths in
      which they put their faith,
   they might have courage.
Your people awaited the salvation of the just
   and the destruction of their foes.
For when you punished our adversaries,
   in this you glorified us whom you
      had summoned.
For in secret the holy children of the good were
      offering sacrifice
   and putting into effect with one accord the
      divine institution.

RESPONSORIAL PSALM
Psalm 33:1, 12, 18–19, 20–22 (12b)

R. Blessed the people the Lord has chosen to
      be his own.

Exult, you just, in the LORD;
   praise from the upright is fitting.
Blessed the nation whose God is the LORD,
   the people he has chosen for his own
      inheritance.   R.

See, the eyes of the LORD are upon those who
      fear him,
   upon those who hope for his kindness,
to deliver them from death
   and preserve them in spite of famine.   R.

Our soul waits for the LORD,
   who is our help and our shield.
May your kindness, O LORD, be upon us
   who have put our hope in you.   R.

READING II   *Hebrews 11:1–2, 8–12*

Longer: Hebrews 11:1–2, 8–19

Brothers and sisters: Faith is the realization of what is hoped for and evidence of things not seen. Because of it the ancients were well attested.

By faith Abraham obeyed when he was called to go out to a place that he was to receive as an inheritance; he went out, not knowing where he was to go. By faith he sojourned in the promised land as in a foreign country, dwelling in tents with Isaac and Jacob, heirs of the same promise; for he was looking forward to the city with foundations, whose architect and maker is God. By faith he received power to generate, even though he was past the normal age—and Sarah herself was sterile—for he thought that the one who had made the promise was trustworthy. So it was that there came forth from one man, himself as good as dead, descendants as numerous as the stars in the sky and as countless as the sands on the seashore.

GOSPEL   *Luke 12:32–48*

Shorter: Luke 12:35–40

Jesus said to his disciples: "Do not be afraid any longer, little flock, for your Father is pleased to give you the kingdom. Sell your belongings and give alms. Provide money bags for yourselves that do not wear out, an inexhaustible treasure in heaven that no thief can reach nor moth destroy. For where your treasure is, there also will your heart be.

"Gird your loins and light your lamps and be like servants who await their master's return from a wedding, ready to open immediately when he comes and knocks. Blessed are those servants whom the master finds vigilant on his arrival. Amen, I say to you, he will gird himself, have them recline at table, and proceed to wait on them. And should he come in the second or third watch and find them prepared in this way, blessed are those servants. Be sure of this: if the master of the house had known the hour when the thief was coming, he would not have let his house be broken into. You also must be prepared, for at an hour you do not expect, the Son of Man will come."

Then Peter said, "Lord, is this parable meant for us or for everyone?" And the Lord replied, "Who, then, is the faithful and prudent steward whom the master will put in charge of his servants to distribute the food allowance at the proper time? Blessed is that servant whom his master on arrival finds doing so. Truly, I say to you, the master will put the servant in charge of all his property. But if that servant says to himself, 'My master is delayed in coming,' and begins to beat the menservants and the maidservants, to eat and drink and get drunk, then that servant's master will come on an unexpected day and at an unknown hour and will punish the servant severely and assign him a place with the unfaithful. That servant who knew his master's will but did not make preparations nor act in accord with his will shall be beaten severely; and the servant who was ignorant of his master's will but acted in a way deserving of a severe beating shall be beaten only lightly. Much will be required of the person entrusted with much, and still more will be demanded of the person entrusted with more."

Practice of Hope

Today's readings ask us to stay vigilant and live as if God were in charge of our lives. This takes courage, but Jesus tells us, "Do not be afraid any longer, little flock, for the Father is pleased to give you the kingdom." ♦ This week examine TV shows, commercials, and/or news reporting with your children. Ask whether fear is being promoted and discuss how hope in Christ's Word answers that fear. ♦ We are not meant to be alone in our faith. As God's "little flock" we are called to act courageously. The program Just Faith forms faith communities as agents of social transformation. Learn more at justfaith.org. ♦ How does being part of Christ's "little flock" reflect our relationship with God?

Download more questions and activities for families, Christian initiation groups, and other adult groups at http://www.ltp.org/ahw.

Scripture Insights

All of today's readings speak about people on the move in search of a new homeland. The reading from Wisdom reminds us of the night of Passover when the people of Israel, trusting in God's promises, journeyed from slavery to freedom in a new homeland God had promised.

In the reading from Hebrews, we hear how Abraham placed his faith and trust in God's promises and journeyed to a land promised him and his descendants. "He went out, not knowing where he was to go." He simply and faithfully trusted in God's guidance. As the reading states, "Faith is the realization of what is hoped for and evidence of things not seen."

The Gospel reading presents us with a parable in which Jesus reminds his followers to trust in the Father's promises: "Do not be afraid any longer, little flock, for your Father is pleased to give you the kingdom." Followers are to be patient as they await the return of their master, who will bring them into their new homeland. Jesus touches on the yearning for this eternal homeland that lies in the human heart. However, Jesus adds that we must be attentive and prepared for the arrival of this homeland. We must do our part and act as faithful stewards of our talents and obligations. "Much will be required of the person entrusted with much, and still more will be demanded of the person entrusted with more."

We do not journey alone. Our journey is united with others also responding to God's call to prepare for the coming of God's kingdom. Ours is the task to support them through lives of service and solidarity.

♦ What impression does the definition of faith in the Letter to the Hebrews have on you?

♦ To what can you compare Abraham's faith?

♦ Jesus tells the disciples that their heart is where their treasure is. What does your heart value?

READING I *Jeremiah 38:4–6, 8–10*

In those days, the princes said to the king: "Jeremiah ought to be put to death; he is demoralizing the soldiers who are left in this city, and all the people, by speaking such things to them; he is not interested in the welfare of our people, but in their ruin." King Zedekiah answered: "He is in your power"; for the king could do nothing with them. And so they took Jeremiah and threw him into the cistern of Prince Malchiah, which was in the quarters of the guard, letting him down with ropes. There was no water in the cistern, only mud, and Jeremiah sank into the mud.

Ebed-melech, a court official, went there from the palace and said to him: "My lord king, these men have been at fault in all they have done to the prophet Jeremiah, casting him into the cistern. He will die of famine on the spot, for there is no more food in the city." Then the king ordered Ebed-melech the Cushite to take three men along with him, and draw the prophet Jeremiah out of the cistern before he should die.

RESPONSORIAL PSALM
Psalm 40:2, 3, 4, 18 (14b)

R. Lord, come to my aid!

I have waited, waited for the Lord,
    and he stooped toward me.   R.

The LORD heard my cry.
He drew me out of the pit of destruction,
    out of the mud of the swamp;
he set my feet upon a crag;
    he made firm my steps.   R

And he put a new song into my mouth,
    a hymn to our God.
Many shall look on in awe
    and trust in the Lord.   R.

Though I am afflicted and poor,
    yet the LORD thinks of me.
You are my help and my deliverer;
    O my God, hold not back!   R.

READING II *Hebrews 12:1–4*

Brothers and sisters: Since we are surrounded by so great a cloud of witnesses, let us rid ourselves of every burden and sin that clings to us and persevere in running the race that lies before us while keeping our eyes fixed on Jesus, the leader and perfecter of faith. For the sake of the joy that lay before him he endured the cross, despising its shame, and has taken his seat at the right of the throne of God. Consider how he endured such opposition from sinners, in order that you may not grow weary and lose heart. In your struggle against sin you have not yet resisted to the point of shedding blood.

GOSPEL *Luke 12:49–53*

Jesus said to his disciples: "I have come to set the earth on fire, and how I wish it were already blazing! There is a baptism with which I must be baptized, and how great is my anguish until it is accomplished! Do you think that I have come to establish peace on the earth? No, I tell you, but rather division. From now on a household of five will be divided, three against two and two against three; a father will be divided against his son and a son against his father, a mother against her daughter and a daughter against her mother, a mother-in-law against her daughter-in-law and a daughter-in-law against her mother-in-law."

Practice of Hope

Jesus clearly states in the Gospel that the Kingdom of God comes with a cost. Jesus will be "baptized" through the fire of his death on a cross. Similarly, as we wait in hope for the kingdom, the author of Hebrews urges us to "rid ourselves of every burden and sin that clings to us and persevere in running the race that lies before us." ◆ Prayerfully meditate on your life this week, asking: Who are the people that incline you toward sin? What circumstances tempt you to give up the race? Pray for the will and guidance to persevere in living the life to which God calls you. ◆ Each morning this week, pray St. Patrick's Breastplate, found at www.ourcatholicprayers.com/st-patricks-breastplate.html. ◆ The author of Hebrews tells us to keep "our eyes fixed on Jesus." This week, try to check in with God by offering short prayers throughout the day. Set an alarm on your watch or phone to remind you.

Download more questions and activities for families, Christian initiation groups, and other adult groups at http://www.ltp.org/ahw.

Scripture Insights

"I have come to set the earth on fire, and how I wish it were already blazing!" These words in the Gospel cause us to take notice. How does Jesus as the Prince of Peace square with Jesus who brings discord and division to the world? Throughout the Old Testament, fire symbolizes God's presence. In the desert, Moses discovers God's presence in the burning bush (Exodus 3:2). In Elijah's great battle with the prophets of Baal on Mount Carmel, God's fire consumed Elijah's sacrifice. At Pentecost, flames of fire appeared over the heads of the Apostles symbolizing the descent of the Holy Spirit.

The symbol of fire also bears with it the power to purify. When the fire of God's Spirit fills our hearts, we are purified of selfishness and whatever is not compatible with a relationship with God. In the process of purification, we experience the pain of separation from what has divided us from God. Commitment to Jesus bears consequences. It brings about division from those who are opposed to Jesus. The heart of Jesus' message is that our relationship with him is the most significant relationship of all.

Today's reading from the Letter to the Hebrews reiterates the Gospel theme that our relationship with Jesus is the most important aspect in our lives. The author compares life's journey to a race we are running. On the race of life, we are called, as any runner is, to keep our eyes fixed on the goal, the prize. We are "keeping our eyes fixed on Jesus."

◆ How does the image of Jesus bringing fire to earth harmonize with Jesus as the "Prince of Peace"?

◆ What does the image of "Jesus as the leader and perfecter of faith" convey to you?

◆ Have there been times when your relationship with God has been tested by the values of your friends and family?

READING I *Isaiah 66:18–21*

Thus says the LORD: I know their works and their thoughts, and I come to gather nations of every language; they shall come and see my glory. I will set a sign among them; from them I will send fugitives to the nations: to Tarshish, Put and Lud, Mosoch, Tubal and Javan, to the distant coastlands that have never heard of my fame, or seen my glory; and they shall proclaim my glory among the nations. They shall bring all your brothers and sisters from all the nations as an offering to the LORD, on horses and in chariots, in carts, upon mules and dromedaries, to Jerusalem, my holy mountain, says the LORD, just as the Israelites bring their offering to the house of the LORD in clean vessels. Some of these I will take as priests and Levites, says the LORD.

RESPONSORIAL PSALM
Psalm 117:1, 2 (Mark 16:15)

R. Go out to all the world and tell the
　　　　Good News.
or: Alleluia.

Praise the LORD, all you nations;
　glorify him, all you peoples!   R.

For steadfast is his kindness toward us,
　and the fidelity of the LORD endures
　　　　forever.   R.

READING II *Hebrews 12:5–7, 11–13*

Brothers and sisters: You have forgotten the exhortation addressed to you as children: "My son, do not disdain the discipline of the Lord or lose heart when reproved by him; for whom the Lord loves, he disciplines; he scourges every son he acknowledges." Endure your trials as "discipline"; God treats you as sons. For what "son" is there whom his father does not discipline? At the time, all discipline seems a cause not for joy but for pain, yet later it brings the peaceful fruit of righteousness to those who are trained by it.

So strengthen your drooping hands and your weak knees. Make straight paths for your feet, that what is lame may not be disjointed but healed.

GOSPEL *Luke 13:22–30*

Jesus passed through towns and villages, teaching as he went and making his way to Jerusalem. Someone asked him, "Lord, will only a few people be saved?" He answered them, "Strive to enter through the narrow gate, for many, I tell you, will attempt to enter but will not be strong enough. After the master of the house has arisen and locked the door, then will you stand outside knocking and saying, 'Lord, open the door for us.' He will say to you in reply, 'I do not know where you are from.' And you will say, 'We ate and drank in your company and you taught in our streets.' Then he will say to you, 'I do not know where you are from. Depart from me, all you evildoers!' And there will be wailing and grinding of teeth when you see Abraham, Isaac, and Jacob and all the prophets in the kingdom of God and you yourselves cast out. And people will come from the east and the west and from the north and the south and will recline at table in the kingdom of God. For behold, some are last who will be first, and some are first who will be last."

Practice of Faith

In beckoning us to enter the kingdom "by the narrow door," Jesus directs us to travel lightly, unburdened by possessions. He also encourages us not to get caught up in the crowd of those merely acquainted with Jesus, but rather to know him intimately. We are to narrow our focus so only Christ fills our vision. ◆ Make a list of ways you and/or your family can simplify your lives to make more room for God, and for the lifestyle of service to which we are called. Pray for the courage to begin taking steps toward this vision. ◆ Ask your family members to consider turning off their phones and electronics next Sunday. At day's end, talk about whether you were able to be more attentive to God, each other, and nature. ◆ This week try walking slower, doing only one task at a time, and buying only what is necessary. At the end of the week, journal about the experience.

Download more questions and activities for families, Christian initiation groups, and other adult groups at http://www.ltp.org/ahw.

Scripture Insights

The journey to Jerusalem is a characteristic feature of Luke's Gospel account. For ten chapters (9:51—19:28), Luke presents Jesus on a journey to Jerusalem with his disciples. The symbolism of a journey was instructive to Luke's audience. They knew that during the course of the Hebrew people's travel from Egypt to the Promised Land, God formed them into his people. Against this background, Luke reminds us that Jesus is the guide leading his disciples purposefully on the path to Jerusalem, where he will bring salvation to them through his death on the cross.

This passage offers a series of sayings through which Jesus instruct his disciples about the conscious decision that must be made to become a member of his kingdom. Jesus also draws attention to the fact that one cannot claim to be a member of his kingdom simply because of Jewish heritage. Consequently, the places at the table in Jesus' kingdom are extended to the Gentiles who "come from the east and the west, and from the north and the south." The Gentiles, who have been called last, will go ahead of those who were first invited, the Jews. God's kingdom is open to all humanity, to everyone who embraces Jesus and his message.

Today's reading from the prophet Isaiah shows how Jesus' message of inclusivity was foretold centuries before by the prophet. Jesus has come to bring God's plan to fulfillment.

◆ How does Jesus fulfill the expectations proclaimed by the prophet Isaiah in the First reading today?

◆ How do you see the Catholic Church as a continuation of the message conveyed by the readings from Isaiah and the Gospel?

◆ Where have you experienced God's presence with you on your journey of faith?

Prayer before Reading the Word

God of the covenant,
whose promises can never fail,
in every age you place your words
on the lips of the prophets.
We children of this age come to you in faith,
longing to be transformed in Christ
as children of the Resurrection.

Give us humility of heart.
Let us cling to your Word
in Moses, the prophets, and the Gospel.
Let each new day be for us
a time to testify to the Gospel.

We ask this through our Lord
        Jesus Christ, your Son,
who lives and reigns with you
in the unity of the Holy Spirit,
one God, for ever and ever. Amen.

Prayer after Reading the Word

O God, author of life and resurrection,
before whom even the dead are alive,
grant that the Word of your Son,
sown in our hearts,
may blossom and bear fruit in every good work,
so that both in life and in death
our hearts may be strengthened
by eternal comfort and good hope.

We ask this through our Lord
        Jesus Christ, your Son,
who lives and reigns with you
in the unity of the Holy Spirit,
one God, for ever and ever. Amen.

Weekday Readings

September 2: *1 Thessalonians 4:13–18; Luke 4:16–30*
September 3: *1 Thessalonians 5:1–6, 9–11; Luke 4:31–37*
September 4: *Colossians 1:1–8; Luke 4:38–44*
September 5: *Colossians 1:9–14; Luke 5:1–11*
September 6: *Colossians 1:15–20; Luke 5:33–39*
September 7: *Colossians 1:21–23; Luke 6:1–5*

September 9: *Colossians 1:24—2:3; Luke 6:6–11*
September 10: *Colossians 2:6–15; Luke 6:12–19*
September 11: Colossians 3:1–11; Luke 6:20–26
September 12: Colossians 3:12–17; Luke 6:27–38
September 13: *1 Timothy 1:1–2, 12–14; Luke 6:39–42*
September 14: Feast of the Exaltation of the Holy Cross
Numbers 21:4b–9; Philippians 2:6–11; John 3:13–17

September 16: *1 Timothy 2:1–8; Luke 7:1–10*
September 17: *1 Timothy 3:1–13; Luke 7:11–17*
September 18: *1 Timothy 3:14–16; Luke 7:31–35*
September 19: *1 Timothy 4:12–16; Luke 7:36–50*
September 20: *1 Timothy 6:2c–12; Luke 8:1–3*
September 21: Feast of St. Matthew, Apostle
and Evangelist
Ephesians 4:1–7, 11–13; Matthew 9:9–13

September 23: *Ezra 1:1–6; Luke 8:16–18*
September 24: *Ezra 6:7–8, 12b, 14–20; Luke 8:19–21*
September 25: *Ezra 9:5–9; Luke 9:1–6*
September 26: *Haggai 1:1–8; Luke 9:7–9*
September 27: *Haggai 2:1–9; Luke 9:18–22*
September 28: *Zechariah 2:5–9, 14–15a; Luke 9:43b–45*

September 30: *Zechariah 8:1–8; Luke 9:46–50*
October 1: *Zechariah 8:20–23; Luke 9:51–56*
October 2: *Nehemiah 2:1–8; Matthew 18:1–5, 10*
October 3: *Nehemiah 8:1–4a, 5–6, 7b–12; Luke 10:1–12*
October 4: *Baruch 1:15–22; Luke 10:13–16*
October 5: *Baruch 4:5–12, 27–29; Luke 10:17–24*

October 7: *Jonah 1:1—2:2, 11; Luke 10:25–37*
October 8: *Jonah 3:1–10; Luke 10:38–42*
October 9: *Jonah 4:1–11; Luke 11:1–4*
October 10: *Malachi 3:13–20b; Luke 11:5–13*
October 11: *Joel 1:13–15; 2:1–2; Luke 11:15–26*
October 12: *Joel 4:12–21; Luke 11:27–28*

October 14: *Romans 1:1–7; Luke 11:29–32*
October 15: *Romans 1:16–25; Luke 11:37–41*
October 16: *Romans 2:1–11; Luke 11:42–46*
October 17: *Romans 3:21–30; Luke 11:47–54*
October 18: Feast of St. Luke, Evangelist
2 Timothy 4:10–17b; Luke 10:1–9
October 19: *Romans 4:13, 16–18; Luke 12:8–12*

October 21: *Romans 4:20–25; Luke 12:13–21*
October 22: *Romans 5:12, 15b, 17–19, 20b–21; Luke 12:35–38*

October 23: *Romans 6:12–18; Luke12:39–48*
October 24: *Romans 6:19–23; Luke 12:49–53*
October 25: *Romans 7:18–25a; Luke 12:54–59*
October 26: *Romans 8:1–11; Luke 13:1–9*

October 28: Feast of Sts. Simon and Jude, Apostles
Ephesians 2:19–22; Luke 6:12–16
October 29: *Romans 8:18–25; Luke 13:18–21*
October 30: *Romans 8:26–30; Luke 13:22–30*
October 31: *Romans 8:31b–39; Luke 13:31–35*
November 1: Solemnity of All Saints
Revelation 7:2–4, 9–14; 1 John 3:1–3; Matthew 5:1–12a
November 2: Commemoration of All the Faithful Departed
(All Souls' Day)
Wisdom 3:1–9; Romans 5:5–11 or Romans 6:3–9;
John 6:37–40

November 4: *Romans 11:29–36; Luke 14:12–14*
November 5: *Romans 12:5–16b; Luke 14:15–24*
November 6: *Romans 13:8–10; Luke 14:25–33*
November 7: *Romans 14:7–12; Luke 15:1–10*
November 8: *Romans 15:14–21; Luke 16:1–8*
November 9: Feast of the Dedication of the Lateran Basilica
Ezekiel 47:1–2, 8–9, 12; 1 Corinthians 3:9c–11, 16–17;
John 2:13–22

November 11: *Wisdom 1:1–7; Luke 17:1–6*
November 12: *Wisdom 2:23—3:9; Luke 17:7–10*
November 13: *Wisdom 6:1–11; Luke 17:11–19*
November 14: *Wisdom 7:22b—8:1; Luke 17:20–25*
November 15: *Wisdom 13:1–9; Luke 17:26–37*
November 16: *Wisdom 18:14-16; 19:6–9; Luke 18:1–8*

November 18: *1 Maccabees 1:10–15, 41–43, 54–57, 62–63;*
Luke 18:35–43
or, for the Memorial of the Dedication of the Basilicas
of Sts. Peter and Paul, Apostles,
Acts 28:11–16, 30–31; Matthew 14:22–33
November 19: *2 Maccabees 6:18–31; Luke 19:1–10*
November 20: *2 Maccabees 7:1, 20–31; Luke 19:11–28*
November 21: *1 Maccabees 2:15–29; Luke 19:41–44*
November 22: *1 Maccabees 4:36–37, 52–59; Luke 19:45–48*
November 23: *1 Maccabees 6:1–13; Luke 20:27–40*

November 25: *Daniel 1:1-6, 8–20; Luke 21:1–4*
November 26: *Daniel 2:31–45; Luke 21:5–11*
November 27: *Daniel 5:1–6, 13–14, 16–17, 23–28; Luke 21:12–19*
November 28: *Daniel 6:12–28; Luke 21:20–28*
or, for Thanksgiving Day, any readings from the Lectionary for Mass (vol. IV), the Mass "In Thanksgiving to God," nos. 943-947
November 29: Daniel 7:2–14; Luke 21:29–33
November 30: Feast of St. Andrew, Apostle,
Romans 10:9–18; Matthew 4:18–22

READING I *Sirach 3:17–18, 20, 28–29*

My child, conduct your affairs with humility,
 and you will be loved more than a giver
  of gifts.
Humble yourself the more, the greater you are,
 and you will find favor with God.
What is too sublime for you, seek not,
 into things beyond your strength search not.
The mind of a sage appreciates proverbs,
 and an attentive ear is the joy of the wise.
Water quenches a flaming fire,
 and alms atone for sins.

RESPONSORIAL PSALM
Psalm 68:4–5, 6–7, 10–11 (see 11b)

R. God, in your goodness, you have made
   a home for the poor.

The just rejoice and exult before God;
 they are glad and rejoice.
Sing to God, chant praise to his name;
 whose name is the LORD.   R.

The father of orphans and the defender
    of widows
 is God in his holy dwelling.
God gives a home to the forsaken;
 he leads forth prisoners to prosperity.   R.

A bountiful rain you showered down, O God,
    upon your inheritance;
 you restored the land when it languished;
your flock settled in it;
 in your goodness, O God, you provided it for
   the needy.   R.

READING II
Hebrews 12:18–19, 22–24a

Brothers and sisters: You have not approached that which could be touched and a blazing fire and gloomy darkness and storm and a trumpet blast and a voice speaking words such that those who heard begged that no message be further addressed to them. No, you have approached Mount Zion and the city of the living God, the heavenly Jerusalem, and countless angels in festal gathering, and the assembly of the firstborn enrolled in heaven, and God the judge of all, and the spirits of the just made perfect, and Jesus, the mediator of a new covenant, and the sprinkled blood that speaks more eloquently than that of Abel.

GOSPEL *Luke 14:1, 7–14*

On a sabbath Jesus went to dine at the home of one of the leading Pharisees, and the people there were observing him carefully.

He told a parable to those who had been invited, noticing how they were choosing the places of honor at the table. "When you are invited by someone to a wedding banquet, do not recline at table in the place of honor. A more distinguished guest than you may have been invited by him, and the host who invited both of you may approach you and say, 'Give your place to this man,' and then you would proceed with embarrassment to take the lowest place. Rather, when you are invited, go and take the lowest place so that when the host comes to you he may say, 'My friend, move up to a higher position.' Then you will enjoy the esteem of your companions at the table. For every one who exalts himself will be humbled, but the one who humbles himself will be exalted." Then he said to the host who invited him, "When you hold a lunch or a dinner, do not invite your friends or your brothers or your relatives or your wealthy neighbors, in case they may invite you back and you have repayment. Rather, when you hold a banquet, invite the poor, the crippled, the lame, the blind; blessed indeed will you be because of their inability to repay you. For you will be repaid at the resurrection of the righteous."

Practice of Charity

True humility is born in our relationship with Christ and his love. To not take the seat of honor, even when we think we deserve it, goes against much of what our culture celebrates. The truth of our being is that we are sinners and are beloved. When able to hold these truths together in our heart, we become free to glorify God, inviting "the poor, the crippled, the lame, the blind" to God's banquet. ◆ While spending time in prayer with Jesus, imagine carrying your concerns, fears, and weaknesses and placing them at his feet. Rest awhile in God's love. ◆ What are your points of pride? How might you introduce humility into these areas of your life? Pick one action to carry out this week. ◆ Early in his pontificate, Pope Francis described himself by saying, "I am a sinner whom the Lord has looked upon." Read a reflection on those words as the basis for humility here at http://www.americamagazine.org/issue/%E2%80%98i-am-sinner%E2%80%99.

Download more questions and activities for families, Christian initiation groups, and other adult groups at http://www.ltp.org/ahw.

Scripture Insights

"My child," writes the author of Sirach, "conduct your affairs with humility, and you will be loved more than a giver of gifts." Humility is a distinctly Jewish virtue and one that Jesus embraces as the foundation of his teaching on the Kingdom of God. Jesus often uses the image of a banquet to offer a teaching about the kingdom. The poor of Palestine could only dream of a banquet. The overflowing abundance of food and wine was beyond their hope. With this image, Jesus promises the poor that they are the chosen guests at God's banquet. God has a preference for the lowly and only those who acknowledge their lowly status in relation to God and to others will be embraced at the banquet of eternal life.

Many places in the Scriptures show that Jesus lived humility: "Learn from me for I am meek and humble of heart; and you will find rest for yourselves" (Matthew 11:29). "The Son of Man did not come to be served but to serve and to give his life as a ransom for many" (Matthew 20:28). Humility defines Jesus' life and teaching and so it should define Christians' lives, too. In relationship with God, humility defines us as dependent on God for everything; in relationship with others, humility defines us as servants to others.

St. Augustine identified humility as the defining virtue of a Christian way of life, "This way consists, first of humility, second of humility, and third of humility. No matter how often you would ask me, I would say the same" (St. Augustine Letter 118).

◆ How do you define humility?

◆ Why would the image of a banquet be so significant to the people who heard Jesus' message?

◆ Why do you think that humility is such a significant virtue for a Christian?

READING I *Wisdom 9:13–18b*

Who can know God's counsel,
 or who can conceive what the LORD intends?
For the deliberations of mortals are timid,
 and unsure are our plans.
For the corruptible body burdens the soul
 and the earthen shelter weighs down the
  mind that has many concerns.
And scarce do we guess the things on earth,
 and what is within our grasp
  we find with difficulty;
 but when things are in heaven,
  who can search them out?
Or who ever knew your counsel, except you
  had given wisdom
 and sent your holy spirit from on high?
And thus were the paths of those
 on earth made straight.

RESPONSORIAL PSALM
Psalm 90:3–4, 5–6, 12–13, 14 and 17 (1)

R. In every age, O Lord,
  you have been our refuge.

You turn man back to dust,
 saying, "Return, O children of men."
For a thousand years in your sight
 are as yesterday, now that it is past,
 or as a watch of the night.   R.

You make an end of them in their sleep;
 the next morning they are
  like the changing grass,
which at dawn springs up anew,
 but by evening wilts and fades.   R.

Teach us to number our days aright,
 that we may gain wisdom of heart.
Return, O LORD! How long?
 Have pity on your servants!   R.

Fill us at daybreak with your kindness,
 that we may shout for joy and gladness
  all our days.

And may the gracious care of the LORD our God
  be ours;
 prosper the work of our hands for us!
 Prosper the work of our hands!   R.

READING II *Philemon 9–10, 12–17*

I, Paul, an old man, and now also a prisoner for Christ Jesus, urge you on behalf of my child Onesimus, whose father I have become in my imprisonment; I am sending him, that is, my own heart, back to you. I should have liked to retain him for myself, so that he might serve me on your behalf in my imprisonment for the gospel, but I did not want to do anything without your consent, so that the good you do might not be forced but voluntary. Perhaps this is why he was away from you for a while, that you might have him back forever, no longer as a slave but more than a slave, a brother, beloved especially to me, but even more so to you, as a man and in the Lord. So if you regard me as a partner, welcome him as you would me.

GOSPEL *Luke 14:25–33*

Great crowds were traveling with Jesus, and he turned and addressed them, "If anyone comes to me without hating his father and mother, wife and children, brothers and sisters, and even his own life, he cannot be my disciple. Whoever does not carry his own cross and come after me cannot be my disciple. Which of you wishing to construct a tower does not first sit down and calculate the cost to see if there is enough for its completion? Otherwise, after laying the foundation and finding himself unable to finish the work the onlookers should laugh at him and say, 'This one began to build but did not have the resources to finish.' Or what king marching into battle would not first sit down and decide whether with ten thousand troops he can successfully oppose another king advancing upon him with twenty thousand troops? But if not, while he is still far away, he will send a delegation to ask for peace terms. In the same way, anyone of you who does not renounce all his possessions cannot be my disciple."

Practice of Hope

In today's reading, the psalmist prays, "teach us to number our days aright." Jesus echoes this in the Gospel, urging us to be intentional about our faith, and not to let habitual relationships or ways of living dissuade us. Reflect on what a faithful Christian looks like to you. With that image in mind, how might you, in hope, take steps toward this vision? ◆ Consider strengthening your relationship with God through more frequent daily prayer, Mass, and adoration of the Blessed Sacrament. Perhaps you could make a retreat or work with a spiritual director. ◆ Look for ways to become more involved in your parish community. Explore a liturgical ministry, community building, or social justice work. ◆ Find an organization that speaks to your heart and take a step toward supporting them financially or by volunteering, even a couple times a year. If you have time and experience to offer, explore organizations such as Ignatian Volunteer Corps at ivcusa.org/.

Download more questions and activities for families, Christian initiation groups, and other adult groups at http://www.ltp.org/ahw.

Scripture Insights

The cost of being a follower of Jesus is demanding. The Second Reading illustrates this in the request Paul makes of his close friend Philemon. (This is the only private letter from Paul that has survived.) Paul, in prison, asks Philemon to receive back a slave, Onesimus, who had run away. Paul had converted Onesimus to Christ and so asks Philemon to receive him back "no longer as a slave but as a brother." Paul asks Philemon to extend forgiveness.

Today's First Reading from the Book of Wisdom reminds us that we do not have answers to everything. Even more so, we must recognize that we cannot understand God's mind. Only through the gift of wisdom and the Holy Spirit can we "know God's counsel."

The Gospel continues the theme of the cost of discipleship. Jesus offers a series of sayings that require a depth of commitment, for example, "Whoever does not carry his cross and come after me cannot be my disciple." Jesus is being provocative and demanding. His unsettling language causes us to sit up and pay attention. When he says we should "hate our family members," Jesus obviously is not to be taken literally. What we hate is what is opposed to our relationship with him. The full meaning of the First Commandment to love God above all things is fleshed out in the examples Jesus gives: neither family members, or possessions, or even one's life can be placed above love and commitment to God. Priority must be given to our relationship with Jesus Christ.

◆ In the Second Reading, why do you think Paul did not condemn slavery?

◆ How do you reconcile the Fourth Commandment with Jesus' statement in the Gospel about hating father and mother?

◆ What demands does your Christian faith make on you?

READING I *Exodus 32:7–11, 13–14*

The LORD said to Moses, "Go down at once to your people, whom you brought out of the land of Egypt, for they have become depraved. They have soon turned aside from the way I pointed out to them, making for themselves a molten calf and worshiping it, sacrificing to it and crying out, 'This is your God, O Israel, who brought you out of the land of Egypt!' I see how stiff-necked this people is," continued the LORD to Moses. "Let me alone, then, that my wrath may blaze up against them to consume them. Then I will make of you a great nation."

But Moses implored the LORD, his God, saying, "Why, O LORD, should your wrath blaze up against your own people, whom you brought out of the land of Egypt with such great power and with so strong a hand? Remember your servants Abraham, Isaac, and Israel, and how you swore to them by your own self, saying, 'I will make your descendants as numerous as the stars in the sky; and all this land that I promised, I will give your descendants as their perpetual heritage.'" So the LORD relented in the punishment he had threatened to inflict on his people.

READING II *1 Timothy 1:12–17*

Beloved: I am grateful to him who has strengthened me, Christ Jesus our Lord, because he considered me trustworthy in appointing me to the ministry. I was once a blasphemer and a persecutor and arrogant, but I have been mercifully treated because I acted out of ignorance in my unbelief. Indeed, the grace of our Lord has been abundant, along with the faith and love that are in Christ Jesus. This saying is trustworthy and deserves full acceptance: Christ Jesus came into the world to save sinners. Of these I am the foremost. But for that reason I was mercifully treated, so that in me, as the foremost, Christ Jesus might display all his patience as an example for those who would come to believe in him for everlasting life. To the king of ages, incorruptible, invisible, the only God, honor and glory forever and ever. Amen.

GOSPEL *Luke 15:1–32*

Shorter: Luke 15:1–10

Tax collectors and sinners were all drawing near to listen to Jesus, but the Pharisees and scribes began to complain, saying, "This man welcomes sinners and eats with them." So to them he addressed this parable. "What man among you having a hundred sheep and losing one of them would not leave the ninety-nine in the desert and go after the lost one until he finds it? And when he does find it, he sets it on his shoulders with great joy and, upon his arrival home, he calls together his friends and neighbors and says to them, 'Rejoice with me because I have found my lost sheep.' I tell you, in just the same way there will be more joy in heaven over one sinner who repents than over ninety-nine righteous people who have no need of repentance.

"Or what woman having ten coins and losing one would not light a lamp and sweep the house, searching carefully until she finds it? And when she does find it, she calls together her friends and neighbors and says to them, 'Rejoice with me because I have found the coin that I lost.' In just the same way, I tell you, there will be rejoicing among the angels of God over one sinner who repents."

Then he said, "A man had two sons, and the younger son said to his father, 'Father give me the share of your estate that should come to me.' So the father divided the property between them. After a few days, the younger son collected all his belongings and set off to a distant country where he squandered his inheritance on a life of dissipation. When he had freely spent everything, a severe famine struck that country, and he found himself in dire need. So he hired himself out to one of the local citizens who sent him to his farm to tend the swine. And he longed to eat his fill of the pods on which the swine fed, but nobody gave him any. Coming to his senses he thought, 'How many of my father's hired workers have more than enough food to eat, but here am I, dying from hunger. I shall get up and go to my father and I shall say to him, "Father, I have sinned against heaven and against you. I no longer deserve to be called your son; treat me as you would treat one of your hired workers.'" So he got up and went back to his father. While he was still a long way off, his father caught sight of him, and was filled with compassion. He ran to his son, embraced him and kissed him. His son said to him, 'Father, I have sinned against heaven and against you; I no longer deserve to be called your son.' But his father ordered his servants, 'Quickly bring the finest robe and put it on him; put a ring on his finger and sandals on his feet. Take the fattened calf and slaughter it. Then let us celebrate with a feast, because this son of mine was dead, and has come to life again; he was lost, and has been found.' Then the celebration began. Now the older son had been out in the field and, on his way back, as he neared the house, he heard the sound of music and dancing. He called one of the servants and asked what this might mean. The servant said to him, 'Your brother has returned and your father has slaughtered the fattened calf because he has him back safe and sound.' He became angry, and when he refused to enter the house, his father came out and pleaded with him. He said to his father in reply, 'Look, all these years I served you and not once did I disobey your orders; yet you never gave me even a young goat to feast on with my friends. But when your son returns, who swallowed up your property with prostitutes, for him you slaughter the fattened calf.' He said to him, 'My son, you are here with me always; everything I have is yours. But now we must celebrate and rejoice, because your brother was dead and has come to life again; he was lost and has been found.'"

Scripture Insights

As we look back over our lives, we recall with embarrassment and guilt sinful events we would rather forget. Each of the readings recalls such moments but these are celebrated instead of forgotten. In the reading from Exodus the people of Israel, whom God had liberated from slavery, have turned away to worship false gods. In prayer, Moses mediates on their behalf and they experience the joy of God's merciful love.

In his Letter to Timothy, Paul recalls his former way of life as he persecuted Christ and his followers. Without excusing himself, Paul celebrates the forgiveness he has experienced through the Risen Christ's call and transformation.

The Gospel offers three parables displaying God's immense love and forgiveness. "There will be more joy in heaven over one sinner who repents than over ninety-nine righteous people who have no need of repentance."

This joy is captured in the parable that could be called the "Parable of the Forgiving Father." After patiently awaiting his son's return, the father sees him in the distance, runs, and embraces him. Such actions may have been extraordinary for a Jewish patriarch. The son begins to ask forgiveness, saying, "Father, I have sinned against heaven and against you," but the father interrupts his prepared speech and throws a party to welcome him back. Forgiveness results in celebration.

The second part of the parable, contrasts the father's joy and forgiveness with the elder son's inability to forgive. He cannot share his father's joy. Undoubtedly, the father portrays the greatest example of God's forgiving and embracing love.

♦ Which of the characters do you identify with most in the parable of the prodigal son?

♦ Why was the elder son unable to share in his father's joy?

♦ How can you imitate St. Paul in celebrating God's loving forgiveness in your life?

READING I *Amos 8:4–7*

Hear this, you who trample upon the needy
and destroy the poor of the land!
"When will the new moon be over," you ask,
"that we may sell our grain,
and the sabbath, that we may display
the wheat?
We will diminish the ephah,
add to the shekel,
and fix our scales for cheating!
We will buy the lowly for silver,
and the poor for a pair of sandals;
even the refuse of the wheat we will sell!"
The LORD has sworn by the pride of Jacob:
Never will I forget a thing they have done!

RESPONSORIAL PSALM
Psalm 113:1–2, 4–6, 7–8 (see 1a, 7b)

R. Praise the Lord, who lifts up the poor.
or: Alleluia.

Praise, you servants of the LORD,
praise the name of the LORD.
Blessed be the name of the LORD
both now and forever. R.

High above all nations is the LORD;
above the heavens is his glory.
Who is like the LORD, our God,
who is enthroned on high
and looks upon the heavens
and the earth below? R.

He raises up the lowly from the dust;
from the dunghill he lifts up the poor
to seat them with princes,
with the princes of his own people. R.

READING II *1 Timothy 2:1–8*

Beloved: First of all, I ask that supplications, prayers, petitions and thanksgivings be offered for everyone, for kings and for all in authority, that we may lead a quiet and tranquil life in all devotion and dignity. This is good and pleasing to God our savior, who wills everyone to be saved and to come to knowledge of the truth.

For there is one God.
There is also one mediator between God
and men,
the man Christ Jesus,
who gave himself as ransom for all.

This was the testimony at the proper time. For this I was appointed preacher and apostle—I am speaking the truth, I am not lying—, teacher of the Gentiles in faith and truth.

It is my wish, then, that in every place the men should pray, lifting up holy hands, without anger or argument.

GOSPEL *Luke 16:1–13*

Shorter: Luke 16:10–13

Jesus said to his disciples, "A rich man had a steward who was reported to him for squandering his property. He summoned him and said, 'What is this I hear about you? Prepare a full account of your stewardship, because you can no longer be my steward.' The steward said to himself, 'What shall I do, now that my master is taking the position of steward away from me? I am not strong enough to dig and I am ashamed to beg. I know what I shall do so that, when I am removed from the stewardship, they may welcome me into their homes.' He called in his master's debtors one by one. To the first he said, 'How much do you owe my master?' He replied, 'One hundred measures of olive oil.' He said to him, 'Here is your promissory note. Sit down and quickly write one for fifty.' Then to another the steward said, 'And you, how much do you owe?' He replied, 'One hundred kors of wheat.' The steward said to him, 'Here is your promissory note; write one for eighty.' And the master commended that dishonest steward for acting prudently.

"For the children of this world are more prudent in dealing with their own generation than are the children of light. I tell you, make friends for yourselves with dishonest wealth, so that when it fails, you will be welcomed into eternal dwellings. The person who is trustworthy in very small matters is also trustworthy in great ones; and the person who is dishonest in very small matters is also dishonest in great ones. If, therefore, you are not trustworthy with dishonest wealth, who will trust you with true wealth? If you are not trustworthy with what belongs to another, who will give you what is yours? No servant can serve two masters. He will either hate one and love the other, or be devoted to one and despise the other. You cannot serve both God and mammon."

Practice of Charity

Speaking of how the master praises the unjust steward for his craftiness, Pope Francis says, "This is praise for bribes! And the habit of bribes is a mundane and extremely sinful habit. . . . It's a habit that does not come from God" (November 8, 2013, Mass). Cunning and corruption are often admired as navigating the system. Yet even as we live and work in the world, we are called to be trustworthy and responsible in obeying God's laws of charity, honesty, and justice. ◆ Read more about the pope's homily at www.catholicnewsagency.com/news/pope-warns-against-unclean-bread-of-corruption/. ◆ 100 Women Who Care is an organization that, through community, turns small amounts of material wealth into powerful charitable action. Find them at www.100wwc.org/. ◆ Students nationwide are learning how to become civic-minded leaders and philanthropists through the Students4Giving program. Find them at Portland Community College (www.pcc.edu/resources/community-based-learning/students4giving/) and Northeastern University (http://www.northeastern.edu/impactlab/ns4g-6/).

Download more questions and activities for families, Christian initiation groups, and other adult groups at http://www.ltp.org/ahw.

Scripture Insights

The liturgy's readings today challenge us to view our world through God's eyes. Paul's Letter to Timothy contains valuable advice worthy of deep reflection. Firstly, Paul calls on Timothy, and by extension us, to pray for our leaders so that we may live a peaceful existence. Their authority has one goal: our peaceful existence. Secondly, Paul reminds us that God wills the salvation of all people: "God our savior, who wills everyone to be saved and to come to knowledge of the truth." Finally, as Son of God and Son of Man, Jesus Christ is the only mediator between God and us. Jesus is the one to whom we owe sole allegiance.

The prophet Amos speaks out against those who oppress the poor. Because the poor have no voice, God becomes their advocate. God is the God of the poor.

The Gospel reading continues the prophet's stance as Jesus draws attention to the dishonest use of wealth. This parable is disturbing since at first it appears that Jesus is praising dishonesty when he says, "I tell you, make friends for yourselves with dishonest wealth." A deeper look at the parable helps us discover its true meaning. The manager is a smart operator and to save his situation, he makes his master's debtors an offer they cannot refuse and acquires the money his master is owed.

Jesus uses this story of the dishonest manager to teach that just as those in our materialistic world work so hard and sacrifice so much, to attain material results that last only a few years, so Jesus' followers should work and sacrifice even more because they have as their goal eternal results. Nothing could be greater than the inheritance promised Jesus' followers so they should be dedicated and willing to sacrifice everything for it.

◆ How would you explain the meaning of the parable of the dishonest manager to a friend?

◆ Why should we pray for our leaders?

◆ What implications do you see in Paul's words that "God wills everyone to be saved"?

READING I   *Amos 6:1a, 4–7*

Thus says the LORD, God of hosts:
Woe to the complacent in Zion!
Lying upon beds of ivory,
   stretched comfortably on their couches,
they eat lambs taken from the flock,
   and calves from the stall!
Improvising to the music of the harp,
   like David, they devise their
      own accompaniment.
They drink wine from bowls
   and anoint themselves with the best oils;
   yet they are not made ill
      by the collapse of Joseph!
Therefore, now they shall be
      the first to go into exile,
   and their wanton revelry shall be done
      away with.

RESPONSORIAL PSALM
Psalm 146:7, 8–9, 9–10 (1b)

R. Praise the Lord, my soul!
or: Alleluia.

Blessed is he who keeps faith forever,
   secures justice for the oppressed,
   gives food to the hungry.
The LORD sets captives free.   R.

The LORD gives sight to the blind;
   the LORD raises up those
      who were bowed down.
The LORD loves the just;
   the LORD protects strangers.   R.

The fatherless and the widow he sustains,
   but the way of the wicked he thwarts.
The LORD shall reign forever;
   your God, O Zion, through
      all generations. Alleluia.   R.

READING II   *1 Timothy 6:11–16*

But you, man of God, pursue righteousness, devotion, faith, love, patience, and gentleness. Compete well for the faith. Lay hold of eternal life, to which you were called when you made the noble confession in the presence of many witnesses. I charge you before God, who gives life to all things, and before Christ Jesus, who gave testimony under Pontius Pilate for the noble confession, to keep the commandment without stain or reproach until the appearance of our Lord Jesus Christ that the blessed and only ruler will make manifest at the proper time, the King of kings and Lord of lords, who alone has immortality, who dwells in unapproachable light, and whom no human being has seen or can see. To him be honor and eternal power. Amen.

GOSPEL   *Luke 16:19–31*

Jesus said to the Pharisees: "There was a rich man who dressed in purple garments and fine linen and dined sumptuously each day. And lying at his door was a poor man named Lazarus, covered with sores, who would gladly have eaten his fill of the scraps that fell from the rich man's table. Dogs even used to come and lick his sores. When the poor man died, he was carried away by angels to the bosom of Abraham. The rich man also died and was buried, and from the netherworld, where he was in torment, he raised his eyes and saw Abraham far off and Lazarus at his side. And he cried out, 'Father Abraham, have pity on me. Send Lazarus to dip the tip of his finger in water and cool my tongue, for I am suffering torment in these flames.' Abraham replied, 'My child, remember that you received what was good during your lifetime while Lazarus likewise received what was bad; but now he is comforted here, whereas you are tormented. Moreover, between us and you a great chasm is established to prevent anyone from crossing who might wish to go from our side to yours or from your side to ours.' He said, 'Then I beg you, father, send him to my father's house, for I have five brothers, so that he may warn them, lest they too come to this place of torment.' But Abraham replied, 'They have Moses and the prophets. Let them listen to them.' He said, 'Oh no, father Abraham, but if someone from the dead goes to them, they will repent.' Then Abraham said, 'If they will not listen to Moses and the prophets, neither will they be persuaded if someone should rise from the dead.'"

Practice of Charity

To pass by Lazarus daily and not extend charity, the rich man had to have been blind to Lazarus as a person. Our culture makes it easy for us to be like the rich man. On our busy streets, it's easy to walk by those asking for a handout. On social media, it's easy to say things we would never say face to face. On our electronic devices, it's easy to watch the basest human tendencies play out as entertainment. Charity begins by seeing others through God's eyes, as persons made in God's image and worthy of our love and care. ◆ This week seek to pause. Pause to notice the man or woman on the street. Pause before firing off the next tweet. Pause before tuning in. Take a moment to see through God's eyes. ◆ Pope Francis tells us to give to panhandlers "without worry" and to connect with them as human beings. ◆ At the center of Catholic Social Teaching is belief in the dignity of every human being. Learn the basics at http://www.usccb.org/beliefs-and-teachings/what-we-believe/catholic-social-teaching/seven-themes-of-catholic-social-teaching.cfm. To learn more, read *101 Questions & Answers on Catholic Social Teaching* by Kenneth R. Himes, OFM (Paulist Press, 2013).

Download more questions and activities for families, Christian initiation groups, and other adult groups at http://www.ltp.org/ahw.

Scripture Insights

"Woe to the complacent," shouts the prophet Amos in the First Reading. Indifference to the needs and plight of those around us challenges the prophet Amos and Jesus in today's readings.

Luke tells the parable in the Gospel in three scenes. In the first, a contrast is drawn between the sumptuous lifestyle of the rich man (who remains unnamed) and the poor man (named Lazarus) covered with sores and lying at the entrance to the rich man's estate. There Lazarus dies, forgotten, with no mention of burial. The rich man also dies and is buried.

The next scene takes place in the afterlife, where the roles are reversed and Lazarus is with Abraham while the rich man is in torment. In the final scene, the rich man begs that his brothers be warned about their fate for overlooking the poor. Like the rich man and his brothers, we have the teachings of Scripture, but we also have the example from this parable and more importantly that of Christ, to remind us of our responsibility to care for the needs of others. Christians can never be indifferent to the needs of and injustices done to others. Pope Paul VI said in *Populorum progressio*, 23, "It is well known how strong were the words used by the Fathers of the Church to describe the proper attitude of persons who possess anything towards persons in need. To quote Saint Ambrose: 'You are not making a gift of your possessions to the poor person. You are handing over to him what is his. For what has been given in common for the use of all, you have abrogated to yourself.'"

◆ Why do you think that the poor man is named but not the rich man?

◆ Why do we have a responsibility to help those who are in need?

◆ How has your life been touched or changed when you have responded to someone in need?

READING I *Habakkuk 1:2–3; 2:2–4*

How long, O LORD? I cry for help
  but you do not listen!
I cry out to you, "Violence!"
  but you do not intervene.
Why do you let me see ruin;
  why must I look at misery?
Destruction and violence are before me;
  there is strife, and clamorous discord.
Then the LORD answered me and said:
  Write down the vision clearly upon the tablets,
  so that one can read it readily.
For the vision still has its time,
  presses on to fulfillment,
    and will not disappoint;
if it delays, wait for it,
  it will surely come, it will not be late.
The rash one has no integrity;
  but the just one, because of
    his faith, shall live.

RESPONSORIAL PSALM
Psalm 95:1–2, 6–7, 8–9 (8)

R. If today you hear his voice, harden not
    your hearts.

Come, let us sing joyfully to the LORD;
  let us acclaim the Rock of our salvation.
Let us come into his presence with thanksgiving;
  let us joyfully sing psalms to him. R.

Come, let us bow down in worship;
  let us kneel before the LORD who made us.
For he is our God,
  and we are the people he shepherds, the flock
    he guides. R.

Oh, that today you would hear his voice:
  "Harden not your hearts as at Meribah,
  as in the day of Massah in the desert,
where your fathers tempted me;
  they tested me though they had seen
    my works." R.

READING II *2 Timothy 1:6–8, 13–14*

Beloved: I remind you, to stir into flame the gift of God that you have through the imposition of my hands. For God did not give us a spirit of cowardice but rather of power and love and self-control. So do not be ashamed of your testimony to our Lord, nor of me, a prisoner for his sake; but bear your share of hardship for the gospel with the strength that comes from God.

Take as your norm the sound words that you heard from me, in the faith and love that are in Christ Jesus. Guard this rich trust with the help of the Holy Spirit that dwells within us.

GOSPEL *Luke 17:5–10*

The apostles said to the Lord, "Increase our faith." The Lord replied, "If you have faith the size of a mustard seed, you would say to this mulberry tree, 'Be uprooted and planted in the sea,' and it would obey you.

"Who among you would say to your servant who has just come in from plowing or tending sheep in the field, 'Come here immediately and take your place at table'? Would he not rather say to him, 'Prepare something for me to eat. Put on your apron and wait on me while I eat and drink. You may eat and drink when I am finished'? Is he grateful to that servant because he did what was commanded? So should it be with you. When you have done all you have been commanded, say, 'We are unprofitable servants; we have done what we were obliged to do.'"

Practice of Hope

As we witness atrocities committed against God's children in all corners of the globe, it is hard not to question God's governance, as we cry out in despair with Habakkuk, "How long, oh Lord?" Today's readings urge us to wait in hope, and remind us that we are equipped by the Holy Spirit not with "a spirit of cowardice, but rather of power and love and self-control." Through God's invitation and grace, we use our gifts to further the Kingdom of God. ◆ Is there a particular injustice that speaks to you? Talk to God about it in prayer. ◆ What is one small step you can take toward spreading God's hope and joy? Can you find support for this in your parish community? ◆ Meditate on David Ogden's song "Christ Has No Body Now but Yours," based on the words of St. Teresa of Avila and found at www.youtube.com/watch?v=zoV6R6qk4vY.

Download more questions and activities for families, Christian initiation groups, and other adult groups at http://www.ltp.org/ahw.

Scripture Insights

"The just one, because of his faith, shall live," says the prophet Habakkuk some six hundred years before Jesus' birth. These words are taken up by St. Paul in his thesis, "In the gospel is revealed the righteousness of God from faith to faith, as it is written, "The one who is righteous by faith will live" (Romans 1:17). The prophet cried out to God to intervene to help his people in their desperation. His cry expresses his faith that God cares for his people and will respond.

Today's readings offer a deeper insight into the nature of Christian faith. In Paul's Letter to Timothy, the Apostle encourages his disciple to "stir into flame the gift of God that you have through the imposition of my hands." Timothy has been entrusted with protecting the faith of his community. Paul reminds him of the gift of the Spirit he received that brings with it a gift of boldness that provides strength to overcome obstacles.

In the Gospel, when the Apostles tell the Lord, "increase our faith," they are not asking for the content of their faith to be increased but for the quality of their faith to be enhanced. In other words, the faith they refer to is their relationship with Jesus Christ. Jesus and the disciples are concerned with the depth of their faith relationship. It is not the quantity of faith that is significant but the quality of the relationship with Christ. After all, as Jesus said, faith the size of a mustard seed could move a tree. Genuine faith, the depth of our genuine relationship with Christ, enables us to perform the impossible.

◆ What does the word "faith" mean to you?

◆ Why is the quality of faith more important than the quantity?

◆ How have you experienced the power of faith at work in your life?

READING I 2 Kings 5:14–17

Naaman went down and plunged into the Jordan seven times at the word of Elisha, the man of God. His flesh became again like the flesh of a little child, and he was clean of his leprosy.

Naaman returned with his whole retinue to the man of God. On his arrival he stood before Elisha and said, "Now I know that there is no God in all the earth, except in Israel. Please accept a gift from your servant."

Elisha replied, "As the LORD lives whom I serve, I will not take it"; and despite Naaman's urging, he still refused. Naaman said: "If you will not accept, please let me, your servant, have two mule-loads of earth, for I will no longer offer holocaust or sacrifice to any other god except to the LORD."

RESPONSORIAL PSALM
Psalm 98:1, 2–3, 3–4 (see 2b)

R. The Lord has revealed to the nations his
     saving power.

Sing to the LORD a new song,
    for he has done wondrous deeds;
his right hand has won victory for him,
    his holy arm. R.

The LORD has made his salvation known:
    in the sight of the nations he has revealed
       his justice.
He has remembered his kindness and
       his faithfulness
    toward the house of Israel. R.

All the ends of the earth have seen
    the salvation by our God.
Sing joyfully to the LORD, all you lands:
    break into song; sing praise. R.

READING II 2 Timothy 2:8–13

Beloved: Remember Jesus Christ, raised from the dead, a descendant of David: such is my gospel, for which I am suffering, even to the point of chains, like a criminal. But the word of God is not chained. Therefore, I bear with everything for the sake of those who are chosen, so that they too may obtain the salvation that is in Christ Jesus, together with eternal glory. This saying is trustworthy:

If we have died with him
    we shall also live with him;
if we persevere
    we shall also reign with him.
But if we deny him
    he will deny us.
If we are unfaithful
    he remains faithful,
    for he cannot deny himself.

GOSPEL Luke 17:11–19

As Jesus continued his journey to Jerusalem, he traveled through Samaria and Galilee. As he was entering a village, ten lepers met him. They stood at a distance from him and raised their voices, saying, "Jesus, Master! Have pity on us!" And when he saw them, he said, "Go show yourselves to the priests." As they were going they were cleansed. And one of them, realizing he had been healed, returned, glorifying God in a loud voice; and he fell at the feet of Jesus and thanked him. He was a Samaritan. Jesus said in reply, "Ten were cleansed, were they not? Where are the other nine? Has none but this foreigner returned to give thanks to God?" Then he said to him, "Stand up and go; your faith has saved you."

Practice of Faith

Today's readings urge us to be as the healed leper, glorifying God with praise and thanksgiving. Jesus tells us that the Kingdom of God is already among us, but to see it we need eyes of faith and a grateful heart. ◆ Count the ways God loves you by starting a gratitude journal. Each day, try to notice and record three things for which you are grateful. ◆ If you are too busy to keep a journal but want to cultivate a grateful heart, tips can be found at CatholicMom.com: catholicmom.com/2011/11/23 /seven-unique-ways-to-keep-a-gratitude-journal -you-can-stick-with/. ◆ For more inspiration on cultivating gratitude, read this article from Our Sunday Visitor: www.osv.com/OSVNewsweekly /InFocus/Article/TabId/721/ArtMID/13629 /ArticleID/16399/Gratitude.aspx.

Download more questions and activities for families, Christian initiation groups, and other adult groups at http://www.ltp.org/ahw.

Scripture Insights

Today's readings offer two examples of people whose lives were transformed through miraculous healings and return to give thanks. In the First Reading, the leper, Naaman, is an army commander who was healed of his disease. Despite his initial reluctance, he followed the prophet Elisha's instructions and bathed in the Jordan River seven times. Instead of returning home, he first sought out Elisha to thank him and offer him a reward. Elisha declined his gift but allowed Naaman to take home some earth to build a shrine to the God of Israel. Naaman found faith as well as healing.

In a similar way, in the Gospel, Jesus heals ten lepers (nine Israelites and one Samaritan) but only one returns to give Jesus thanks, "Where are the other nine? Has none but this foreigner returned to give thanks to God?" Not only does this foreigner, a Samaritan, find healing, he finds faith.

In both readings, a foreigner returns to give thanks. In both readings, their healings lead to thankfulness that generates faith. Their physical healing is an external manifestation of their spiritual healing. Jesus deliberately drew attention to the faith of this Samaritan to illustrate that faith and salvation in Jesus Christ extend beyond the borders of Israel to all people. As Paul states in the Second Reading, "The word of God is not chained."

Faith, salvation, thanksgiving, all are intimately connected in today's readings as they are in the Eucharist that we celebrate.

◆ Read the full account of the healing of Naaman in 2 Kings 5:1–17. What do you notice about the gradual transformation of Naaman's faith?

◆ While imprisoned, Paul says that the "word of God is not chained." What does he mean?

◆ The two healings illustrate how God is found in suffering. Have you experienced a deepening of God's presence during suffering?

READING I *Exodus 17:8–13*

In those days, Amalek came and waged war against Israel. Moses, therefore, said to Joshua, "Pick out certain men, and tomorrow go out and engage Amalek in battle. I will be standing on top of the hill with the staff of God in my hand." So Joshua did as Moses told him: he engaged Amalek in battle after Moses had climbed to the top of the hill with Aaron and Hur. As long as Moses kept his hands raised up, Israel had the better of the fight, but when he let his hands rest, Amalek had the better of the fight. Moses' hands, however, grew tired; so they put a rock in place for him to sit on. Meanwhile Aaron and Hur supported his hands, one on one side and one on the other, so that his hands remained steady till sunset. And Joshua mowed down Amalek and his people with the edge of the sword.

RESPONSORIAL PSALM
Psalm 121:1–2, 3–4, 5–6, 7–8 (see 2)

R. Our help is from the Lord, who made heaven
and earth.

I lift up my eyes toward the mountains;
    whence shall help come to me?
My help is from the LORD,
    who made heaven and earth.   R.

May he not suffer your foot to slip;
    may he slumber not who guards you:
indeed he neither slumbers nor sleeps,
    the guardian of Israel.   R.

The LORD is your guardian;
        the LORD is your shade;
    he is beside you at your right hand.
The sun shall not harm you by day,
    nor the moon by night.   R.

The LORD will guard you from all evil;
    he will guard your life.
The LORD will guard your coming and
        your going,
    both now and forever.   R.

READING II *2 Timothy 3:14—4:2*

Beloved: Remain faithful to what you have learned and believed, because you know from whom you learned it, and that from infancy you have known the sacred Scriptures, which are capable of giving you wisdom for salvation through faith in Christ Jesus. All Scripture is inspired by God and is useful for teaching, for refutation, for correction, and for training in righteousness, so that one who belongs to God may be competent, equipped for every good work.

I charge you in the presence of God and of Christ Jesus, who will judge the living and the dead, and by his appearing and his kingly power: proclaim the word; be persistent whether it is convenient or inconvenient; convince, reprimand, encourage through all patience and teaching.

GOSPEL *Luke 18:1–8*

Jesus told his disciples a parable about the necessity for them to pray always without becoming weary. He said, "There was a judge in a certain town who neither feared God nor respected any human being. And a widow in that town used to come to him and say, 'Render a just decision for me against my adversary.' For a long time the judge was unwilling, but eventually he thought, 'While it is true that I neither fear God nor respect any human being, because this widow keeps bothering me I shall deliver a just decision for her lest she finally come and strike me.'" The Lord said, "Pay attention to what the dishonest judge says. Will not God then secure the rights of his chosen ones who call out to him day and night? Will he be slow to answer them? I tell you, he will see to it that justice is done for them speedily. But when the Son of Man comes, will he find faith on earth?"

Practice of Faith

Prayer is the basis for our relationship with God. Pope Francis says that it is to be "our daily bread, our powerful weapon and the staff for our journey." "The goal of the prayer is of secondary importance; what matters above all is the relationship with the Father" (May 25, 2016, General Audience in St. Peter's Square). ◆ Recall a time when you prayed persistently. Did you feel there was an outcome or effect? ◆ Is God inviting you to draw closer through prayer? The following are prayer resources that you can receive daily on your phone or computer: from Notre Dame, faith. nd.edu/s/1210/faith/pray.aspx?sid=1210&gid=609 &pgid=10745; from the United States Conference of Catholic Bishops, www.usccb.org/bible/reflec tions/. ◆ St. Monica, patron saint of wives and mothers, is recalled for her persistent and unfailing prayer. Learn more about her at www.catholic newsagency.com/saint.php?n=572.

Download more questions and activities for families, Christian initiation groups, and other adult groups at http://www.ltp.org/ahw.

Scripture Insights

Today's liturgy celebrates the virtue of perseverance. In the reading from Exodus, the Israelites face an attack from the Amalekites, a nomadic tribe they encountered in their wanderings through the desert. Through Moses' perseverance, as he interceded with God in prayer, the people of Israel finally triumph over their enemy.

In the Gospel reading, a widow's perseverance wins as well. Three groups of people were considered the most vulnerable and in need of support: the widow, the orphan, and the stranger. In the justice system in Israel, a judge was expected to give special attention to each of these groups. This makes the judge's lack of attention to the widow's pleas even more outrageous. Despite his rejection, the widow persists. Finally, the judge gives in, not because of the justice of her cause but because she had worn him out.

The message of these two accounts could be easily mistaken. They both advocate persistence in prayer. A literal reading of these accounts may convey that persistence in prayer will change God's mind, but this is nonsense. The God we believe in is a God of love, who promises fidelity to his covenant people. God's love for us never fluctuates (see James 1:16–17). God's love is always constant. Persistence in prayer is for our benefit. Through persistence in prayer, we change and deepen our faith and trust in God, his promises, and his love for us.

Paul also calls on his coworker, Timothy, as he exercises his ministry of proclaiming the word, to "be persistent, whether it is convenient or inconvenient, convince, reprimand, encourage through all patience and teaching."

◆ Why are we called to persevere in prayer?

◆ Who are the people that we are called to champion and support in our world?

◆ Where is God calling you to persevere?

READING I *Sirach 35:12–14, 16–18*

The LORD is a God of justice,
  who knows no favorites.
Though not unduly partial toward the weak,
  yet he hears the cry of the oppressed.
The Lord is not deaf to the wail of the orphan,
  nor to the widow when she pours out
      her complaint.
The one who serves God willingly is heard;
  his petition reaches the heavens.
The prayer of the lowly pierces the clouds;
  it does not rest till it reaches its goal,
nor will it withdraw till the Most High
      responds,
  judges justly and affirms the right,
and the Lord will not delay.

RESPONSORIAL PSALM
Psalm 34:2–3, 17–18, 19, 23 (7a)

R. The Lord hears the cry of the poor.

I will bless the LORD at all times;
  his praise shall be ever in my mouth.
Let my soul glory in the LORD;
  the lowly will hear me and be glad. R.

The LORD confronts the evildoers,
  to destroy remembrance of them from
      the earth.
When the just cry out, the LORD hears them,
  and from all their distress
      he rescues them. R.

The LORD is close to the brokenhearted;
  and those who are crushed in spirit he saves.
The LORD redeems the lives of his servants;
  no one incurs guilt who takes refuge
      in him. R.

READING II *2 Timothy 4:6–8, 16–18*

Beloved: I am already being poured out like a libation, and the time of my departure is at hand. I have competed well; I have finished the race; I have kept the faith. From now on the crown of righteousness awaits me, which the Lord, the just judge, will award to me on that day, and not only to me, but to all who have longed for his appearance.

At my first defense no one appeared on my behalf, but everyone deserted me. May it not be held against them! But the Lord stood by me and gave me strength, so that through me the proclamation might be completed and all the Gentiles might hear it. And I was rescued from the lion's mouth. The Lord will rescue me from every evil threat and will bring me safe to his heavenly kingdom. To him be glory forever and ever. Amen.

GOSPEL *Luke 18:9–14*

Jesus addressed this parable to those who were convinced of their own righteousness and despised everyone else. "Two people went up to the temple area to pray; one was a Pharisee and the other was a tax collector. The Pharisee took up his position and spoke this prayer to himself, 'O God, I thank you that I am not like the rest of humanity—greedy, dishonest, adulterous—or even like this tax collector. I fast twice a week, and I pay tithes on my whole income.' But the tax collector stood off at a distance and would not even raise his eyes to heaven but beat his breast and prayed, 'O God, be merciful to me a sinner.' I tell you, the latter went home justified, not the former; for whoever exalts himself will be humbled, and the one who humbles himself will be exalted."

Practice of Hope

This week we celebrate All Saints' Day, a holy day of obligation dedicated to those whose lives are examples of our hope. ◆ To learn more about the Communion of Saints, and for a summation on the Church's process of beatification and canonization, visit www.usccb.org/prayer-and-worship/prayers-and-devotions/saints/. ◆ All Souls' Day is a time to remember someone close to you or your family who has died. You might recall them by preparing a meal of their favorite food and setting a place for them at the table with their picture. You might retell stories about the person, and share what you loved about them or do an activity that this person loved. At the end of the day, light a candle and say prayers for your loved one. ◆ Pray with the music and images of John Becker's Litany of the Saints, found here at www.youtube.com/watch?v=kId0NBvNiCk.

Download more questions and activities for families, Christian initiation groups, and other adult groups at http://www.ltp.org/ahw.

Scripture Insights

The psalmist's proclamation, "The Lord hears the cry of the poor" reflects the message of today's readings. The Book of Sirach expresses the fundamental Israelite understanding that God champions the oppressed, the poor, the widow, the orphan, and the lowly. Their prayer "pierces the cloud."

From his prison cell, Paul writes to his fellow missionary Timothy as he foresees his imminent death. Looking back over his life, he expresses with conviction his trust in the Lord's love and mercy: "I have finished the race; I have kept the faith. From now on the crown of righteousness awaits me."

The parable in the Gospel is one of Jesus' most concise and forceful. Luke conveys its purpose in the introduction, "Jesus addressed this parable to those who were convinced of their own righteousness and despised everyone else." The prayer of the Pharisee expresses this attitude. In fact, the Pharisee was not praying to God, he was talking to himself as he listed all his great virtues. He considered himself to be better than the rest of humanity. Contrasted to the Pharisee, is the tax collector, one of the most despised members of society. In his encounter with God, he recognized his unworthiness by uttering the simple prayer, "O God, be merciful to me a sinner."

Luke captures the parable's message succinctly in Jesus' ending, "whoever exalts himself will be humbled, and the one who humbles himself will be exalted."

The humble person, as all the readings illustrate, is the one who acknowledges that all is grace. Everything comes from God. In our encounter with God, we recognize our sinfulness and need of God's forgiveness.

◆ What is Paul's mood as he foresees his execution as close at hand? What does this tell you about Paul?

◆ How did the tax collector miss the point of pray?

◆ How have deep experiences of prayer affected your life?

READING I *Wisdom 11:22—12:2*

Before the LORD the whole universe is as a
>grain from a balance
>>or a drop of morning dew come down upon
>>the earth.
But you have mercy on all, because you can do
>all things;
>>and you overlook people's sins that they
>>may repent.
For you love all things that are
>and loathe nothing that you have made;
>>for what you hated, you would not
>>have fashioned.
And how could a thing remain, unless you
>willed it;
>>or be preserved, had it not been called forth
>>by you?
But you spare all things, because they are yours,
>O LORD and lover of souls,
>>for your imperishable spirit is in all things!
Therefore you rebuke offenders little by little,
>warn them and remind them of the sins they
>are committing,
>>that they may abandon their wickedness and
>>believe in you, O LORD!

RESPONSORIAL PSALM *Psalm 145:1–2, 8–9, 10–11, 13, 14 (see 1)*

R. I will praise your name for ever, my king
>and my God.

I will extol you, O my God and King;
>and I will bless your name forever and ever.
Every day I will bless you;
>and I will praise your name forever
>>and ever. R.

The LORD is gracious and merciful,
>slow to anger and of great kindness.
The LORD is good to all,
>and compassionate toward all his works. R.

Let all your works give you thanks, O LORD,
>and let your faithful ones bless you.
Let them discourse of the glory of your kingdom
>and speak of your might. R.

The LORD is faithful in all his words
>and holy in all his works.
The LORD lifts up all who are falling
>and raises up all who are bowed down. R.

READING II *2 Thessalonians 1:11—2:2*

Brothers and sisters: We always pray for you, that our God may make you worthy of his calling and powerfully bring to fulfillment every good purpose and every effort of faith, that the name of our Lord Jesus may be glorified in you, and you in him, in accord with the grace of our God and Lord Jesus Christ.

We ask you, brothers and sisters, with regard to the coming of our Lord Jesus Christ and our assembling with him, not to be shaken out of your minds suddenly, or to be alarmed either by a "spirit," or by an oral statement, or by a letter allegedly from us to the effect that the day of the Lord is at hand.

GOSPEL *Luke 19:1–10*

At that time, Jesus came to Jericho and intended to pass through the town. Now a man there named Zacchaeus, who was a chief tax collector and also a wealthy man, was seeking to see who Jesus was; but he could not see him because of the crowd, for he was short in stature. So he ran ahead and climbed a sycamore tree in order to see Jesus, who was about to pass that way. When he reached the place, Jesus looked up and said, "Zacchaeus, come down quickly, for today I must stay at your house." And he came down quickly and received him with joy. When they all saw this, they began to grumble, saying, "He has gone to stay at the house of a sinner." But Zacchaeus stood there and said to the Lord, "Behold, half of my possessions, Lord, I shall give to the poor, and if I have extorted anything from anyone I shall repay it four times over." And Jesus said to him, "Today salvation has come to this house because this man too is a descendant of Abraham. For the Son of Man has come to seek and to save what was lost."

Practice of Charity

Today is the feast day for St. Martin de Porres. Born in Peru in 1579, Martin was of mixed race and abandoned by his father, a Spanish knight. Martin's holiness flourished despite his difficult life circumstances. First apprenticed as a barber-surgeon, he later become a Dominican lay brother. Celebrated for miraculous healings, he is especially known for his abundant charity, humility and devotion to God. ◆ St. Martin was known for approaching the humblest tasks with great love and charity. Reflect on the humble things you do each day. To which tasks could you bring greater love? Throughout the week, pray: "God, give me the spirit for the life that is in front of me right now." ◆ The workers at St. Martin de Porres House of Hospitality in San Francisco aim to reflect St. Martin's spirit by "serving food with as much love as possible." They offer free breakfast and lunch, and additional services to the homeless daily. Find them at www.martindeporres.org/. ◆ To learn more about St. Martin de Porres, visit www.catholic.org/saints/saint.php?saint_id=306.

Download more questions and activities for families, Christian initiation groups, and other adult groups at http://www.ltp.org/ahw.

Scripture Insights

In an amusing account, Luke tells the story of Zacchaeus, a well-known tax collector, short in stature, who climbs a tree in his excitement to catch a glimpse of Jesus passing through Jericho on his way to Jerusalem. His loss of dignity must have been amusing to the crowds. As Jesus passes by, he looks up and says to Zacchaeus, "Come down quickly, for today I must stay at your house." Zacchaeus welcomes Jesus with joy. This encounter transforms Zacchaeus and he promises to give away half his possessions to the poor and to pay restitution to anyone he harmed. Jesus accepts Zacchaeus' faith, saying, "Today salvation has come to this house because this man too is a descendant of Abraham."

Every encounter with Jesus brings with it the challenge to make a free decision. Zacchaeus seizes the moment and his encounter with Jesus changes his life. His experience also demonstrates the true attitude toward wealth: to give away one's surplus to those in need and not to defraud another of what is rightfully theirs.

This story is another example in which Luke's Gospel account presents Jesus turning social expectations upside down. The people are shocked that Jesus is inviting himself to the home of a tax collector, a sinner. Jesus goes further and acknowledges that Zacchaeus has been granted salvation and that he "too is a descendant of Abraham." Zacchaeus' ability to change his way of life is an example of how Abraham's descendants should act. Abraham is among those in the Old Testament who are heirs to God's promises.

◆ What does Jesus mean when he says that "this man too is a descendant of Abraham"?

◆ How does Zacchaeus' attitude toward riches demonstrate the right approach to wealth?

◆ What aspects of this story strike you as significant for your relationship with Jesus?

READING I *2 Maccabees 7:1–2, 9–14*

It happened that seven brothers with their mother were arrested and tortured with whips and scourges by the king, to force them to eat pork in violation of God's law. One of the brothers, speaking for the others, said: "What do you expect to achieve by questioning us? We are ready to die rather than transgress the laws of our ancestors."

At the point of death he said: "You accursed fiend, you are depriving us of this present life, but the King of the world will raise us up to live again forever. It is for his laws that we are dying."

After him the third suffered their cruel sport. He put out his tongue at once when told to do so, and bravely held out his hands, as he spoke these noble words: "It was from Heaven that I received these; for the sake of his laws I disdain them; from him I hope to receive them again." Even the king and his attendants marveled at the young man's courage, because he regarded his sufferings as nothing.

After he had died, they tortured and maltreated the fourth brother in the same way. When he was near death, he said, "It is my choice to die at the hands of men with the hope God gives of being raised up by him; but for you, there will be no resurrection to life."

RESPONSORIAL PSALM
Psalm 17:1, 5–6, 8, 15 (15b)

R. Lord, when your glory appears, my joy will
     be full.

Hear, O LORD, a just suit;
     attend to my outcry;
     hearken to my prayer from lips
          without deceit. R.

My steps have been steadfast in your paths,
     my feet have not faltered.
I call upon you, for you will answer me, O God;
     incline your ear to me; hear my word. R.

Keep me as the apple of your eye,
     hide me in the shadow of your wings.
But I in justice shall behold your face;
     on waking I shall be content in
          your presence. R.

READING II *2 Thessalonians 2:16—3:5*

Brothers and sisters: May our Lord Jesus Christ himself and God our Father, who has loved us and given us everlasting encouragement and good hope through his grace, encourage your hearts and strengthen them in every good deed and word.

Finally, brothers and sisters, pray for us, so that the word of the Lord may speed forward and be glorified, as it did among you, and that we may be delivered from perverse and wicked people, for not all have faith. But the Lord is faithful; he will strengthen you and guard you from the evil one. We are confident of you in the Lord that what we instruct you, you are doing and will continue to do. May the Lord direct your hearts to the love of God and to the endurance of Christ.

GOSPEL *Luke 20:27–38*

Shorter: Luke 20:27, 34–38

Some Sadducees, those who deny that there is a resurrection, came forward and put this question to Jesus, saying, "Teacher, Moses wrote for us, *If someone's brother dies leaving a wife but no child, his brother must take the wife and raise up descendants for his brother.* Now there were seven brothers; the first married a woman but died childless. Then the second and the third married her, and likewise all the seven died childless. Finally the woman also died. Now at the resurrection whose wife will that woman be? For all seven had been married to her." Jesus said to them, "The children of this age marry and remarry; but those who are deemed worthy to attain to the coming age and to the resurrection of the dead neither marry nor are given in marriage. They can no longer die, for they are like angels; and they are the children of God because they are the ones who will rise. That the dead will rise even Moses made known in the passage about the bush, when he called out 'Lord,' the God of Abraham, the God of Isaac, and the God of Jacob; and he is not God of the dead, but of the living, for to him all are alive."

Practice of Charity

Today's Scriptures affirm that this life is not the end. Through grace we have "eternal comfort and good hope," and when we pass through death into everlasting life we will be "equal to angels." Ministering in charity to the dying reflects our belief that the "God of the living," provides hope and comfort. ◆ To better understand the Catholic perspective on suffering and death, and our practice of ministering to the dying, read a theologically based vision of care from The Catholic Health Association of the U.S.: www.chausa.org /publications/health-progress/article/june-1993 /care-of-the-dying-a-catholic-perspective. ◆ If you are experiencing the pain of a loss, pray this week with a photo of your loved one, remembering the special qualities of the person and the joy and happiness shared. Thank God for all these blessings. Tell God of your sadness and sorrow and ask God to enter into the pain you are feeling over this loss. ◆ Pray with the hopeful hymn "On Eagle's Wings," by J. Michael Joncas, based on Psalm 91: www .youtube.com/watch?v=oXP-FsNUWOc.

Download more questions and activities for families, Christian initiation groups, and other adult groups at http://www.ltp.org/ahw.

Scripture Insights

Today's readings reinforce our faith that beyond death there is life with God forever. In the First Reading, taken from the Book of Maccabees, a mother and her seven sons are put to death because of their loyalty to their Jewish faith. The mother is forced to watch as her seven sons are put to death on the day before she is killed. The sons' conviction in the resurrection of the dead enables them to remain faithful to their beliefs.

Not all Jews at the time of Jesus believed in the resurrection of the dead. The Sadducees were one such group and that is the pretext for posing their absurd question to Jesus in today's Gospel. Jesus' answer is concise and to the point, "The God of Abraham, the God of Isaac, and the God of Jacob; and he is not God of the dead, but of the living, for to him all are alive." Jesus is referring to the story of Moses, who encounters God in the burning bush. God reveals his name to Moses as "I am . . . the God of Abraham, the God of Isaac, the God of Jacob." The point Jesus makes is that God did not say, "*I was* their God," but that "*I am* their God." They are still alive because God is the God of the living, not of the dead. The very name of God "I AM" continues to hold them in existence. They are eternally alive because of God's eternal "I AM." God's name is the assurance that our *faithful* departed are alive in God.

◆ How does God's name, "I AM," assure us that our faithful friends and relatives are alive in God?

◆ How does your belief in the resurrection of the dead give meaning to your life?

◆ How does Paul's prayer for encouragement speak to you in your life?

READING I *Malachi 3:19–20a*

Lo, the day is coming, blazing like an oven,
  when all the proud and all evildoers will
    be stubble,
and the day that is coming will set them on fire,
  leaving them neither root nor branch,
    says the LORD of hosts.
But for you who fear my name, there will arise
  the sun of justice with its healing rays.

RESPONSORIAL PSALM
Psalm 98:5–6, 7–8, 9 (see 9)

R. The Lord comes to rule the earth with justice.

Sing praise to the LORD with the harp,
  with the harp and melodious song.
With trumpets and the sound of the horn
  sing joyfully before the King, the LORD. R.

Let the sea and what fills it resound,
  the world and those who dwell in it;
let the rivers clap their hands,
  the mountains shout with them for joy. R.

Before the LORD, for he comes,
  for he comes to rule the earth;
he will rule the world with justice
  and the peoples with equity. R.

READING II *2 Thessalonians 3:7–12*

Brothers and sisters: You know how one must imitate us. For we did not act in a disorderly way among you, nor did we eat food received free from anyone. On the contrary, in toil and drudgery, night and day we worked, so as not to burden any of you. Not that we do not have the right. Rather, we wanted to present ourselves as a model for you, so that you might imitate us. In fact, when we were with you, we instructed you that if anyone was unwilling to work, neither should that one eat. We hear that some are conducting themselves among you in a disorderly way, by not keeping busy but minding the business of others. Such people we instruct and urge in the Lord Jesus Christ to work quietly and to eat their own food.

GOSPEL *Luke 21:5–19*

While some people were speaking about how the temple was adorned with costly stones and votive offerings, Jesus said, "All that you see here—the days will come when there will not be left a stone upon another stone that will not be thrown down."

Then they asked him, "Teacher, when will this happen? And what sign will there be when all these things are about to happen?" He answered, "See that you not be deceived, for many will come in my name, saying, 'I am he,' and 'The time has come.' Do not follow them! When you hear of wars and insurrections, do not be terrified; for such things must happen first, but it will not immediately be the end." Then he said to them, "Nation will rise against nation, and kingdom against kingdom. There will be powerful earthquakes, famines and plagues from place to place; and awesome sights and mighty signs will come from the sky.

"Before all this happens, however, they will seize and persecute you, they will hand you over to the synagogues and to prisons, and they will have you led before kings and governors because of my name. It will lead to your giving testimony. Remember, you are not to prepare your defense beforehand, for I myself shall give you a wisdom in speaking that all your adversaries will be powerless to resist or refute. You will even be handed over by parents, brothers, relatives and friends, and they will put some of you to death. You will be hated by all because of my name, but not a hair on your head will be destroyed. By your perseverance you will secure your lives."

Practice of Hope

At first glance, this week's readings seem incongruous. The words of Psalm 98 call the whole earth to shout with joy to the Lord, whereas the readings in 2 Thessalonians and Luke urge us to put our heads down, work hard, mind our business, and persevere through trial and tribulation. Yet true joy, born of hope in Christ, transcends circumstance, and transforms our encounters, so we can live in gratitude and joy no matter what life brings.
◆ Can you discover how God is in the midst of the people and activities that bring you joy? How might making time for things and people that bring you joy bring you closer to God? ◆ Start each day this week listening to the joyful hymn "Lift Up Your Hearts," by Roc O'Connor, SJ, at www. youtube.com/watch?v=SK41kpLNG7I. ◆ Read *Between Heaven and Mirth*, by Rev. James Martin, SJ, a book said to sanctify laughter. For a lighthearted talk by Martin on how joy, humor, and laughter are needed in our spiritual lives and in the life of the Church, watch this lecture from Boston College: www.youtube.com/watch?v =Ys5Uxy7qjmY.

Download more questions and activities for families, Christian initiation groups, and other adult groups at http://www.ltp.org/ahw.

Scripture Insights

Central to the readings are Jesus' words in the Gospel: "By your perseverance you will secure your lives."

In the Gospel reading, Jesus predicts the Temple's destruction. For the Jewish people, this would be disastrous since the Temple was where God dwelt among his people and the people carried out their religious sacrifices. Yet the words of Jesus came true. In AD 70, the Roman army destroyed the Temple and Jerusalem. As Jesus said, "not a stone will be left upon another stone that will not be thrown down."

The Church came to interpret the destruction of the Temple as a sign that the world will come to an end. Jesus' words here are not meant to be taken literally as though he is offering a blueprint for what will occur at the end of the world. The foundational message is that, just as God brought our world into existence, so God will bring the world as we know it to an end. Jesus warns his followers not to be afraid and not to be deceived by people who claim to read the signs of the times and foretell when the end will happen. As we experience natural disasters, deceptions, and persecution, the virtue that should be the hallmark of our lives is perseverance. Trust in the Lord's guidance and protection.

In the First Reading, the prophet Malachi offers further advice regarding the end of time. When God's judgment occurs, those who are faithful and "fear the name" of the Lord will experience God's healing and salvation.

◆ Why does Paul, in the Second Reading, tell us that he worked to pay for his keep?

◆ What are some of the virtues that today's readings speak of today and how significant are they in your life?

◆ Are you at all influenced by the belief that the world will come to an end?

READING I *2 Samuel 5:1–3*

In those days, all the tribes of Israel came to David in Hebron and said: "Here we are, your bone and your flesh. In days past, when Saul was our king, it was you who led the Israelites out and brought them back. And the LORD said to you, 'You shall shepherd my people Israel and shall be commander of Israel.'" When all the elders of Israel came to David in Hebron, King David made an agreement with them there before the LORD, and they anointed him king of Israel.

RESPONSORIAL PSALM
Psalm 122:1–2, 3–4, 4–5 (see 1)

R. Let us go rejoicing to the house of the Lord.

I rejoiced because they said to me,
    "We will go up to the house of the LORD."
And now we have set foot
    within your gates, O Jerusalem.   R.

Jerusalem, built as a city
    with compact unity.
To it the tribes go up,
    the tribes of the LORD.   R.

According to the decree for Israel,
    to give thanks to the name of the LORD.
In it are set up judgment seats,
    seats for the house of David.   R.

READING II *Colossians 1:12–20*

Brothers and sisters: Let us give thanks to the Father, who has made you fit to share in the inheritance of the holy ones in light. He delivered us from the power of darkness and transferred us to the kingdom of his beloved Son, in whom we have redemption, the forgiveness of sins.

He is the image of the invisible God, / the firstborn of all creation. / For in him were created all things in heaven and on earth, / the visible and the invisible, / whether thrones or dominions or principalities or powers; / all things were created through him and for him. / He is before all things, / and in him all things hold together. / He is the head of the body, the church. / He is the beginning, the firstborn from the dead, / that in all things he himself might be preeminent. / For in him all the fullness was pleased to dwell, / and through him to reconcile all things for him, / making peace by the blood of his cross / through him, whether those on earth or those in heaven.

GOSPEL *Luke 23:35–43*

The rulers sneered at Jesus and said, "He saved others, let him save himself if he is the chosen one, the Christ of God." Even the soldiers jeered at him. As they approached to offer him wine they called out, "If you are King of the Jews, save yourself." Above him there was an inscription that read, "This is the King of the Jews."

Now one of the criminals hanging there reviled Jesus, saying, "Are you not the Christ? Save yourself and us." The other, however, rebuking him, said in reply, "Have you no fear of God, for you are subject to the same condemnation? And indeed, we have been condemned justly, for the sentence we received corresponds to our crimes, but this man has done nothing criminal." Then he said, "Jesus, remember me when you come into your kingdom." He replied to him, "Amen, I say to you, today you will be with me in Paradise."

Practice of Faith

This Sunday points us in the direction toward which all time is moving: Christ, King of the Universe. Jesus comes to us without earthly glory but on a cross, crowned by thorns. As Pope Francis said in his November 20, 2016, homily, "the grandeur of his kingdom is not power as defined by this world, but the love of God, a love capable of encountering and healing all things." ◆ Reflect on how you can honor God through compassionate encounter. Perhaps this means reaching out to an estranged friend or family member, or direct service to the poor or needy. ◆ Pray this week with the words of the thief crucified with Christ: "Jesus, remember me when you come into your kingdom." A Taizé chant version can be found at www.youtube.com/watch?v=r6tVReXsioM. ◆ Talk with your children about their images of a king, contrasting the images with Christ's way of being a king. Discuss what this teaches us about God and God's kingdom. Tie these ideas to the Lord's Prayer, and what it means to pray "thy kingdom come, thy will be done."

Download more questions and activities for families, Christian initiation groups, and other adult groups at http://www.ltp.org/ahw.

Scripture Insights

On this final Sunday of the liturgical year, the Church invites us to celebrate the kingship of Jesus Christ. All the readings provide an insight into the true nature of this kingship. The First Reading reminds us that all kingship ultimately comes from God. God promised that the kingdom of David would endure forever. The Gospel accounts proclaim that Jesus is David's descendant and heir to his kingdom. God's plan for the salvation of humanity is celebrated in the hymn of today's Second Reading from Paul's Letter to the Colossians. God's Son become man is the image of the invisible God. God's plan is to "reconcile all things for him, making peace by the blood of his cross."

The Gospel illustrates the fulfillment of God's plan. The irony is that the kingship of Christ is revealed through his Cross, not through power and majesty, but in the humiliation of the Crucifixion. Today's Gospel presents a memorable scene where the innocent Jesus is crucified between two criminals. The first criminal mocks Jesus, while the other admits his guilt and recognizes Jesus' innocence. In what must be the clearest acknowledgment of Jesus' kingship in the Gospel accounts, the criminal confesses, "Jesus, remember me when you come into your kingdom." Jesus embraces this criminal's sincerity and faith and promises him, "Today you will be with me in Paradise." To be with Jesus in his kingdom is the destiny for every Christian who confesses with this criminal, "Jesus, remember me when you come into your kingdom." The death of Jesus on the Cross establishes his kingdom and brings salvation to all who call on the name of the Lord.

◆ How is the kingship of Jesus different from that of all other kings?

◆ What virtues does Luke's account of Jesus' death between two criminals teach us?

◆ In the Second Reading, which images of Jesus most appeal to you?

God Speaks in the Liturgy

Celebrating Advent

Kristopher W. Seaman

During elementary school, I did not understand what Advent celebrated until one of my teachers, a Benedictine woman religious, helped me not only to understand something about Advent, but also to appreciate the season itself. She went all out for Advent, much like some of my neighbors do for Christmas decorations. Our teacher decorated our homeroom with an Advent wreath made with fragrant cedar branches and beautiful pillar candles. Bluish purple fabric covered the bulletin boards and the table on which the Bible was displayed. Every morning during Advent, Sister had us gather around the Advent wreath to participate in a 10-minute prayer service. She would then give us a five-minute reflection on one aspect of Advent. Her reflection could be as simple, though profound, as discussing one of the symbols of the Jesse tree, or having us engage our senses to think about why cedar was used for the ring of the wreath. From that period, Advent became one of my favorite times of the liturgical year.

Advent has two purposes. The first, and most obvious, is that it helps us prepare for Christmas when Christ became human. The readings for the Fourth Sunday of Advent, in particular, relate to Mary's conception. Mary responded to God's invitation to bear Jesus. The time from her conception until Jesus's birth nine months later was one of expectancy and hope. Advent has this same aspect for us: a time of joyful expectation for Christ's coming into our lives. Christ is the Redeemer and Savior whom we, like Mary, bear in our very beings. In the waters of Baptism, we began to be called "Christian" but it was the Father's gift of the Spirit who was bestowed on us that we, too, might bear Christ. Like Mary, Christ lives within us. Christ is "Emmanuel"—"God-with-us." God continues to be with us, even after Baptism, especially through the Eucharist when Christ enters us to transform us more and more into his image.

From December 17 through the 24th, Advent begins to focus intensely on Christmas. These days are often referred to as the "O" Antiphons. Each day between these dates is geared toward one of the titles for Christ: "O Wisdom," "O Lord," "O Root of Jesse," "O Key of David," "O Dayspring," "O King of All Nations," "O Emmanuel." Thus, the chant "O Come, O Come, Emmanuel" is particularly appropriate during these days of Advent. The Book of Isaiah, prophesied about the Messiah whom Israel expected to arrive to liberate them. The O Antiphons come from Isaiah's prophecies of the Messiah and these are used prior to Christmas as a way to recall that Christ is the Messiah, the long-awaited one who is the bringer of hope.

Secondly, during Advent "minds and hearts are led to look forward to Christ's Second Coming at the end of time (*Universal Norms on the Liturgical Year and Calendar*, 39). This second focus is most noticeable in the first few weeks of Advent. For those of us in the northern hemisphere, winter days grow shorter and nights become longer as we progress through Advent. The natural rhythm of life evokes the mystery of Christ. One of the titles for Christ is the Morning Star. The morning star generally refers to the rising sun at dawn. This ancient title is an analogy. Christ as the Son (like the sun) of God rises to dispel the darkness of sin and death. While we look to Christ's final coming at the end times, we are not necessarily waiting for a day of doom; rather, we are awaiting a day of hope. This future is the future God intends for the world. We continue to journey toward that future, but we cannot do it on our own. It is in the present where both themes of Advent are connected: past (Christ's birth) and future (Christ's final coming).

In liturgy, Christ comes into the present through the power of the Spirit. In the proclaimed Scriptures, Christ speaks to us; and in the Eucharist, Christ enters us so that we might be transformed into his body. The power of Christ is that he is not confined to either the past or the future, but he comes into the present to nourish us in Word (Scriptures) and Eucharist so that we will continue to wait joyfully for the consummation of Christ's final coming.

Advent is a season when the Church prepares for Christ's coming (1) at Christmas, (2) in the final coming, and (3) through the sacraments. Past and future are mediated in the present. It is God's transforming invitation to accept his promises and to journey in hope toward Christ's final coming.

KRISTOPHER W. SEAMAN, DMIN, is currently a PHD student at King's College, University of London. He is the former director of the Office of Worship for the Diocese of Gary and the Office for Liturgy in the Diocese of Juneau. He earned an MA in liturgical studies from Saint John's University (Collegeville), an MA in Systematic Theology from Catholic Theological Union (CTU), Chicago, and a DMIN from CTU.

Lent: A Time for Inner Cleansing

Kathy Kuczka

Every year my mother would rearrange the furniture in the living room and family room and change the drapes. Then she would open the cupboards and drawers in the kitchen, remove all the dishes, glasses, cups, goblets, plates, pitchers, platters, bowls, casseroles, china, and silverware to clean them. It was as if we were preparing for the biggest banquet of the year. She called this cleansing fury "spring cleaning."

Every year at this time the Church gives us the opportunity to do some inner spring cleaning. In fact, the word *Lent* is derived from the Anglo-Saxon word meaning "spring." Lent is a prime time to rearrange our priorities, to open the cupboards of our hearts and hold our egos to the light to see those areas that need to be cleaned and polished. Inner cleansing, or conversion, has always been at the heart of Lent. In the early Church, Lent was the final leg of the journey for the catechumens preparing for Baptism. It was also a time when already baptized penitents, isolated from the assembly because of their sins, would prepare to be reconciled to God and the community. The journeys of the catechumen and the penitent were related in that both embraced conversion. As the catechumen looked forward to Baptism, the penitent looked forward to reconciliation. To this day, the focus of Lent remains both baptismal and penitential.

Return, repent, reconcile, and renew are words that we hear in the liturgies of Lent. A common factor among these words is the prefix *re-*. That prefix expresses the meaning "again," as in words such as *redo*, *remake*, and *revise*; but it also indicates withdrawal or backward motion, as in words such as *return*, *revert*, and *remember*. During Lent, we are called to change by going back to childlike innocence, simplicity, and joy.

Prayer helps us to return to childlike innocence. Prayer prompts us to withdraw. As Jesus said, "When you pray, go to your inner room, close the door, and pray to your Father in secret" (Matthew 6:6, *New American Bible, Revised Edition*). Prayer nurtures our relationship with God. Prayer also nurtures our relationship with ourselves. Prayer peels away the masks we wear and the layers of ego defenses we think we need to survive. Prayer tells us that it's okay to be who we really are. Prayer changes us.

Fasting helps us to return to childlike simplicity. Fasting challenges us to trust that God will provide all that we need. Fasting helps us to sort our priorities. Because the digestive system doesn't have to work as hard when we fast, we have

Prayer helps us to return to childlike innocence.

more energy to focus on what matters. Fasting creates a hunger for God. Fasting changes us.

Almsgiving helps us to return to childlike joy. Almsgiving moves us to acknowledge how much we have been given and that fills us with gratitude and praise. Almsgiving frees us from fear by compelling us to surrender what we have and who we are to others. Almsgiving requires humility. As Jesus said, "When you give alms, do not let your left hand know what your right is doing, so that your almsgiving may be secret" (Matthew 6:2). True humility always leads to joy. Almsgiving changes us.

It is God who calls us to conversion, and it is God's transforming grace that accompanies us on the Lenten journey as we pray, fast, and give alms. Let us pray for the courage to be open to this grace that we might come to Easter, the biggest banquet of the liturgical year, with hearts cleansed and spirits renewed.

Text by Kathy Kuczka. Art © Julie Lonneman. © 2017 Archdiocese of Chicago: Liturgy Training Publications, 3949 South Racine Avenue, Chicago, IL 60609; 800-933-1800; www.LTP.org. *Pastoral Liturgy*® magazine, January/February 2018, www.PastoralLiturgy.org.

How Does Baptism Change Us?

Kristopher W. Seaman

During the Litany of the Saints at the Easter Vigil, the bishop invited Jenifer and her family to come to the font. This mother and her children had been awaiting Baptism for nearly two years. Jennifer decided she would go first, to show the children (ages eight to fifteen) how she would enter the waters into which they would follow. After the Blessing of the Water, the bishop helped her into the large, deep baptismal font. He then stepped in himself. All of a sudden, the smallest child ran to the bishop, waving his finger and exclaiming, "Do not drown my mom!" The bishop was quite surprised. He reassured this child that he would not drown the mother. Then, turning to the assembly, the bishop said, "Did everyone hear that? He gets what Baptism is about—death, but also, we need to add, new life." Then, the mother was baptized, followed by her children, and, of course, the most eager to be baptized, the young boy.

This story illustrates the power of sacramental symbols to evoke meaning at a deeply human or cosmic level. The child's experience of water meant that he knew the destructive quality of water—it can unleash floods or quench one's breath in drowning. But there is another side to water—it sustains life. The human body needs water to stay alive, specifically for the continual activity of the cells within the human body. The production of food requires water. Life at its fundamental is dependent on water. Baptism changes us to see the human and the cosmic as imbued with life-giving and death-wielding power.

Baptism immerses us in Christ's person and mission.

DYING AND RISING

But there is also a theological significance to water. The theological meaning is tied to death and life, but particularly to the life, Death, and Resurrection of Christ Jesus. His life, Death, and Resurrection give meaning to Baptism. The baptized enter cosmically and bodily into the very life, Death, and Resurrection of Christ. The blessed water ritually cleanses the person, provides access to Christ's renewed life, and gives entrance into the Body of Christ, the Church. From the waters of Baptism, one receives the Holy Spirit, is washed clean from sin, and is renewed in the life and mission of Christ, a life and mission the Church promises to serve. Baptism changes us in such a way we are given a new mission, a new calling, and a new body because of the work of Christ's Spirit in the font.

The anointing that may go along with the Baptism is also tied to Christ's life, which is given in Baptism.

St. Augustine remarked that the anointing with the Cross, a symbol of Christ's Death and life, is tied to the person and mission of Christ. (The word *Christ* is Greek for *anointed one*.) To be anointed, therefore, is to be marked a Christian, a person dedicated and joined to the person and mission of Christ.

These baptismal waters are sometimes referred to as waters of regeneration. The waters not only drown our old selves but regenerate, or recreate, us into disciples of Christ. If Baptism immerses us into Christ's person and mission, the rest of life is potentially a response to that baptismal call. Each day we are to discern how we might live as Christ. Baptism changes not only how we see the world but how we live according to Christ's mission.

Text by Kristopher W. Seaman, DMIN. Art by Steve Erspamer. © 2017 Archdiocese of Chicago: Liturgy Training Publications, 3949 South Racine Avenue, Chicago, IL 60609; 800-933-1800; www.LTP.org. *Pastoral Liturgy*® magazine, May/June 2017, www.PastoralLiturgy.org.

A Day for Prayers, Remembering

Kristopher W. Seaman

When I first arrived in Dublin, Ireland, to study, it was suggested that I visit the National Leprechaun Museum. Sure that I would not enjoy it, I didn't give it much thought. In a few months, I was given a research desk with other doctoral students, including one whom I later discovered worked in the Leprechaun Museum. When I asked about the museum, he told me it was created to preserve and catalog the old Irish folktales before they were lost or forgotten.

A couple of months later, a storyteller from the museum made a presentation to the university's Theological Society on how the Irish celebrated and understood Halloween. He told us it was the day when it was considered that the souls were the closest to the physical realm, and households would perform certain rituals so the souls would be at peace. The rituals also acknowledged the closeness of death. When the nights are growing longer, and light seems momentary, a culture turns to nature as a way of reminding themselves of death. Halloween, the Solemnity of All Saints, and the Commemoration of All the Faithful Departed (All Souls' Day), it seems to me, are popularly held closely together. We remember those who have gone before us: the good, the holy (the saints), and the seemingly ordinary person (all souls). This memory is alive in the Church, perhaps in household customs (such as those in parts of Ireland), and in nature itself.

In some ways, the close connection makes a lot of sense. On November 1, we remember all those who have gone before us who imitated and participated in Christ's holiness. They now remind us, pray for us, show us that holiness is obtainable and that we are called to imitate and participate in Christ's holiness. On All Souls' Day, we pray for all the faithful who have passed before us. We also recognize the need presently to pray to God for empowerment to live Christ's holiness.

A good lens to the day is either of the options of the Second Reading (Romans 5:5–11 or Romans 6:3–9). Sin prevents us from flourishing, prevents unity with God and with one another. Both readings address the need to turn away from sin, to turn to God who in Christ saved us from sin so that we may live imbued with God's holiness. We live in hope that we might, like the saints, live in true unity with God and one another.

From the day when the Commemoration for the All the Faithful Departed was first celebrated in the tenth century,

On the Commemoration of All the Faithful Departed (All Souls' Day), we pray for and remember those who have gone before us.

there has been a focus on prayers for all who have died. Unlike a funeral liturgy, during which prayers are for a particular person as he/she transitions to renewed life in Christ, All Souls' Day is about *everyone* who has gone before us. This feast, then, is both a reminder of our need to pray for and be healed by God's merciful love and a day to be reminded of those of us who have died, asking for the healing of all who await the fullness of unity with God's merciful love.

While we may not always think of leprechauns on All Souls' Day, we may be reminded of the importance of keeping the memory alive of the significant stories and people who have gone before us—whether saints or other souls. As Christian disciples, our important heritage is always rooted in the call toward God's holiness, shown to us by Christ Jesus, his holiness imitated by the saints, and which, it is hoped, we are empowered to imitate and participate in.

Text by Kristopher W. Seaman, DMin. Art by Suzanne Novak. © 2016 Archdiocese of Chicago: Liturgy Training Publications, 3949 South Racine Avenue, Chicago, IL 60609; 1-800-933-1800; www.LTP.org. *Pastoral Liturgy*® magazine, September/October 2016, www.PastoralLiturgy.org.

Why Is Incense Used at Mass?

Kristopher W. Seaman

While walking from home to college recently, I saw large, spiraling smoke rising from a building on fire. The smell of smoke awakened childhood memories. As a youth, I lived close to a reservation where Native Americans burnt areas of the land to renew it and make it fertile for crops. I loved the smell of the burning fields of grass and flowers, but I was afraid of the fire and was sorry to see the colorful fields being destroyed.

Something both beautiful and terrifying was at work in the burning at the reservation that is akin to the notion of the "numinous" that theologian Rudolph Otto described in his writing. Briefly, this notion contends that something both mysterious and fascinating is at the foundation of faith. In Christianity, this something is the Paschal Mystery: Christ's Passion, Death, Resurrection, Ascension, and subsequent gift of the Holy Spirit, who incorporates us into God's deepest purposes. The Paschal Mystery is about death and life (the Cross).

The smoke that came both from the fiery building and the burning of the land frightened and fascinated while also evoking death and life. Christ's gift of himself on the Cross for the world was both terrifying (death) and fascinating (life) because through Christ Jesus, God brought about mercy, forgiveness, and compassion for the world. The Cross evokes, just as does smoke or incense, death and life, especially the death and life of Christ.

Like all created materials used within the liturgy, the power of incense to "speak," or to convey meaning, is dependent upon our experience of it. Because I am aware of the damaging effects of fire, I know to call the emergency number when I see smoke rising from a building. In liturgy, incense takes on a *theological* significance in addition to its daily experience. Incense in liturgy evokes images from Scripture: the cloud of smoke God sent to liberate the Israelites from Egyptian slavery; the incense used in the Jerusalem Temple (Exodus 30:34–38), God's instruction to Moses to make a mixture to burn like incense as a sign of God's presence; prayers rising to God like incense (Psalm 141); the gift of incense that one of the Magi presented to Jesus.

In the liturgy, incense evokes God's presence, inviting the assembly to engage with God in new ways through prayer. In its numinous quality, incense conveys the renewed life that Christ's presence offers in the midst of death, or those experiences in which God's purposes are extinguished, numbed, evaded, or rejected. While not reducing incense to any of a number of meanings, incense concerns encountering a God who repeatedly invites us to "smell" his purposes, despite our often resistant ways.

At funerals, the priest incenses the casket of the deceased person, enveloping the casket in smoke and fragrance, portraying the invitation into God's presence and purpose in a new way of life.

Incense evokes God's presence, inviting the congregation to engage with God in new ways.

Text by Kristopher W. Seaman, DMin. Art by Vicki Shuck. © 2016 Archdiocese of Chicago: Liturgy Training Publications, 3949 South Racine Avenue, Chicago, IL 60609; 1-800-933-1800; www.LTP.org. *Pastoral Liturgy*® magazine, July/August 2016, www.PastoralLiturgy.org.

Baptismal Symbols at Funerals

Kristopher W. Seaman

At the beginning of a funeral, the body is greeted at the church's entrance, which often is nearby the baptismal font. The entryway is a threshold, a place of transition that is neither inside nor outside. In funeral liturgies, the space marks the transition of the deceased person from earthly life to eternal life. The symbols of Baptism, symbols that mark the transition of the person from non-faith to new life in Christ, are also present at the beginning of the funeral rites. There, we see holy water, white in the pall that will be placed over the coffin, the Paschal candle, and possibly the use of incense.

SPRINKLING WITH HOLY WATER

On Easter Sunday, we renew our baptismal promises as we are sprinkled with holy water. During funeral liturgies, the casket is likewise sprinkled with holy water. The person who began life as a Christian disciple in Baptism, is, even in death, still a disciple, though his/her life has changed by a deeper participation in Christ's eternal life. Just as Baptism was not an end to growing deeper in faith, so too in death, the disciple will continue to grow deeper in Christ's life. Death is not end, but a transition.

CASKET/COFFIN

The font is a place of transition, a transition from death to new life, which means that the font is literally a coffin, a place where one is buried in the hope of rising just as Christ rose from the dead. Christ's victory over death is our path to new life in Christ. The casket/coffin is "a new font," a place of transition from earthly death to eternal life with Christ. The coffin is a symbol of being born into eternal life. After the coffin is sprinkled with holy water at the threshold, a pall is placed over the casket.

PALL

The pall, the long, white cloth that covers the casket at funerals, is another baptismal symbol. During the baptismal rite, a white gown, a symbol of new life in Christ, is worn. The placement of the pall recognizes that the deceased person is clothed with Christ.

PASCHAL CANDLE

During the Entrance Hymn, the casket is processed forward and placed near the sanctuary, where the Liturgies of the Word and the Eucharist occur. Baptism leads to new life in Christ, which is directed to the Word and Table of Christ. His words are proclaimed in the hope that disciples will be comforted and consoled by his teachings and will seek to live his Word. In the Eucharist, Christians unite their prayers and

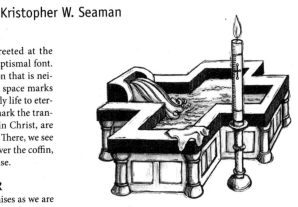

During the baptismal rite, the symbols of water, light, and a white garment symbolize new life in Christ. Those same symbols at the funeral signify the eternal life that awaits those baptized in Christ.

lives to Christ in thanksgiving and receive Christ's Body and Blood. Baptismal new life is renewed and strengthened in Eucharistic participation. By placing the casket close to the altar, those gathered remember that the person who has entered eternal life continues to be a member of the Church and continues to pray around the heavenly banquet.

Next to the casket is the Paschal candle, a symbol of Christ, the light that dispels darkness, sin, and death. At Baptism, the newly baptized is given a baptismal candle lit from the Paschal candle. The baptized have not only found new life but are called to be Christ's light within the world.

INCENSE

Incense is not necessarily associated with Baptism but provides baptismal imagery. The body/casket is incensed, perfumed, and enfolded with misty smoke. The body, even in death, still has dignity because the person was not only created in God's image, but also through baptismal waters, is named, marked, and called as Christ's own, Christian. The baptismal symbols at funerals signify not only one's eternal life in Christ but the Church's reverence and care of the human body.

KRISTOPHER W. SEAMAN, DMIN, is a doctoral student at Trinity College, Dublin, Ireland. He is the former director of the Office of Worship for the Diocese of Gary, Indiana. He earned a master of arts degree in liturgical studies from St. John's University, Collegeville, Minnesota, and a master of arts degree in systematic theology and a doctorate of ministry from Catholic Theological Union.

The Holy Oils

Kristopher W. Seaman

OIL OF THE SICK   OIL OF THE CATECHUMENS   SACRED CHRISM

Many of us well know the story of the Lord's calling and anointing David as king. Having been told that one of Jesse's sons was to be the king, Samuel went to Bethlehem. When the eighth of Jesse's sons was presented to Samuel, the Lord said, "Rise and anoint him." In the Old Testament, those whom God called to be kings, priests, and prophets were anointed with an oil that was to be regarded as "holy to the Lord" (Exodus 30:37).

For Christians, anointing is significant because it is closely tied to who Christ is. *Christos* is the Greek word for the Hebrew *messiah*. Both words mean "anointed one." Jesus as the Christ is anointed by God, that is, he is the perfect embodiment of God's purpose and mission. He is the perfect Priest, Prophet, and King. In Baptism, Christians share in Christ's perfect identity as God's Son. We hear in the Rite of Baptism for Children, "He now anoints you with the chrism of salvation, so that, united with his people, you may remain for ever a member of Christ who is Priest, Prophet, and King."

During Holy Week or shortly before, the bishop of a diocese gathers with his priests and some of the laity to bless the oils for the sick and catechumens and to consecrate the chrism. This is indeed a rich liturgy.

The first oil to be blessed is the oil for the sick. The prayer of blessing recalls Christ's ministry of healing the sick. The Holy Spirit is invoked upon the oil so that all those anointed will be healed in body, mind, and soul. The oil is principally used for the sacrament of the Anointing of the Sick.

Next, the oil for catechumens is blessed. Catechumens are those who are preparing to become Christians. This oil will be used, then, for catechumens as they journey toward Baptism, Confirmation, and Eucharist at the Easter Vigil. It is also used in the Baptism of infants. The prayer asks that those who are anointed will be strengthened in faith, grow in their understanding of the Gospel, and live more fully Christian discipleship.

The final oil, chrism, is a mixture of olive oil and balsam, a fragrance from the Holy Land. Chrism receives its name from Christ, as do we who are Christians, because we have been anointed with this oil. The prayer is quite rich as it recalls the song of David and the anointing of Aaron as priest; creation that brought forth the olive tree; and the dove that returned to Noah with an olive branch. Next, the prayer asks the Father to bless the oil so that those who are anointed with it might bear the image of Christ, be freed from sin, and share in eternal life. This oil is used for Baptism, Confirmation, and Holy Orders, the sacraments that are not repeated.

The oils are all used for the spiritual health of disciples so that as Christians journey deeper into faith, they might be healed from sin and live within and according to the loving, healing, and prophetic presence of Christ, whose name we bear and with whom we were anointed.

KRISTOPHER W. SEAMAN, DMIN, is a doctoral student at Trinity College, Dublin, Ireland. He is the former director of the Office of Worship for the Diocese of Gary, Indiana. He earned a master of arts degree in liturgical studies from St. John's University, Collegeville, Minnesota, and a master of arts degree in systematic theology and a doctorate of ministry from Catholic Theological Union.

May the Bride and Groom Process up the Aisle Together?

Kristopher W. Seaman

During the past six years, I have been involved in the wedding liturgies of four family members: two brothers, a nephew, and a niece. I was struck by how the ceremonies were shaped and also by the inspiration for the celebration of the liturgies. The couples' ideas on the wedding liturgy had been formed by television, movies, and their participation in the weddings of friends and members. In most of the wedding liturgies, the bride processed up the aisle last (following the bridesmaid and the maid of honor) along with her father. The groom did not walk up the main aisle but was already standing with the priest and the groomsmen near the altar. In one brother's wedding, the bride and the groom walked down the main aisle together, and the bride was not "given away" by her father.

Couples' ideas about their wedding ceremonies often are inspired by popular culture. The *Rite of Marriage* describes a procession in which the couple processes up the aisle together.

May the bride and groom process up the aisle together? A simple answer is yes. In fact, the *Rite of Marriage* describes a procession with the bride and bridegroom walking together.

The present *Rite of Marriage* suggests the order of and the persons who should be part of the procession. The rite states:

> If there is a procession to the altar, the ministers go first, followed by the priest, and then the bride and the bridegroom. According to local custom, they may be escorted by at least their parents and the two witnesses. (20)

Note that the rite presupposes a liturgical procession. As a rite of the Church the marriage rite is prepared as a liturgical act. The rite, then, takes for granted that the procession follows what we ordinarily participate in on Sundays, with the addition of the couple and with the possible inclusion of parents and witnesses. Another important element of the procession is not only the inclusion of the liturgical ministers but also the placement of the couple after the priest. Typically, the priest is the last to process up the aisle, but the *Rite of Marriage* calls for the couple to be last. Why is this? It is because the ministers of the Sacrament of Matrimony are the bride and bridegroom together, while the priest witnesses the exchange of vows.

Theologically and also liturgically, if both the bride and the bridegroom are the ministers of the Sacrament of Matrimony, then both should have equal roles and should participate similarly within the rite, including the wedding procession. The procession in which the bride walks down the aisle with her father, with the groom awaiting her, suggests the groom is not only incidental, but theologically, that his role in the rite itself is marginal. The rite presents that the couple share in growing in their union with Christ Jesus and his Church, as well as the coming together of two families, that is, two domestic churches. The bride and bridegroom have been reared in the family, the domestic church, where it is hoped that faith was nurtured. Now, in and through this rite, these two members of the Church and members of their respective domestic churches will be uniting, in faith. The marginalization of the groom, even in the procession, may communicate that one member of the domestic church is more significant than the other.

The official *Rite of Marriage* is prophetic in regard to how the marriage rite is prepared and executed. It may be challenging to our popular imaginations, but it speaks to the depth of faith that should be a part of not only the rite but the entire marriage.

Text by Kristopher W. Seaman, DMin. Art by Luba Lukova. © 2016 Archdiocese of Chicago: Liturgy Training Publications, 3949 South Racine Avenue, Chicago, IL 60609; 1-800-933-1800; www.LTP.org. *Pastoral Liturgy*® magazine, May/June 2016, www.PastoralLiturgy.org.